Culinary Gardens

'Sunshine' lettuce. (Photo courtesy of Territorial Seed)

Culinary Gardens

FROM DESIGN TO PALATE

Susan McClure

FULCRUM PUBLISHING

To Millie Adams and Lori Zaim, whose culinary creativity
and good taste are a source of continual inspiration.

Library of Congress Cataloging-in-Publication Data

McClure, Susan, 1957–
    Culinary gardens : from design to palate / Susan McClure.
        p.   cm.
    Includes bibliographical references (p.   ) and index.
    ISBN 1-55591-311-3 (hardcover)
    1. Edible landscaping. 2. Gardens—Design.   3. Vegetable gardening.
4. Herb gardening. 5. Plants, Edible.   I. Title.
SB475.9.E35M38   1997
712'.6—DC21   97-11850
                                                         CIP

Printed in Korea
0 9 8 7 6 5 4 3 2 1

Fulcrum Publishing
350 Indiana Street, Suite 350
Golden, Colorado 80401-5093
(800) 992-2908 • (303) 277-1623

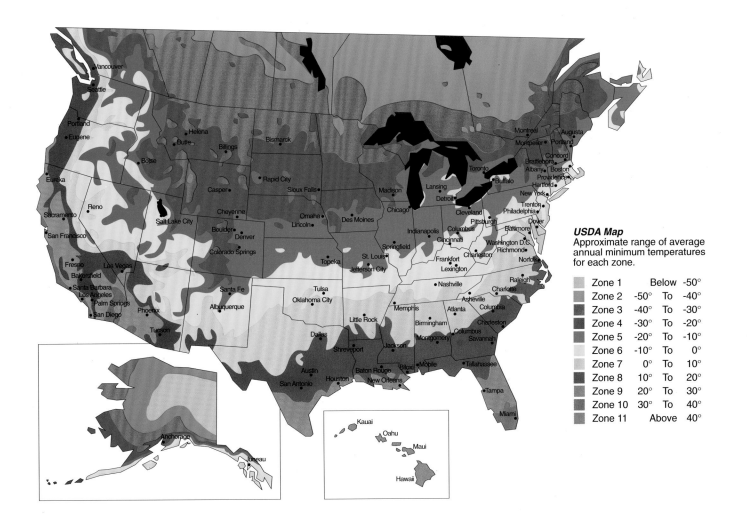

USDA Map
Approximate range of average
annual minimum temperatures
for each zone.

Zone 1	Below	-50°
Zone 2	-50°	To	-40°
Zone 3	-40°	To	-30°
Zone 4	-30°	To	-20°
Zone 5	-20°	To	-10°
Zone 6	-10°	To	0°
Zone 7	0°	To	10°
Zone 8	10°	To	20°
Zone 9	20°	To	30°
Zone 10	30°	To	40°
Zone 11	Above	40°

Contents

Ruby-colored 'Red Sails' leaf lettuce with dianthus and petunias.

ÍNTRODUCTION

Fresh ingredients—grown at home and harvested when bursting with flavor—make any meal special. A slice of a sweet, full-flavored, garden-fresh tomato in a simple sandwich adds a world of cheer. Gourmet gardening offers even more perks. It eliminates frustrating shopping for good, tender carrots, and hard-to-find foods such as aromatic French thyme and juicy lemon cucumbers. It also saves money. Exquisite and pricey mesclun (baby greens) can be grown for pennies and save you dollars. A gourmet garden can look great, beautifying your landscape and even increasing your property value. What better reasons could there be for starting your own gourmet garden?

This book is here to help you. It features eleven garden designs—ready to be made a reality in any yard. They are stocked with handsome and delicious food, showcased in carefully designed gardens with beds, paths, fences, arbors, and more. Recipes accompany each garden so you'll never be at a loss for what to make next. The only challenge will be to decide which wonderful garden to try first. Will it be a Casual Country Garden or a Freeform, Better Vegetable Garden? Or would you rather take a stroll back in time through an American Heirloom Garden or a Victorian Courtyard Garden? Travel to another part of the world with a formal Italian Villa Garden or a Mexican Sun Garden. You may decide to follow these garden designs and plant lists exactly or to experiment with other spaces and plant varieties. When you have thoroughly enjoyed one, try another, and another, and another … .

Heirloom tomatoes such as 'Brandywine', 'Marmande', and 'Green Grape' are grown for their exceptional flavor.

how to use THIS BOOK

Culinary Gardens is a book to enrich all seasons. On a cold winter day, use it for inspiration, planning, and organizing an exciting new garden. When spring arrives, it will help you get your garden in place and your new plants off to a healthy start. On a sunny summer day, it will help you harvest baskets full of food and provide great ideas for using all the bounty. In late summer, it will help you schedule late plantings for those precious autumn and early winter harvests.

Consult Basics—The Heart of the Matter (Chapter 1) to learn how to develop your garden so it grows rich and lush. Fashioning Your Garden (Chapter 2) lets you identify the right garden style for your property.

Eleven great gardens follow, including detailed plans, plant lists, instructions, and recipes. Contemporary Gardens features the best of what modern garden technology has to offer. An expansive Casual Country Garden (Chapter 3), tailored after my own, can provide enough produce to feed a family of four. For the newest in high-tech vegetables, there's a Freeform, Better Vegetable Garden (Chapter 4). People with small yards and gourmet tastes should check out the Small Garden of Baby Vegetables (Chapter 5). Gourmet gardens can also be grown on patios or balconies, like the Creative Container Garden (Chapter 6).

Gardens of History takes a step back into the richness of culinary history. Set up an American Heirloom Garden (Chapter 7) filled with food enjoyed by American colonists. Venture even further back in time with an Elizabethan Knot Garden (Chapter 8), interwoven with old-fashioned herbs and produce. Another alternative is a Victorian Courtyard Garden (Chapter 9), boasting flamboyant edible flowers patterned after L'Auberge Provençale, an award-winning bed-and-breakfast in Virginia.

Gardens Around the World provides even more culinary adventures. A formal Italian Villa Garden (Chapter 10) is full of tomatoes, eggplant, and aromatic herbs planted according to classic Roman traditions. A Cook's Garden of Fine French Favorites (Chapter 11) combines French thyme, tarragon, leeks, and more in a romantic formal garden. The Geometric Garden from Great Britain (Chapter 12) blends English favorites in a beautiful garden inspired by Montague Inn, a bed-and-breakfast in Saginaw, Michigan. The spiciest garden, a Mexican Sun Garden (Chapter 13), blends chili peppers and tasty Mexican specialties in a small but intensive garden.

For design and growing specifics—colors, textures, spacing, timing, tending, and other tips—consult Appendix A: Encyclopedia of Crops, a comprehensive growers' guide.

Multicolored 'Sweet Pickle' peppers blend handsomely with annuals such as scarlet sage and will brighten any salad.

Gardening Background

Any garden can be great when you know how to coax vegetables, herbs, and fruits to grow lush and sweet. Basics—The Heart of the Matter supplies you with the background necessary to develop a prolific green thumb.

Design considerations also merit advance consideration. Learn what garden size, style, structure, and decorations will look best in your yard by reading Fashioning Your Garden.

The National Arboretum's children's gardens in Washington, D.C., grow bountiful produce for city-bound youngsters.

1
βASICS—THE HEART OF THE MATTER

Children may enjoy tending to their own pet tomato plants.

When starting a new garden, as when decorating a room or buying a new house, a little advance planning goes a long way. This chapter will help you with this important first step—planning a garden that will grow great plants. Plants need certain basic elements to grow—sun, moisture, and a fertile soil. You need to find out which of the three elements are readily available in your yard and which ones need to be added before planting can begin. The more attention paid to finding a sunny location and preparing rich, fertile soil, the better harvests will be in the coming weeks, months, and years.

A good way to start is by opening your mind to the many possible sites your yard contains. Don't assume you should place the garden in the middle of your backyard. Let your imagination wander and consider a variety of other alternatives. A garden can look great set in a curving bed near the perimeter of your property, which leaves the middle of the yard open for ball games or croquet. If your backyard is crowded with shade trees, consider whether a handsomely designed garden might be more appropriately situated in a bright front courtyard. Browsing through the designs in following chapters will help you visualize new possibilities.

Remember any site you choose must have plenty of sun, moisture, and good soil—essential elements that high-performance vegetables, fruits, and herbs need. Read through the discussion of these important basics, then consider how various places in your yard would work for a garden. When you've tallied up availability of sun and moisture with suitability of soil, the growing potential of each area will suddenly become quite clear.

SUN

Most high-performance culinary gardens need to be bathed in full sun, which translates to at least six hours of sun a day. Plants transform the rays of the sun into energy—fuel to power photosynthesis which then turns carbon dioxide and water into sugars—creating food. Culinary crops need photosynthesized food to grow and survive—a top priority. Then, any extra food they produce goes into making sweet tomatoes, plump potatoes, and fragrant edible flowers which are important for a good harvest. You can grow a few vegetables—primarily salad crops such as lettuce and spinach (unburdened by fruits and flowers) with less than full sun—but why limit the garden? Sunshine is free and natural; there is no need to skimp. If you're going to have a great culinary garden—one to brag about—give it the ultimate fuel, full sun.

The best way to identify how much sun a garden site receives is the old-fashioned way: count the number of hours the sun shines directly on it. When spending a day at home, check the site regularly and note when the sun reaches it in the morning and when it leaves in the afternoon or evening. The best season for observing sun exposure is in spring or fall, when the sun is low, shadows are long, and days are short. If you count more than six full hours of sun under these conditions, you can be confident the garden will have plenty of sun throughout the long days of summer. But if you count six hours of sun in mid-June, when days are longest, don't be surprised if the garden comes up a little short of sunlight in April or September.

A garden set in the middle of an open space, untouched by shadows, will have full sun; it's not necessary to count the hours. But a garden located near trees, buildings, fences, or hedges is likely to be shaded part of the day. The timing of the sun exposure, which varies according to the direction the garden faces, can influence how plants grow.

Garden sites that face south will be exposed to sun through-out the day. They will be great performers during cool growing seasons, but in the heat of summer it may take extra water and mulch to keep the soil moist and its temperature moderate.

Sites on the east side of a house, wall, or hedge will have plenty of mild morning sun, plus some shade during the heat of the afternoon. This is great for plants that thrive in cool weather; they can continue to be productive into summer. It also works well for tomatoes, sweet peppers, cucumbers, and beans grown in midsummer in hot climates.

West-facing sites will have warm afternoon sun which encourages quick growth from spring crops and allows fall crops to continue to mature even in cool weather. But it also hastens the summertime decline of lettuces, radishes, arugula, and other crops that prefer cool temperatures.

Sites that face north, for example, those situated on the north side of a two-story house, may be shaded much of the time and therefore unsuitable for a gourmet garden.

In south- or west-facing gardens, chives, sorrel, and other early-emerging perennials get off to a good start.

This sunken garden at Dunbarton Oaks will reap the benefits of maximum sun exposure if it faces south.

3

If the first site you consider does not have ideal sun, look around for a brighter location, perhaps on the south side of your house, beyond the reach of the shade trees, or beside the patio. Alternatively, you could prune or remove trees or shrubs to allow more light to filter down to a garden. Have an arborist remove the lower limbs from nearby shade trees so the sun can shine in below. Cut out any tangled shrubs or wild growth that no longer serves a purpose in your yard, and you may uncover an ideal spot for a culinary garden. Replace a tall fence with a short wall that the sun can shine over the top of to the garden beyond. Prune back a tall, overgrown hedge for similar benefits.

SOIL

Soil is more than a dark mass of dirt that lies below the lawn. It holds nutrients and moisture for all plants and, like the floor under our feet, it supplies support. In its dark recesses roots are always growing, reaching between particles in the soil and drinking in oxygen and moisture. The need of roots for both air and moisture is one reason gardeners must prepare the soil carefully. Both elements must squeeze into open pores between mineral particles and organic matter such as compost and other plant and animal remains. An ideal soil stays moist but not soggy, with water and air sharing pore spaces. But the distribution of both elements is not always equal, and this can create problems. A soil saturated with water lacks air; rotting often results. A soil full of air lacks water and leads to wilting.

SOIL COMPOSITION

The composition of the soil in your yard will determine the size of pore spaces and availability of moisture and air. Soils are made up of different-sized mineral components, broken down roughly by size into sand (coarse particles easily seen with the naked eye), silt (particles about the size of white flour), and clay (microscopic-sized particles). Clay soils, made up of tightly fitted clay particles and tiny pore spaces

between them, are likely to hold more water than air. Sandy soils have large pore spaces that allow moisture to drain out freely, leaving mostly air.

Most soils are called loams, a blend of these different-sized particles. Loams high in sand are lean, with limited moisture and nutrients. Sandy loams are ideal for many herbs and root crops such as carrots and parsnips. A good way to improve sandy soil is to add compost, decayed livestock manure, or rotten leaves, applying a 4-inch layer the first year and at least 1 to 2 inches every subsequent year. This makes sandy soils suitable for growing most gourmet crops.

Loams that are higher in silt or clay tend to be moister and more fertile than sandy loams. They can be great for fruiting crops and leafy greens. These soils, however, can form hard surface crusts that few seedlings can tolerate, and clay can be low on oxygen. These problems can be corrected by adding extra organic matter, similar to sandy soil. It's best to avoid walking on or working in these soils when wet, which can cause them to compress

JUDGING SOIL

Look closely and feel your soil to judge its qualities.

Clay soil: forms bricklike clods when dry; when moist, it has a slick, plastic feel when rubbed between finger and thumb; it will mold into a ribbon, like modeling clay.

Silt blends: dry clods can be broken up in your hand; if squeezed when moist, a small ribbon may be formed; a few scratchy sand grains may be visible.

Sandy blends: scratchy sand grains are easy to feel and see—dry clods don't form, wet clods barely cling together, no ribbon forms.

Sand: like at the beach, sand is visible, loose, shifting, and won't cling when dry.

into bricklike masses, better for building houses than growing plants.

More details on your soil conditions are easy to obtain through a professional soil test. For details contact the nearest Cooperative Extension Service, which is usually listed in the phone book under federal or county offices.

SOIL DRAINAGE

Water must be able to move freely through the garden soil—a condition called good drainage. It allows a soil to be well aerated and brings extra perks as well. Well-drained soil warms up and dries out quickly in spring, allowing for early planting. It is essential for winter gardening—a fun alternative in warm climates. Well-drained soil also harbors beneficial soil microorganisms—root-extending fungi, nutrient-releasing bacteria, tunneling earthworms, and other beneficials that encourage productive growth.

Just how quickly water needs to drain through the soil depends somewhat on which plants you grow. A lily bulb will only stand submersion in soggy soil for an hour or two before it begins to rot. Likewise, many culinary herbs—sage, rosemary, and thyme—are particularly sensitive to wet soils and require sharp drainage if they are to survive wet winter or spring weather. Alternatively, daylilies (which have edible flowers and buds) will tolerate a clay soil in which water moves more slowly. Poor drainage is difficult—if not impossible—to correct once the garden is planted, so put it on the top of the list of basics for consideration before any planting begins.

Give your soil a percolation test to determine how quickly moisture moves through soil pores. When the soil is dry, dig a hole 1 foot deep and 2 feet wide in your future garden site. Fill it with water and let the water drain out. Time its disappearance to make assumptions about your soil.

In a well-drained soil, the water should disappear within an hour.

If it drains in less than 10 minutes, the soil is likely to be too dry for most crops and will need 4 to 6 inches of organic matter worked in to slow moisture loss.

In soil with moderate drainage—suitable for many moisture-loving vegetables—the hole should be empty within six hours.

If the water is still there after six hours, the area is poorly drained and will require some attention.

The soil in my garden originally failed the drainage test—water in the percolation hole didn't budge.

Cucumbers benefit from a raised bed.

The problem is widespread. In some cases, good topsoil near the house has been removed by construction crews, leaving only subsoil clay

Zucchini and melons, which are related and require rich moist soil, can be grown together and rotated to a new site as a team.

CREATING COMPOST

Compost—the great equalizer—is an almost magical ingredient that makes any soil good for gardening. Compost is the decayed remains of leaves, twigs, salad scraps, grass clippings, cow manure, and other stable and garden leftovers. What the concept lacks in romance, it makes up for in good results. These recycled remains provide a broad spectrum of nutrients for nourishing growth. Coarse fibers—the slow-decaying veins of oak leaves or tough corn stalks, for example—help to break up tight soils. Humic acids released during decay modify the soil by clumping small particles into larger crumbs that make the soil work more efficiently. Sheaths of moisture that cling to compost help keep dry soils moister.

It's difficult to go wrong with compost—add as much as you can. (The one exception is compost rich in animal manure which is best limited to an inch or two a year to avoid overfertilizing plants.) To maintain a healthy soil, add at least an inch layer of compost each year (more in warm climates where decay progresses more quickly), working it in before planting or layering it over the bed as mulch. With sandy or clay soils that need an attitude adjustment, even more compost is beneficial. The only problem with compost may be getting enough for your needs. Here are some ideas.

1. Collect fall leaves—your own, your neighbors. Shred them and work them into your garden in the fall. They will be mostly decayed by spring.

2. Pile up all your extra organic vegetable matter— including corncobs and husks, cabbage leaves, coffee grounds, guinea pig bedding, and also seed-free weeds—in an unobtrusive corner of the yard. Once the pile reaches about 3 feet high, let it sit for a year before adding it to your garden.

3. Look around for local stables that may have old manure piles just waiting to be hauled away. If you ask nicely, they may even deliver them to your garden.

4. Find a cattle farm and harvest their stable leftovers. Unlike horse manure, cows digest their food twice so it seldom contains weed seeds. You can put it straight into your garden in the fall and be ready to plant in the spring.

5. Find out where your city stores the leaves they collect in the fall. Many communities compost them for municipal plantings or free residential giveaways.

6. Invest in a fast composting program. Buy a compost-making bin or barrel in which you can spin old leaves and grass clippings to promote extra rapid decay. In a couple of weeks or months, you'll have a fresh batch of compost.

7. Look in the yellow pages of your telephone book for bulk soil dealers that sell truckloads of compost. One big load every couple years should have you sitting pretty.

below. Adding a 6-inch-deep layer of good topsoil can remedy that.

In my region, the predominant soil is pure, stiff, gray clay—great for molding into pots but not so hot for growing a great garden, unless modified. I chose to garden in timber-supported beds, raised 6 inches high so plants can grow up above the sticky clay. I lightened the garden soil with 2-inch layers of coarse sand and 4-inch layers of leaf compost, available in bulk from my city recycling department. After this, the clay begins to look and act like soil, with porous openings for air and moisture to move through and support healthy roots.

Other areas, even ordinarily well-drained sandy soils, may have hard, underground layers that prevent water from draining out. This is especially common in a site that trucks, tractors, or heavy equipment has passed over repeatedly. Dig deeply with a spade or garden fork to break up this layer allowing water to move freely again.

Low areas of a yard also may be prone to poor drainage simply because rainwater, snowmelt, and runaway irrigation water will collect there. During extended rainy spells, this could spell problems for garden plants. One answer is to install underground drainage pipes or dig a little drainage ditch to carry the excess moisture away. Or add a big load of extra soil—build it up into a raised bed if you wish—to turn a low area into a high area that won't become saturated.

SOIL ROTATION

In many of the gourmet gardens in this book, crops that are related or have similar soil needs are grown together in the same bed. For example, pumpkins, zucchini, squash, melons, and cucumbers all need a rich, moist soil with plenty of nutrients, while carrots and radishes grow better in a lean soil of moderate fertility. One way to provide for both requirements is to develop a rotation system. Apply abundant compost and fertilizer, if necessary, to the cucumber bed before planting. When the cucumber crop is through, the compost

has decayed, and many nutrients have been consumed, use the same bed to plant carrots. Then add compost and fertilizer to the bed used for carrots to make it ready for greedier crops. Altering demands on the soil is a great way to keep it healthy.

OTHER SITE-EFFECTING FACTORS

Just like sun and soil, air surrounds your plants and can move in ways that hinder or help your garden. A preferred garden site won't be swept by strong wind, which can flatten, whip, or otherwise damage plants, and pull moisture from them like a magnet, which amplifies water shortages on hot and dry days. But the garden should have free air circulation—don't enclose it within four solid walls—to reduce problems of plant diseases.

The elevation in relation to the rest of the yard is also important. Low sites can get swamped during rainy weather. They are also the first place to be hit by frost in fall and the last to feel frosts bite in spring, even while the frost misses a nearby garden just 3 feet higher on a slope. Avoiding these low-frost pockets is particularly important if you grow early-flowering fruit trees and bushes or like to sneak heat-loving crops in extra early.

Garden siting can influence how warm or cool the garden stays. If you live in a cool climate but want to grow plants such as chili peppers that love heat, situate your garden accordingly. Put it beside a south-facing wall, which will absorb the sun's heat and release it to nearby areas of the garden. If you want to keep a garden in a hot climate slightly cooler, place it in light afternoon shade, which will cut the worst of the sun's heat.

PROPAGATION

When you've finally found the right site and decided which garden plan to try first, you'll want to gather together all the plants you need for a delicious culinary garden. Some you may be able to find at local greenhouses.

If not, check with specialty growers who are more likely to carry gourmet cultivars. If you ask them early enough in the season, they may agree to grow your favorite cultivar especially for you. To find these nurseries, ask at a local botanical garden, farm market, garden club, or Cooperative Extension Service.

But to save money or expand your selection, you may opt to start some of your own plants from seed, cuttings, or divisions. Here's how.

Direct Sowing: Planting seed directly out in the garden as indicated on the seed packet is especially easy and particularly effective for the crops (see "How to Start Favorite Crops"), which start fast and prefer to avoid root disturbance.

1. Work the soil well into a fine texture that seeds enjoy.

2. Plan to sow seeds when the weather is warm enough for them to germinate readily. For example, carrots, which thrive in cool weather, won't sprout if the soil is cooler than 45°F, and even then will sprout slowly. They germinate most quickly in warmer soil, about 75°F, which you might experience if you planted the seeds in summer for a fall harvest. Corn, a warm-season crop, won't sprout well if the soil is less than 60°F, but practically jumps out of its seed shell at 80°F.

3. Create furrows, wide beds, or shaped plantings as indicated on the garden plan.

4. Follow ideal planting depth and spacing guidelines indicated on seed packets. (Spacing is also included in Appendix A: Encyclopedia of Crops.) If set too deep, seeds won't reach the surface; if too shallow, the soil may dry out and they won't sprout. If set too close, they'll emerge in a dense thicket that discourages good growth; if too sparse, your yields will diminish.

5. Label the planting site using a water- and weatherproof marker on plastic tags or soft zinc tags on aluminum legs that indent as you write the plant name.

HOW TO START FAVORITE CROPS

Grow gourmet crops from seeds if you want to choose from a huge selection of excellent crops available from seed catalogs. Quick growers for direct seeding are good for beginning gardeners who can work up to slower starting seeds as they gain experience. But some special cultivars—for example, mints, variegated thymes, and fruit bushes—won't grow from seeds. They must be cloned from cuttings or divisions taken from a parent plant. For many perennial plants, cuttings or divisions work much faster than seeds, making this option even more desirable. Dwarf fruit trees are propagated by grafting—a complicated process best left to the nurseryman.

DIRECT SEEDING

Suitable as Cool-Season Crops: peas, carrots, beets, lettuce, arugula, cilantro, spinach, mustard, broccoli, chives, scallions, parsnips, radishes, turnips, and chicory.

Suitable as Warm-Season Crops: beans, sunflowers, squash, cucumbers, pumpkins, melons, basil, dill, fennel, and nasturtiums.

Prestarting Seedlings: Suitable for tomatoes, eggplant, peppers, broccoli, cabbage, cauliflower, cucumbers, squash, melons, basil, anise hyssop, nasturtiums, parsley, and sage.

Stem Cuttings: scented geraniums, basil, lavender, rosemary, bee balm, catnip, marjoram, mint, oregano, winter savory, tarragon, and thyme.

Division: rhubarb, asparagus, thyme, marjoram, oregano, bee balm, mint, and Jerusalem artichokes.

6. Keep the soil moist, even after the seedlings sprout. Most seedlings take at least a few weeks to develop deep roots that can sustain them when the surface of the soil dries out.

Starting Seedlings Indoors: Some seeds germinate so slowly or erratically outdoors that it's better to start them inside, or buy them at a greenhouse. To experiment with indoor seed starting, buy a sterile, peat-based potting mix and find a warm and bright spot—ideally a south-facing window—in your house. It's easiest to start with trays containing individual pockets for each plant and to use a fluorescent grow light that you can put down snugly near the seedlings.

Begin with plants that need just a short period (three to four weeks) indoors such as melons, cucumbers, squash, basil, and sunflowers. Then, if you find the nursery area has

Broccoli seedlings benefit from a head start indoors.

enough light to keep the seedlings stocky and thriving, move up to crops that require longer periods indoors. These include tomatoes, peppers, and eggplant which are best with an eight-week head start, and even onions that don't mind a whopping twelve-week head start. Here's how to start seeds indoors.

Jerusalem artichokes grow from edible tubers that arise on plant roots.

1. Fill sterile, plastic six-pack trays with moist, peat-based, seed-starting mix (not real topsoil). If you are recycling old trays from last year, wash them out well in soapy water then dip in a 10 percent bleach solution (1 part bleach in 9 parts water). Rinse and use.

2. Set one or two seeds in each opening, sinking them to the recommended depth.

3. Cover the tray with clear plastic wrap and leave in a warm location.

4. Check daily for the first sprouts to appear, then move immediately to a brightly lit spot.

5. Keep the mix moist—not wet or dry. It helps to keep the tray covered with clear plastic as long as possible, at least until the seedlings push up against it and beg to be set free. After that, check daily to see if the soil needs more water.

6. A week before the outdoor transplanting date, begin to set the seedlings outside for a short time in a little shade. Gradually work up to all day in full sun. This is called hardening off and, like kids in college, gets the seedlings ready to go off on their own in the big garden outside. If the plants wilt or yellow with

sunburn, return the seedlings to shade until they perk up, then begin again.

Cuttings and Division: Plants such as fruit bushes and trees, special flavored herb cultivars, Jerusalem artichokes, raspberries, blackberries, potatoes, rhubarb, and asparagus don't grow well from seeds or grow more easily from cuttings or divisions. It's best, initially, to get these from the nursery or from a plant in a friend's garden. You can propagate more from your first plant as follows.

Chives are easily propagated by division.

Divide healthy plants that have multiple stems arising from a well-rooted cluster; bee balm, for example, is an ideal candidate. The ideal time is spring or late summer in cold climates, or fall in mild climates. Use a shovel to slice off a wedge of an existing plant or unearth the entire plant and divide it into several pieces, each of which has its own roots. Replant immediately, either in the garden or in a pot. Keep the soil moist for several weeks until the plant begins to grow vigorously again.

Another way to clone plants is to take cuttings, which works well with many herbs (see "How to Start Favorite Crops" on page 8).

Cut off new shoots—the tender ones of early summer—for thyme, sage, and tarragon; cut firmer shoots of late summer for scented geraniums and basil. If the first cuttings don't root right away, experiment by taking different length cuttings at different times—the firmness and size can make a difference. Here's the easy process.

1. Prepare sterile plastic cell packs, as for seed sowing, or larger plastic foam cups with a hole punched in the bottom for drainage. Fill them with moist, sterile, peat-based mix. Or for herbs such as rosemary, lavender, and sage that prefer a drier soil, fill the containers with perlite. Set the containers aside momentarily while making the cuttings.

2. Remove a healthy shoot (without flowers or fruit) that is 3 to 4 inches long, or includes at least four sets of leaves.

3. Pinch off the lower two or three sets of leaves, using care not to damage the stem.

4. You could treat the cutting with rooting hormones, which may encourage root formation but are not always essential to success. They are available at some garden centers or through mail-order garden supply catalogs. Dip the bottom of the cutting in a small heap of powdered hormone and tap any extra powder off by flicking the stem gently with your finger.

5. Use a pencil or your finger to make a hole in the rooting mix and slip in the bottom of the cutting. Firm the mix around the cutting.

6. Set the cuttings in bright, indirect light. If they begin to wilt, cover with clear plastic wrap and make sure the rooting mix stays moist, but not wet.

7. Within several weeks, when the cuttings stop wilting and begin to grow, roots are probably forming. You'll know for sure when they begin to peek out of the drainage holes in the bottom of the pot. Once well rooted, transplant the cutting into a larger pot or harden it off like a seedling and plant it in the garden.

COMPLETE SHOPPING LIST

As the season progresses, you'll need a few supplies to keep your garden thriving. Here's a shopping list of what to keep on hand.

Fertilizers: Compost added to improve the soil also doubles as a gentle fertilizer. But sometimes newly planted seedlings or heavy-feeding crops need even more nutrients. Try a water-soluble fertilizer with extra nitrogen (look for nutrient ratios on the label that have slightly higher first numbers such as 10-5-5, 8-2-2, or 4-1-1, for example), to get transplants off to a fast start. Mix the fertilizer in water according to the label directions, then use it to soak around the planting hole, adding a little more to the foliage for quick absorption.

When crops flower or prepare to resprout after a first harvest, they may do well with a sprinkle of balanced, granular fertilizer (a product with similar levels of nutrients such as 4-4-4, 8-8-8, or 10-10-10). Apply the fertilizer at least one foot away from the plant (a technique called side-dressing), which encourages roots to grow outward and provide a broader base. Use a hoe to work the fertilizer granules lightly into the soil so they can dissolve down into the earth rather than splashing up on the plant or running off in heavy rainfall.

Organic fertilizers, which are made from natural products, generally are released gradually providing a more natural approach to fertilizing than quick-acting synthetics. Organic fertilizers usually have a lower percentage of nutrients than synthetics but may contain a wider variety of minor elements which can be beneficial. Synthetic fertilizers can pack a powerfully high percentage of nutrients—as much as 30 percent of an element. Stick with those listing under 10 or at the most 12 percent on the nutrient label and use these with care to avoid burning roots or encouraging excessive growth.

Support: Some crops will need supports to climb toward the sun and save space that would be consumed if allowed to sprawl at random in the garden. Here are some options.

Stakes: Use wooden stakes to hold up tomatoes. Start with 6-foot-high stakes, if you have full-size tomatoes. Pinch the tomato plant back to a single stem and secure gently, with strips of nylon stocking or floral tape, to the stake as it grows. A staked tomato will produce earlier and larger tomatoes but fewer of them.

Cages: Tomatoes can also be caged in wire mesh or wood with twine supports they can lean on.

Trellises: You can grow vining crops such as pole beans, peas, cucumbers, melons, and raspberries or blackberries on trellises. For vigorously climbing legumes such as pole, lima, or runner beans, you can set up individual teepees for then to twine up. Set poles 1 or 2 feet apart in a circle and tie them together at the top. Plant the beans or peas around the base of each pole, and they'll do the rest.

top: Staked tomatoes can form a tall row in the garden. bottom: Extra tall tomatoes can be tied to an arbor as in Longwood Gardens.

‹Compact
tomatoes fit well
inside a
cylindrical wire
cage.

Be creative when
configuring
trellises to add an
element of art to
the garden.(right
and bottom right)

Make teepees of sticks or poles, creating a vertical feature in the garden.

FAMILIES THAT SHARE PESTS

The members of the cabbage family, which includes cabbage, broccoli, broccoli raab, cauliflower, and kohlrabi, may be troubled by similar problems. Finding a solution to them now will help you in every case.

Cabbage worms—Which is Which? Two caterpillars commonly attack cabbage, broccoli, cauliflower, and related plants. One is the imported cabbage worm, common in Canada and the northeast United States. It's velvety green and is produced by a white and yellow butterfly. The first butterflies of the season emerge in May and new generations are produced all through the summer. The second is the cabbage looper—light green with lighter racing stripes on each side of its body. An American native, it winters in the warm southern states and migrates north in midsummer. The caterpillars emerge from eggs laid by a brown moth.

Both can be controlled by covering plants with floating row covers, which prevent female moths from laying eggs on the plants, or by spraying with Bt, a bacterial disease of caterpillars that kills existing caterpillars.

Clubroot Club: Members of the cabbage family also share a common predisposition for certain diseases. Among them is clubroot, a soilborne fungus that attacks young roots and causes them to swell until they can no longer function. Upon pulling up a sluggishly performing plant, you might find a huge, hard, bulbous root, a symptom of clubroot. Should this occur, avoid planting susceptible plants in that area again—the fungus can lie dormant as long as 10 years waiting for a suitable host.

Most Susceptible: cabbage, Chinese cabbage, brussels sprouts, some turnips, and some candytuft species.

Medium Susceptible: kohlrabi, kale, cauliflower, collards, broccoli, rutabaga, sea kale, some turnips and radishes, and some candytuft.

Mildly Susceptible: rape, black mustard, some turnips and radishes.

Very Resistant: wintercress, horseradish, wallflowers, peppergrass, garden cress, stock, and some radishes.

Labels: To keep track of all the plants so you know which ones to harvest for any particular recipe, (or so you can send someone else out into the garden to gather anything you need for dinner), use labels. By far, the most common labels are plastic tags you can push into the soil beside each plant or row of plants. Unfortunately, even so-called permanent inks will wash off of these tags in a matter of months, usually before you are ready to harvest that crop.

For more reliable results in the long run, spend a little more money and get metal tags that rest on long legs you can stab into the ground. Write on them with a ball point pen or hard lead pencil (which also will wash off but leaves the name indented in the soft zinc).

Mulch: In nature, soil is seldom found lying brown and exposed, open to the elements. In a woodland, for example, it is protected by a carpet of fallen leaves. This protects it from erosion, abrupt temperature changes, and from drying out quickly. Gardeners can offer the same protection to their gardens by applying mulch. In the garden, mulch has another important role—it limits the germination of weed seeds.

Organic mulch, such as compost, weed-free straw, and shredded leaves, breaks down adding organic matter to the soil. Applying an inch or more a year will help maintain a healthy soil. Another alternative is inorganic mulch, such as black or green plastic. Although plastics won't improve the soil, they can warm the soil more quickly in spring and eliminate problems with weeds.

Use mulch only on well-drained soil. Apply just enough to cover and shade the soil completely. Finer textured mulches such as grass clippings or shredded leaves should be put on thinly so they won't pack and smother the soil. Fluffy mulches such as hay can be applied more thickly.

IRRIGATION

Every gardener, at some time or another, will need to water the garden. A drought could strike or new seedlings could need extra moisture to get started. Be prepared to irrigate, having the equipment necessary to keep the soil moist so plants can grow steadily.

Irrigation lines moisten the soil near crops, not the rest of the surroundings.

Water often and lightly around young plants until they begin to grow vigorously and develop a root system large enough to be self-supporting. Once new plants are well established, you can leave the irrigation system on longer to drench the soil and encourage deep root growth. Occasionally, close to harvest time, crops such as potatoes and onions, berries, and melons are best left without irrigation (as long as they don't wilt) to concentrate flavor and firm up flesh.

The best way to water is with drip or trickle irrigation, ground-hugging waterlines that deliver moisture directly to the soil and the roots below. Pick from permanent or semipermanent types, set up around perennials, or fruit trees and shrubs, or stretched along a garden bed. You can also substitute canvas or rubber soaker hoses, which are not as precise, but also deliver water directly to the ground, soaking it deeply if you leave the water running long enough. For more information on these irrigation systems, look under Irrigation in the telephone book's yellow pages or consult suppliers in the Index.

Overhead sprinklers can get the job done, but they are inefficient. Much of the water they spray up into the air evaporates, bounces down and compresses planting areas, and runs off, carrying away good soil. Still more falls on uncultivated areas—benefiting the weeds. Only a small amount actually reaches plant roots.

TROUBLESHOOTING

Just like people, plants are prone to attack by insects or diseases. To avoid this, keep your plants healthy by providing great soil, plenty of sun, and lots of fresh air—a useful prescription for anything that ails greenery. What makes this work even better is starting with a plant that has a robust disposition—a hearty grower that has been bred to resist common disease problems and to be unappetizing to pests. You'll learn more about these options in Appendix A: Encyclopedia of Crops.

You can help eradicate minor problems that may crop up from time to time with several easy techniques.

Clean up foliage hopelessly infested with pests such as aphids and fallen plant parts that are covered with disease, spots, blots, and rots. Toss these into the trash, not the compost pile, so they won't return to haunt you.

Thin out overgrown plants so they won't crowd themselves out and harbor diseases. This also allows wet foliage to dry quickly, preventing germination of moisture-loving disease spores.

Rotate crops, switching to unrelated plants from year to year so that pests and diseases won't build up and soil nutrients won't be depleted.

Use environmentally friendly, pest-control products, which can handle almost anything that comes up. Try insecticidal soap for aphids, whiteflies, spider mites, scale, leafhoppers, and others. Use Bt (*Bacillus thuringiensis,* a bacteria that kills pests within a day or two of consumption) for caterpillars, potato beetles, and elm leaf beetles. Try sticky yellow, blue, and white traps for plant bugs such as aphids, thrips, leaf miners, leafhoppers, and other pests. Try light oil sprays for in-season control of scale, mites, aphids, lace bugs, mealybugs, whiteflies, beetles, and other pests. Check out a new garlic repellent that prevents insects from landing. For more information on specific pest problems to watch for, see individual entries in Appendix A.

2
*f*ASHIONING YOUR GARDEN

Eleven gardens that you can pull out of this book and put into your yard are presented here. All have been designed to look great and provide a bountiful harvest. All that remains is for you to choose which one to use and where to put it. Consider the size and style of each garden to determine which suits you best. Then think about what you'd like to add on your own.

HOW TO USE GARDEN SIZE TO YOUR ADVANTAGE

The best way to begin is to analyze your present yard. In a large yard, it is appropriate to install a large culinary garden—a bountiful spread such as the Casual Country Garden. Large gardens are big and impressive, able to hold their own in an expansive yard; but remember, the larger the garden, the more time it requires to tend and harvest. To limit time demands, try a garden with paved walks and more moderate-sized planting beds such as the Italian Villa Garden. Another option is to put a smaller garden near the house that can serve as another room of the house, albeit an outdoor one. A good example of this is the Victorian Courtyard Garden.

In a small yard, a petite garden of containers or baby vegetables looks great alongside the lawn. Another option is to eliminate the lawn and use the entire yard for one of the larger gardens.

Grass walks, herbal edgings, and neat rows add structure to a gourmet garden, as at Mount Vernon.

FASHIONING YOUR GARDEN

How will your garden style affect your yard? A wide variety of garden styles are available throughout this book, most of which would look lovely in any location. Pick the one that appeals to your own sense of beauty and that grows the cuisine you love. Or choose the garden style that best complements your home design.

Formal gardens such as the Elizabethan Knot Garden, the Geometric Garden from Great Britain, and the Italian Villa Garden utilize symmetrical geometrical planting beds. They complement homes of formal architecture such as colonial, French provincial, and Georgian. Symmetrically

This formal garden utilizes symmetrical, matched beds and conveys an air of precision. (Twinsburg Ohio Library)

balanced, formal gardens would use the same plants in the same locations on both sides of the garden.

Semiformal gardens such as the Mexican Sun Garden and Victorian Courtyard Garden combine a strong sense of rhythm and structure with graceful, natural plantings. Use semiformal gardens for Cape Cod or ranch houses. Or try one such as the Casual Country Garden in a wild and rugged place where its formality is a bold reminder of human presence and order where nature rules. The contrast is dramatic.

Informal gardens such as the Better Vegetable Garden feature softly curving beds and sweeping clusters of plants. They look good with casual farmhouses, cottages, Tudor, or

A formal raised bed with attention paid to plant height is combined with rambling vines to render this garden semiformal. (Sea World of Ohio)

modern, contemporary houses. But you can also use them to soften a formal home and yard in a way that is both comfortable and appealing. In an informal bed, both sides of the garden would be equally powerful but might include a large cluster of bright-fruited plants on one side to balance out a taller fruit tree on the other.

FINDING THE RIGHT LOCATION

A culinary garden will be handiest if placed close to the house. You can step out and gather what you want in seconds. The garden also becomes easier to maintain simply because you're

A blend of different shapes, colors, and textures in a naturalistic planting plan makes this garden informal.

always walking by, spotting weeds when they sprout, and pulling them out. It's also easy to turn on the hose if the weather is dry or to toss a blanket over a tender plant if frost threatens.

Aesthetically, building a garden close to your house has another advantage. You can blend the garden into the structure of your home, transforming it into an outdoor room, an extension of your living space. Just like in your home, enclose the garden with symbolic walls—hedges, fences, or rows of sunflowers. Repeat construction material used elsewhere in the yard and home, perhaps a brick wall for a brick house or a white picket fence for a white colonial house. Likewise, create floors—walks, sitting areas, and garden paths—from the same material as your patio or front walk. These repetitions create a rhythm that draws the entire yard together into one big, beautiful picture.

But not everyone can nestle a culinary garden near their house. Maybe the existing landscaping is in the way or there isn't enough room to grow all the food needed. If this is the case, move the garden farther out in the yard. You could have a culinary garden softly outline the perimeter of the property, as in the Small Garden of Baby Vegetables. Or make it a freestanding island bed such as the Freeform, Better Vegetable Garden.

You may be tempted to plop the garden down in the middle of the yard—which is often the sunniest spot and

Add a bench at one end of a walk to serve as an attention-catching focal point and a pleasant place to rest or read.

thus a logical choice. But from a design perspective, this can look awkward. It breaks up the smooth sweep of lawn with an alien form that is tied neither to the house nor to the perimeter of the property. So if this is your only choice, make sure to blend the garden into the rest of the landscaping. One way to do this is to surround the garden with a fence, put a patio in the center, and build a walk out from the house so that the garden becomes an extension of your living space.

The structure of the culinary garden will play an important role in its beauty—perhaps more so than in any other kind of garden. This is because fruits, vegetables, and herbs come and go throughout the growing season. All have their moments of beauty, but soon after they may be harvested and gone. Because these plants are ephemeral, a solid garden structure keeps things interesting, year-round. At the same time, structure makes the space more useful and productive.

A handsome fence will elicit gasps of appreciation from visitors regardless of the season. It is beautiful in itself and it adds to the structure of the garden, while setting limits and giving a feeling of privacy. Meanwhile, it's also doing a job—it can keep out frisky neighborhood dogs or remind children where ball games must stop.

Garden paths—made of grass, mulch, stones, or brick—create a network of lines that are as much a part of the design as the plants. Softly curving lines add grace. Straight or angular lines appear civilized, even regal. Paths also provide a place to walk—regardless of the weather and without concern for stepping on important plants. Paved walks can double as edges that define the perimeter of the bed and the shape of the garden. If used between the lawn and garden, they'll keep grass from invading and provide another benefit—less weeding.

YOUR OWN FLOURISHES

If you like a particular design but need to change the size, location, or outline a little, by all means, do it! Add or subtract extra beds, keeping the integrity of the garden design. Use the organization of the plants—the planned edgings and the preexisting color combinations. Or expand or contract the size of the entire garden so it maintains the original form and balance. If broadening a bed, plan to add an access walk so you can reach the center easily. No matter how large the garden is, you'll still need to be able to walk

An entryway arbor is another nice touch that helps define the garden space and welcomes visitors to the garden. (Photo courtesy of Rodale Institute)

Leathery purple sage leaves contrast with orange nasturtium flowers.

through it without losing your balance or tripping over creeping vines. When making a garden smaller, don't skimp on garden width. Two to three feet wide should be the minimum to allow enough space to be productive. Main walkways should be at least 3 feet wide, but secondary paths can be cut to 2 feet wide or less. If you want to add one of your favorite crops, try substituting it for a plant of similar size and color.

Organize your changes on paper. Sketch the garden, make a few adaptations, and try to imagine how it would look in your yard. While planning, keep these principles of design in mind.

Form: The shape of the garden is one of its most powerful design elements—plan thoughtfully. If adding some curves to the form, make sure they are large, sweeping, and graceful—not small and squiggly. Within the bed itself, you

will also employ a more subtle show of form—the various shapes of the plants. These gardens are designed to display a pleasant variety of shapes, including upright, mounding, and spreading, with a rhythm and flair all their own.

Color: Green will be the most prominent color in your garden. Enjoy subtle variations of green—blue green of cabbage, emerald green of bush beans, yellow green of golden variegated sage. Add to that splashes of brighter colors—ripe red tomatoes and bee balm, orange pot marigolds and peppers, gold nasturtiums, and blue pansies. Other colors are contributed by walks, fences, sitting areas, and arbors—carefully coordinated with each other and the rest of the yard.

Texture: These gardens play artistically with leaf texture, blending big, broad, bold, coarse-textured leaves such as angelica with soft, delicate, finely textured leaves such as

The focal point of this garden is a colonial bee skep placed in the center. (Chicago Botanic Garden)

ferny carrots and dill. Some variety and repetition in texture adds to garden interest.

Focal Point: While crops are coming and going, you'll need an anchor of stability—something permanent that draws the eye every time you look out at the garden. It may be a statue, arbor, center point where two paths cross, or potted fruit tree. This lends to your garden drama.

Balance: These gardens are designed to be balanced. If you would draw an invisible line down the center, there would be as much interest on one side as there is on the other, preventing a lopsided look. Different sides of a garden can have matched plantings or different plantings, carefully juggled according to color, size, and texture.

Proportion: The size of the garden should appear to be in proportion to your yard. If you have a large yard, you'll need a larger garden to look substantial. In a small yard, a smaller garden may be necessary so it doesn't overwhelm the space. In a very small yard, however, very good results can come from replacing the lawn area entirely with one of these gardens.

Rhythm: This is what makes the garden come alive. The rhythm of repeating colors, textures, and forms as well as walkways and raised beds pulls the garden together into one beautiful picture. One easy way to create rhythm is to use the same low-growing plants to edge each bed. Another way is to repeat height sequences; putting taller plants toward the rear or center of the bed and shorter plants toward the front or around the edges.

These are the beginnings of a wonderful new garden experience. Plan ahead now to make one or more of these culinary gardens perfect for you. Remember that design planning doesn't end with garden installation. Continue to adapt the garden style as time goes by, occasionally returning to these design basics and giving your garden a thorough reevaluation.

This handsome garden has subtle rhythm created by the woodwork used to raise garden beds and the repeated blue of broccoli foliage. (San Antonio Botanical Garden)

Contemporary Gardens

There is no time like the present, especially when it comes to gardening. Gourmet gardens are springing up all over the city and country, making the most of innovative modern cultivars. A Casual Country Garden (Chapter 3) caters to those who want super fresh, organic food—enough for today and a surplus to freeze for tomorrow.

A Freeform, Better Vegetable Garden (Chapter 4) blends the best of modern plant breeding into a sweep-ing contemporary garden. A Small Garden of Baby Vegetables (Chapter 5) is ideal for people who relish tender miniatures and have only a small amount of space to devote to gourmet gardening.

Your patio or balcony will never be the same after reading Chapter 6, Creative Container Gardens. Without putting a single root into the ground, your gourmet garden will grow plump and flavorful in an assortment of pots.

Evaluations of cultivars and organic gardening methods are ongoing at the Rodale Institute Research Center in Kutztown, PA.

3
CASUAL COUNTRY GARDEN

On a farm, a vegetable garden is as natural as spring rain and the flowers that blossom in its wake. While lilacs and peonies bloom, succulent lettuce swells. During the warmth of summer, tomatoes ripen in the sweet summer sun and crisp snap beans delight inquisitive barefoot children. Fall brings pumpkins—giant kid-pleasers for carving and small tender pumpkins for pies. In winter, while crusty herb bread is baking in the oven, a glance out the kitchen window to the snow-shrouded garden ignites a thrill of anticipation for the new gardening season to come.

Owning a farmhouse is not a prerequisite for experiencing these pleasures. Anyone with acreage or a large, sunny yard can have a big garden and grow a wide assortment of delicious food. A big garden allows plenty of space for

A country garden has room to spread but also needs to have some boundaries.

Casual Country Garden Design

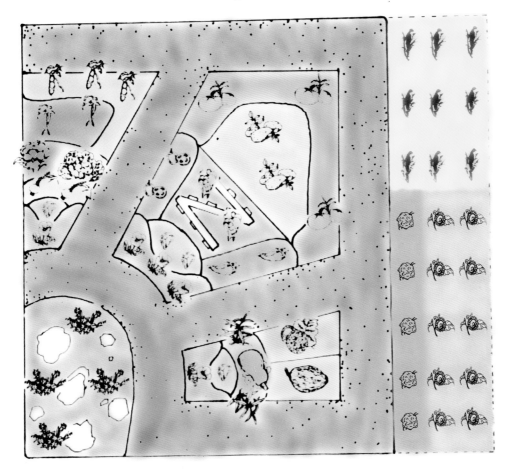

PLANT LIST

Left Bed

- Pansy
- Lettuce
- Onions
- Broccoli
- Cauliflower
- Snap beans
- Lima beans

Center Bed

- Sweet pepper
- Peas
- Potatoes
- Tomatoes

Bottom Bed

- Summer squash
- Savory
- Winter squash
- Muskmelon

Side Plot

- Jerusalem artichoke
- Corn
- Sunflowers

rambling vines and needs not rely on compact vegetable plants, bred for small spaces. Prolific, full-sized plants yield bountiful harvests—enough for everyday meals and plenty of surplus for freezing, canning, and drying.

Yards with woods, stables, and other resources are replete with their own garden-making resources. Saplings from a nearby woodlot provide ideal rustic fencing. Larger logs are used to raise the beds. Livestock manure and landscape leftovers can be turned into compost to enrich the soil or mulch the beds.

A GREAT GARDEN DESIGN

A big garden (28 by 32 feet) demands a strong design to make it stand out in a large yard. It will need walls, walks, and raised beds to create an impression as large as its size. The garden can be enclosed by a two-tier sapling fence for a rustic look appropriate to a country garden. The fence can double as a trellis for fragrant morning glories or pole beans. An entryway arbor, made of curved saplings, exudes magic

A two-tier sapling fence.

SAPLING FENCING

Part of the charm of this garden lies in its homemade version of a split-rail fence. It is composed of two horizontal tiers of 2-inch-diameter sapling trunks set between fence posts made of stouter 4-inch-diameter trunks. The fence reaches 4 feet high and stretches along the front edges of the raised bed. It allows full sun to shine through to the garden but clearly warns children and dogs that a protected area lies within.

Making this fence begins with visiting a woodlot and harvesting young trees with 2- to 4-inch-diameter trunks. This fence was made of sugar maple, which flourish abundantly in a beech maple forest, but any hardwood will do. Each tree harvested may be cut into one or two horizontal pieces and the broader trunk base can serve as one fence post.

Fence posts should be 6 feet long, set 2 feet deep in the ground, and 8 to 10 feet apart. Fence rails should be 8 to 10 feet long, plus a little extra to allow the rails to overlap slightly beside each fence post. Tan twine used for binding boy scout knots will hold the rails to the posts. Small 1-inch-diameter branches can be arched and tied to create entryway arbors. To keep out rabbits, enclose the garden entirely and tack wire mesh over the fence as well as sinking it 6 inches underground.

to welcome visitors to the garden as surely as a stone hearth fireplace beckons guests inside on a cold winter day.

A rock garden of low (edible or otherwise) flowers, herbs, or alpine strawberries forms a neat focal point in a front corner of the garden. With its handsome outcroppings of rocks and steady bloom of flowers, it creates a soothing diversion from the comings and goings of the harvestable feast in the beds beyond.

This Casual Country Garden encompasses symmetry and rhythm, created by flaring rectangular beds that radiate out from the front rock garden. Three-foot-wide gravel walkways divide beds raised with cedar ties, a naturally rot-resistant wood ideal for gourmet gardens. The walks allow garden access in any weather and prevent passersby from compacting growing areas. The entire layout incorporates the ideal conditions for plants and gardeners alike *and* looks great.

Pansies, petunias, dianthus, or other low-growing annuals edge the front corners of each bed and are repeated in the rock garden, lending rhythmic color to the garden as a whole. Lower-growing vegetables such as bush beans can edge the garden, sometimes filling several beds.

Most beds pair related plants—tomatoes with peppers and potatoes, for example—so they can easily be rotated the following year to a new bed. In some beds, vining squash and cucumbers flow over the edge and out on to the path to luxuriate in the bright sun and open spaces. Golden sunflowers, Jerusalem artichokes, and corn fill an optional rear bed, drawing deserved attention with their height and grandeur. The overall effect is one of lush bounty with distinct order—a pleasing combination.

YOUR COUNTRY FAVORITES

High-yielding plants of good character are the ideal residents of a Country Garden. The following cultivars can please crowds of hungry farmhands (or even hungry soccer players) and provide homegrown extras to freeze for winter.

BEANS, LIMA

Bland, store-bought limas cannot compare to the flavor of homegrown lima beans. Sweet and tender with an almost nutty flavor, they are well worth the time they take to grow. To enjoy fresh lima beans at their best, cook them very

Sunflowers for cutting are naturals for this garden.

lightly and use mild butter sauces, if any, to let the subtle flavor and firm texture shine through. Bush lima beans form neat, lime green mounds that serve as a handsome edging. Choose from large-seeded or baby limas but stick with early-producing cultivars in cool climate areas.

'Eastland': This baby lima bean, ready early in about 68 days, produces many pods of sweet, little seeds per plant.

BEANS, SNAP

A wide variety of productive beans are available that are well suited

'Provider' snap beans can edge raised beds.

FREEZING GARDEN FOOD

The freezer can be more than just a place for storing leftovers—it can capture food at its harvest-fresh best. Pick vegetables, fruits, and herbs at their stage of perfection, prepare them promptly, and tuck them into the freezer immediately to suspend them in ideal condition. Here's how.

Harvest vegetables, fruits, and herbs in the morning when they are cool, plump, and fresh. Take them immediately indoors and wash them well.

Herbs can be dried on a clean towel and frozen whole, packed in freezer bags. When ready to use, chop them up and drop into a dish. Herbs that will be used for soups or stews can be chopped in advance and frozen in water in an ice cube tray. When needed, pop out an ice cube and drop it into the soup tureen.

Vegetables need to be blanched, or lightly cooked, before freezing to prevent them from overripening and losing quality. Wash and pare off stems, then boil for the following blanching times.

Snap beans: 2 minutes

Lima beans (shelled): baby, 1 minute; large, 3 minutes

Broccoli, individual florets: 3 minutes

Carrots: small pieces, 2 minutes; large pieces, 3 minutes

Corn, on cob: small ears, 7 minutes; large ears, 11 minutes

Peas, shelled: 1-1/2 minutes

Spinach: 2 minutes

Tomatoes: no blanching required

Remove from boiling water as soon as the time has expired and chill in ice water. Dry well and pack into freezer bags.

Berries such as strawberries and raspberries can be frozen whole or sliced without blanching. You can also coat them with granular sugar before freezing, which helps preserve flavor and color. Apples and pears can be dipped in lemon or pineapple juice before freezing to prevent darkening.

for microwaving, steaming, boiling, or baking, and blending into salads, side dishes, casseroles, and stir-fries. If you like to can, look for cultivars that are firm and hold up well to processing. If you prefer to freeze beans, any good cultivar will do but stringless beans (which don't require snapping and peeling of tough strings) will make the project go much faster. Since you'll have plenty to play with, you can let your imagination be your guide.

This Country Garden calls for bush beans, which produce a concentrated harvest in a short period of time. In contrast, pole beans produce abundant yields over a longer period and can supply vegetables for dinner for a month or more. Pole beans can be added to this garden by planting them on the pea trellis or letting them climb up mesh tacked on the perimeter fence.

'Blue Lake 274': This is a wonderful bush bean that bears melt-in-your-mouth tender pods and high yields about 55 days after sowing.

'Provider': This bush bean starts off strong in late spring because it sprouts readily despite slightly cool soil. It's reliable and quick maturing (50 days from seed to harvest), so you can plant at least two crops each year in most parts of the country.

'Kentucky Blue': An award winner, this pole bean combines the big harvests of parent 'Kentucky Wonder' with the sweet, tender pods of 'Blue Lake', another parent. Harvests start about 58 days after sowing.

BROCCOLI

Mild, sweet broccoli grows best in the cool conditions of spring and fall, even winter in warm climates. It blends well into many casseroles, is great as a side dish, and freezes without fail. Harvest the full heads promptly and freeze any extras. After the first big harvest, plants can be fertilized and allowed to produce small side shoots for salads. Alternatively, they could be replaced with broccoli seeds or seedlings for a higher yielding fall crop.

'Green Comet Hybrid': According to All America Selections (a testing program for new flower and vegetable varieties), this cultivar is America's second favorite vegetable of all time. When you consider the thousands of vegetables people grow, this is a lofty claim. 'Green Comet Hybrid' earns its reputation by producing an early harvest of large heads, reliably about 55 days after planting seedlings.

'Saga': This plant is a good performer that really stands out when nature turns up the heat. When other cultivars struggle in summer, 'Saga' just keeps on growing. Harvest begins about 56 days after transplanting seedlings.

CAULIFLOWER

Creamy white heads of cauliflower are especially fun to watch as they swell from tiny flower buds to large curds. When plump and full, use cauliflower raw in salads of all kinds or steam it to eat dabbed with butter or smothered with mild sauces. Stick with easy-to-grow cultivars to ensure high yields. Early producers work best in areas with limited mild spring and fall weather.

'Milky Way': Large heads, reaching 8 inches wide, appear early, about 45 days from transplanting seedlings.

'Cashmere': This cultivar puts on a grand show about a week after 'Milky Way'. It has foliage that partly encloses the white heads helping to protect them from turning green in the sunlight.

Bicolor sweet corn includes 'Sugar Dots', which is both sweet and early.

CORN

In keeping with the theme of this garden, the cultivars recommended here are good, old-fashioned sweet corn varieties (instead of the sugar-enhanced types discussed in the Encyclopedia of Crops). These varieties of corn are at their best when eaten immediately after harvesting as they lose their sweetness quickly. If you have more than you can eat at one sitting, blanch (parboil quickly) and freeze the excess right away to preserve the great flavor.

'Silver Queen': This is the ideal against which all newcomers are judged. Long ears bear white kernels that are sweet and full of rich corn flavor. The plants are late bearing, producing 91 days after sowing, but that gives them plenty of time to stock great flavor into the ears.

'Early Sunglow': While you're waiting for 'Silver Queen', enjoy this early yellow corn, ready just 62 days after sowing.

JERUSALEM ARTICHOKES

Country gardeners blessed with abundant space can enjoy this unique vegetable. It's a hardy sunflower, with a tendency to spread enthusiastically, producing starchy, underground tubers that can be eaten like potatoes. You can shred them raw into coleslaw or lightly stir-fry them in sesame oil. Extra tubers will keep in the refrigerator for a month or more.

Fall is the ideal time to harvest Jerusalem artichoke tubers.

LETTUCE AND OTHER GREENS

In this Country Garden, leafy lettuce blends handsomely with bright flowers near the front of the garden. Grow leaf lettuce, head lettuce, spinach, or arugula, and in the summer try Swiss chard. Plant new seeds every couple weeks—a technique called "succession planting"—to have fresh leaves to harvest throughout the season.

MUSKMELONS

Let melon vines ramble, producing sweet melons as they go. Muskmelons with orange flesh and netted skin can be left to ripen until the stem slips off the vine and the melons are dripping and sweet. Use them right away or keep less-than-perfectly-ripe melons on the kitchen counter for several days. You can freeze extra melon pieces then puree them to add to tropical coolers.

'Ambrosia Hybrid': Here is a classic muskmelon—everything you ever imagined a melon would be. It takes 86 days from the time of planting to ripening, but that time is spent packing the melon with flavor. Another plus is that these vines resist attack from powdery mildew.

'Fastbreak Hybrid': This is an early muskmelon that produces flavorful, moderate-sized melons just 67 days from sowing—a real record breaker!

ONIONS

Aromatic onions are a must for most country gardens and are invaluable companions to meat, vegetables, soups, or used just by themselves. Be sure to start with onions appropriate for your part of the country. In northern areas, choose long-day onions that develop bulbs during long, northern summer days. Many of the long-day onions available from sets (miniature bulbs) are pungent and good for storing in mesh bags in a cool, dry, airy place during the winter. 'Sweet Sandwich' is unique for its ability to grow milder as it waits in storage.

For southern gardens, mild, succulent short-day onions grow in fall and winter. The most famous of these is 'Granex', the source of Vidalia onions. Mild southern onions are perfect for slicing on a sandwich or layering on a salad. Since they don't store long, you can peel, chop, and freeze the extras. (The flavor may change slightly with freezing, so sample and adjust quantities when adding frozen onions to a recipe.)

PEAS

Like lima beans, super fresh peas are exceptional especially when eaten fresh, straight from the pod in the garden. Peas are great solo, eaten with a mint-margarine sauce, or blended with lamb, beef, chicken, or potatoes. Plant peas in spring for summer harvest and in summer for fall harvest. Shell, blanch, and freeze any extras immediately to preserve their flavor.

'Maestro': This early pea, producing long, plump pods 57 days from sowing, is a reliable producer with vines up to 36 inches long. A trellis isn't essential for this cultivar. It will grow on branched twigs pushed into the ground 4 to 6 inches apart all along the row.

'Multistar': Given a total of 70 days from sowing, 'Multistar' provides more than twice the harvest of 'Maestro'. This is because a pair of pods sprouts on the vine everywhere a single pod would ordinarily grow. Because the vines can reach over 50 inches high, these peas will need a trellis.

POTATOES

Hearty country fare begins with great potatoes—which seem to have extra rich flavor when homegrown. You can choose from fluffy, white potatoes for baking, buttery, golden potatoes for potato salad, and even waxy, blue-fleshed potatoes to surprise your guests. Store extras in a cold corner of your basement.

'Desiree': This is a great red-skinned potato with creamy flesh and the potential to grow big enough to bake. Some smaller potatoes generally accompany the large ones and are wonderful for cooking whole, blending with peas, and drizzling with vinaigrette.

'Yukon Gold': This golden-fleshed potato packs so much flavor it needs little butter. The medium-sized, round potatoes have light brown skin and can be baked or boiled.

'Kennebec': What country garden would be complete without a big baking potato? This late-maturing spud gets

Flowering potato vines have a charm all their own.

'All Blue' potato is purple outside and blue inside.

so big that a single tuber stuffed with cheese and sausage can constitute an entire meal.

SUMMER SQUASH

The image of a bountiful garden is often linked to mounds of summer squash—the ultimate in a productive vegetable. Harvest young squash while they are firm and tender to use in salads, stir-fries, and side dishes. Shred and freeze any extras to drop into quick breads or toss into casseroles. Be sure to plant a number of different types for variety.

'Seneca Prolific': This is the classic, straight-necked, golden squash, ready for harvest 51 days from sowing.

'Sunburst': Here's an award-winning, golden-skinned hybrid (a specially bred high performer) that grows in a scalloped saucer shape. The harvest season begins 52 days after sowing seed.

'Burpee Hybrid Zucchini': This American-made zucchini bears slender green fruit, borne one after another 50 days after sowing.

SUNFLOWERS

There are two kinds of sunflowers—grow one or both in your country garden. Large-headed sunflowers, which produce one flower per stem, have nutritious seeds and attract beautiful birds from miles around. Multistemmed sunflowers bear sprays of smaller golden, yellow, russet, or cream-colored flowers, ideal for cutting and arranging in a big vase. The best cut flowers are pollen free and don't shed messy, golden pollen powder when cut.

'Mammoth Russian': This classic, grown on Russian farms, reaches 7 feet tall and has flowers up to 10 inches across. The top-quality seeds are striped gray and white.

'Sunspot': Huge, 10-inch-wide heads emerge on small plants just 2 feet tall.

'Lemon Queen': Clusters of pale yellow flowers with dark centers stand 5 to 7 feet high.

'Velvet Queen': These cutting sunflowers stand at least 6 feet tall and bloom in shades of dark burgundy, bronze, and mahogany.

TOMATOES

Big, beefy tomatoes on long vines are a classic element in country gardens. Let the fruit grow sweet and ripe before harvesting. If necessary, store on the kitchen counter for a day or two before using, but don't refrigerate. Tomatoes lose their flavor when chilled (although they freeze fine).

'Big Beef': This award winner produces huge beefsteak tomatoes earlier than other beefsteaks, just 73 days from transplanting the seedlings. It also boasts an extra dose of disease resistance, making it a winner even if the weather is uncooperative. Tomatoes weigh up to one pound each.

WINTER SQUASH

Large, sweet, hard-shelled squash are worth growing by the bushel basket. You can store them in your basement for months and enjoy them all winter. Butternut and hubbard squash are among the most flavorful and longest keeping.

'Waltham Butternut': Given 105 days from transplanting seedlings, this vine produces pear-shaped squash with wonderful flavor. They can reach five pounds each and have smooth, orange flesh.

'Blue Hubbard': Here's a monster that can feed all hands on deck. The blue-shelled squash, usually growing one per vine, can swell up to 20 pounds, bearing lightly sweet, yellow flesh. Plan on 100 days from transplanting seedlings to harvest.

THE RECIPES

These hearty recipes enhance the rich, natural flavor of garden-fresh vegetables and offer you plenty of ways to utilize your large harvests.

Salad

POTATO AND LIMA BEAN SALAD

4 small red-skinned potatoes, quartered

1 cup or 8-ounce package imitation crab chunks

1 cup fresh baby lima beans

1 jalapeno pepper, seeds removed and minced

1-1/2 tablespoons margarine, softened

1/4 teaspoon salt

1 tablespoon fresh basil, chopped

Boil potatoes about 10 minutes, until just tender. Cut cooked potatoes and crab chunks into bite-sized pieces. Boil baby lima beans 4 minutes, or until tender. Drain. Combine potatoes, crab, lima beans, basil, and jalapeno. Mix in margarine and salt, and stir gently until margarine melts.

YIELD: Serves 4

Soup

DILLED CHEESE AND POTATO SOUP

Recipe courtesy of Lori Zaim

This hearty soup is the perfect warm-up for a cold winter day.

2 tablespoons butter

2 tablespoons olive oil

2 cups onions, chopped

2 cups carrots, chopped

1 cup celery, chopped

5 sprigs of parsley

1 bay leaf

5 cups chicken broth

3 cups white potatoes, peeled and chopped

1-1/4 cups fresh dill, chopped

salt and pepper to taste

2-1/2 cups cheddar cheese, grated

Heat the butter and oil in a large soup kettle over moderately low heat. Cook the onions, carrots, and celery in the butter-oil mixture for about 25 minutes. Keep the kettle covered, stirring occasionally.

Add chicken broth, potatoes, parsley sprigs, and bay leaf. Bring to a boil then reduce heat to moderately low; cover and simmer the soup until the potatoes are tender, 25 to 30 minutes.

Stir in the chopped dill and remove from heat.

Remove the bay leaf and strain the soup into a heat-proof bowl. Place the vegetables in a food processor fitted with the metal blade. Add 1 cup of the cooking liquid and process until well blended and fairly smooth.

Return the processed vegetables to the soup kettle and slowly stir in the remaining broth. Warm over low heat. Taste and add salt and pepper as needed. When heated through, stir in the grated cheese. Serve immediately.

YIELD: Serves 4 to 6

Side Dishes

GRILLED TOMATOES

——

2 firm beefsteak tomatoes

1 teaspoon fresh basil leaves, minced

1 tablespoon olive oil

2 teaspoons Parmesan cheese, grated

freshly ground pepper

sprinkle of salt

Slice tomatoes in half, crosswise, and brush sides and bottoms with oil. Sprinkle cut tops with basil, salt, pepper, and Parmesan cheese. Place on warm—not hot—grill, cut side up, until the skin loosens and cheese melts, which takes several minutes. Serve immediately.

YIELD: Serves 4

STEWED TOMATOES

——

4 beefsteak tomatoes

1/4 cup green pepper, chopped

2 tablespoons onion, chopped

2 tablespoons celery (1 stalk), chopped

1 teaspoon salt

1-1/2 teaspoons sugar (or to taste)

1 tablespoon fresh basil, chopped

Peel tomatoes after dipping them in boiling water for 15 to 30 seconds, or until skins crack. Set aside to cool, then peel off skin. Chop into large pieces.

Combine all ingredients except basil and sugar in a large saucepan and simmer for 20 minutes or until the mixture is soft and juicy. Stir often to prevent burning and sticking. Add sugar (which may not be necessary if starting with sweet tomatoes) and chopped basil. Warm 5 more minutes. Serve.

YIELD: Serves 6

CARAWAY POTATOES

——

4 medium potatoes

1/4 cup caraway seeds

1 clove garlic, peeled and sliced in half

salt to taste

dill butter (see recipe following)

Cut potatoes in quarters and combine with caraway seeds and garlic in medium-sized sauce pan. Add just enough water to cover and bring to a boil. Simmer until the potatoes are tender. Drain off water. Transfer potatoes with a helping of caraway seeds to serving platter. Drizzle with dill butter and add salt to taste. Serve immediately.

YIELD: Serves 6

DILL BUTTER

——

1 tablespoon dill leaves, chopped

1-1/2 tablespoons margarine

Melt margarine and sauté dill leaves for 1 minute. Set aside for 5 minutes before serving.

HERBED MASHED POTATOES

——

Recipe courtesy of Millie Adams

6 medium potatoes

1 cup buttermilk or regular milk

1 tablespoon each: fresh sage, rosemary, and thyme, chopped

1/4 cup margarine

1 tablespoon fresh parsley, chopped

salt and freshly ground pepper to taste

Peel potatoes and cut into six chunks each. Place in cold, salted water. Bring to a boil, reduce heat to simmer, and cook until potatoes are tender, 15–20 minutes. Meanwhile, in a small saucepan over medium heat, heat milk, sage, rosemary, thyme, and margarine. Cover and turn off heat, allowing flavors to blend until potatoes are done. Drain potatoes.

Using a mixer, mash potatoes until all chunks are blended. Slowly pour in milk until potatoes are the desired consistency. (You may not need all the milk.) Stir in parsley, season with salt and pepper. Serve hot.

YIELD: Serves 4

Main Course

LIMA BEAN BAKE

1-1/2 cups fresh, shelled baby lima beans

1 large clove garlic, minced

3 cups rice

1/2 pound lean pork short ribs, cut in cubes

1/4 cup garden sorrel, sliced

1 tablespoon lemon thyme

2 tablespoons Italian salad dressing

1/2 cup Parmesan cheese

Prepare rice. Sauté pork with garlic. When done drain off fat. Add lima beans, sorrel, and lemon thyme. Sauté 3 minutes. Put rice in bottom of oiled 2-1/2-liter casserole dish. Drizzle with Italian salad dressing. Top with bean and pork mixture. Add Parmesan cheese. Cover and bake at 325°F for 20 minutes.

YIELD: Serves 6

Seasoning

DRIED TOMATOES

If you have a big country garden with more tomatoes than you can eat fresh, dry some for concentrated flavor and easy storage.

2 large tomatoes, washed and stemmed

Slice tomatoes about 1/2-inch thick and place in a food dehydrator. Set dehydrator to 135°F and let the tomatoes dry about 12 hours or until the tomato slices are leathery. If your dehydrator takes longer than 12 hours to dry the tomatoes, start with only one tomato next time. Store in freezer bags in the freezer. To use, crumble into dishes before, during, or after cooking or rehydrate in water, wine, or herbal vinegar and use like fresh.

CASUAL COUNTRY GARDEN

Beverage

HEARTY MELON REFRESHER

1/2 cup vanilla nonfat yogurt

1 cup watermelon or muskmelon, peeled and seeds removed, cubed

1 cup strawberries, washed and stemmed

Combine all ingredients in a food processor and blend until smooth. Serve immediately.

YIELD: Serves 4

VARIATION: For more complex flavor, add a peeled banana before blending.

Melons, shown growing on a trellis, are easy to blend into fruit drinks.

4
fREEFORM, BETTER VEGETABLE GARDEN

This vegetable garden caters to the person who is always looking for something better. (What a surprise it will be to find the rainbows end right here!) Plant breeders, focused on building disease resistance or earliness into new crops, occasionally also come up with better tasting and more nutritious vegetables—the qualifications for getting into this chapter. When combined into one great garden, the results are absolutely revolutionary … and delicious!

Some of the exciting vegetables included in this Better Vegetable Garden are smooth 'Regal Salad' beans (perfect for slicing raw into a salad), sugary 'Sweetheart' beets, extra sweet and vitamin A-enriched carrots, broccoflower (a blend of broccoli and cauliflower), cucumbers free of any bitterness, and handsome, pink flowering 'Pink Panda' strawberries.

'Pink Panda' strawberry is a breakthrough in ornamental edibles.

Freeform, Better Vegetable Garden Design

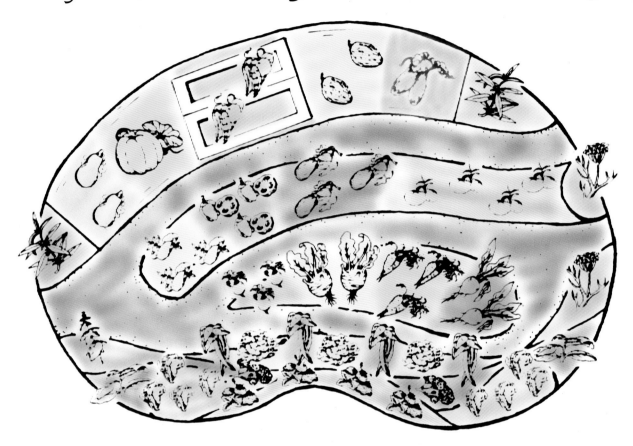

PLANT LIST

Front Bed
Marjoram, sweet
Basil
Lettuce
Strawberries
Parsley
Broccoflower
Beans
Dill

1st Center Bed
Radishes
Kohlrabi
Carrots
Beets

2nd Center Bed
Potatoes
Peppers
Eggplants
Tomatoes
Dill

Rear Bed
Savory, summer
Summer squash
Winter squash
Pumpkins
Cucumbers
Peas

A GREAT GARDEN DESIGN

The Better Vegetable Garden flows into a curving, two-lobed bed traditionally described as a kidney shape. If you can put the name aside, the shape is perfect for setting into a sunny corner of the yard. If a perimeter hedge or fence threatens to shade the garden, move the Better Vegetable Garden slightly closer to the center of the yard where it will be free of shadows. This move also helps the garden avoid woody roots, which can steal moisture and nutrients from smaller gourmet crops.

A substantial 20 by 15 feet, this garden is big enough to provide a steady supply of vegetables all summer. It is made up of four beds, which range from 2 to 4 feet wide and are mounded about 4 inches high. The mounded growing areas can be built up by raking soil out of the paths between the beds and adding a thick layer of compost, several inches

MAKING GRAVEL PATHS

Gravel paths are an easy way to add a little elegance to a Better Vegetable Garden and make it convenient to walk beside the plants even after a heavy rainfall. Light-colored gravel will highlight the meandering paths and provide contrast to the green foliage and brown earth. If you prefer more subtle paths, use darker gravel that will blend in with the soil.

Following the plan on page 39 and using a measuring tape for accuracy, mark out the location of the paths with stakes and strings. Excavate the paths to about 4 inches deep, removing the loose topsoil and adding it to the garden beds. Scrape the bottom of the paths smooth and level with a flat-topped spade. Cover the paths with black plastic mulch, which will keep weeds from sprouting up from the soil below. Then top with a 3-inch-deep layer of gravel, selecting the color of your choice.

deep. The paths can be covered with gravel to be suitable for all-weather traffic.

The garden, as seen from the house or patio, is handsomely edged with interwoven leaf lettuce, parsley, and 'Pink Panda' strawberries—a perky, welcoming combination. Garden entrances are guarded by a mixture of delightful culinary herbs which release their aroma when brushed in passing and display varying hues of green.

Within each bed, several different crops are grown in intermingled clusters providing a satisfying harvest of a variety of foods and a colorful combination of foliage. The central bed contains root crops—carrots, beets, kohlrabi, and radishes—which do best in a deep, light, but moderately fertile soil. These can be planted in spring and mid to late summer for summer and fall harvesting. Another central bed contains botanical relatives—potatoes, peppers, eggplants, and tomatoes—which need rich, fertile soil and grow during the frost-free summer season.

The root crops and the tomatoes, potatoes, peppers, and eggplants can be rotated between the two central beds each year. Plant as the plan dictates this year. Next year, add extra compost to the old root crop bed and use it for the tomatoes and their associates; and vice versa, moving root crops over to take the tomatoes' place. This rotation system keeps crops from sapping soil nutrients or feeding a growing population of subterranean pests or diseases.

In the rear bed, vining peas are set on an A-frame trellis and surrounded by billowing vines of a different set of botanical relatives—cucumbers, squash, and pumpkins. Lay the vines atop a moisture-conserving, black plastic mulch to eliminate weeding.

Another time-saving trick is to surround the garden with plastic or fiberglass edging, set slightly above the soil surface to keep the lawn from intruding into the garden. Using a string trimmer periodically also helps to cut back any marching grass sprigs and prevents them from climbing over the edging barrier.

YOUR BETTER VEGETABLE FAVORITES

Meet the stars of this Better Vegetable Garden—a fun and flavorful cast of characters. Here are some of their vital statistics to help you decide when and how to use them.

BEANS

Easy-to-grow bush beans of many colors—green, purple, and gold—are the basis for a bevy of lively dishes (although the purple-podded kinds fade to green when cooked). Contemporary beans are stringless and tender podded. Some are so tender that they're delicious raw.

'Regal Salad': This bean cultivar has slightly curled pods, mottled with purple on a green background. When young they are so smooth, tender, mild, and sweet that they're best eaten raw. Larger pods are good lightly steamed or sautéed.

The beans are ready for harvesting in 52 days.

'Purple Teepee': When decked with burgundy-colored beans, this climbing cultivar makes a decorative garden addition. The beans mature in about 55 days and look lovely in a harvest basket. But they change to green when cooked. This makes freezing simple, because they're done blanching the moment the color changes.

'Goldkist': This yellow wax bean is ready for harvesting at the same time as the previous

'Purple Teepee' beans add color to a rustic trellis.

USING PLASTIC MULCH

Black plastic mulch can be a great time-saver in a vegetable garden. When laid atop a garden bed, it prevents weed seeds from germinating so there is no need to hoe or weed. Plastic mulch is particularly helpful with vining plants, which can emerge from a relatively small opening in the plastic and stretch out, lounging on the plastic with their big pumpkins and squash resting high and dry.

- Black plastic mulch is available in rolls 4 feet wide that can be cut to the length of the garden bed. But before applying, prepare the soil well since you won't be able to get to it once the plastic is in place. Here is a step-by-step guide.

- Add plenty of compost or decayed manure to the garden—squash and pumpkins like rich, fertile soil

- If you live in an arid or drought prone climate, put a soaker hose under the plastic for easy, undercover watering.

- Lay the plastic mulch over the bed, holding the edges in place with soil or stones.

- Cut circular holes in the plastic mulch where you want to plant seeds or seedlings, then sow the seeds as directed.

- Relax and enjoy.

beans, so it makes a colorful combination. The pods are tender and have a fuller flavor than most wax beans.

BEETS

If you've only tasted canned beets, you'll be surprised by how much better fresh beets taste. You can harvest them young and eat them raw, shredded into salads. Or let them reach full size and bake, boil, or microwave them until tender. You can also eat the leaves, which have a sweet, mild flavor.

'Sweetheart': This extra sweet beet has a sugar beet in its ancestry. It matures about 58 days after sowing.

'Cylindra': The easy-slicing, cylindrical shape of this beet sets it apart from the others. The root gets to be 6 to 8 inches long and up to 3 inches wide. It's ready to harvest about 60 days after planting.

BROCCOFLOWER

'Alverda' is a recent innovation that blends the smooth heads of cauliflower with the easy-growing nature of broccoli. The result is an engaging lime green vegetable with a mild flavor, suitable for eating like either broccoli or cauliflower. Try it raw in salads or with dips. Or steam it lightly and top with butter or a creamy dill sauce. Heads are ready to harvest about 85 days after planting seedlings.

CARROTS

America's original carrots were fodder fit only for livestock. And many of our commercial carrots are only slightly more refined—they're long and tough with hardly any flavor. Fortunately, new generations of carrots are available for home gardeners. These are bred to be tender, so handle them gently. Some have an elevated vitamin A content, which makes them more nutritious and also surprisingly extra sweet. Even those who are not impressed by carrots will give a shout when they bite into one of yours. Look for cultivars such as the following.

'Healthmaster' contains 30 percent more vitamin A than most carrots. (Photo courtesy of Territorial Seeds)

'Altona': This cylindrical carrot reaches about 8 inches long approximately 60 days after planting. It has a strong top so it is easy to pull free from the ground.

'Lindoro': This cultivar can grow as long as 10 inches in 60 days if your soil is deep and loose.

'Artist': If you want a carrot with extra vitamin A and sweetness, look no further. This cultivar also boasts a deep orange color and roots to 8 inches long. It is ready to harvest about 65 days after sowing.

CUCUMBERS

Cucumbers have undergone a revolution in recent years—they now are more productive, milder flavored, and have fewer seeds. Some of the newest cucumbers have a bitter-free trait—they'll stay sweet and mild even in hot, dry weather. Without the bitter chemical, vines are hidden from detection by striped cucumber beetles, which are attracted to the bitter compound. Parthenocarpic cucumbers, which produce fruit without pollination, have few seeds and can be grown safe from pests beneath floating row covers. You can find similar cucumbers in the store, but you'll have to look for them in the gourmet section. One other advance is the emergence of the all-female cucumber. This appeals to more than just women's rights activists because with all-female flowers, cucumber vines can produce more fruit.

With all of these choices, it's well worth growing a few vines of cucumbers. When fresh and crisp off the vine, cucumbers taste wonderful and make wonderful pickles. Grow them alongside peas or set them on the pea trellis when the spring crop is done. Here are some cultivars to try.

'Sweet Success': This award-winning cultivar produces 14-inch-long slicing cucumbers in about 55 days. The skin is thin and dark and the fruit is bitter-free.

'Euro-American': Here's a cultivar with thin-skinned, foot-long cucumbers and few seeds. It's ready to pick just 45 days after planting.

'Little Leaf': This is a pickling cucumber that produces 20 to 30 cucumbers per vine, doesn't require pollination, and is bitter-free. You can gather the first cucumbers about 60 days after planting.

EGGPLANT

Gone are the days when all eggplants had a deep purple skin and needed soaking in salted water to remove bitterness.

One brand-new cultivar to try is 'Neon', which has exciting, pink skin and mild, white flesh. You can cook the eggplant with the skin on or peel it off. Fruits begin to be ready to harvest 65 days after planting sizable seedlings.

'Bride' eggplant shows off slender, shapely, purple-striped fruit. (Photo courtesy of Territorial Seeds)

HERBS

Fresh herbs are welcome in any garden and are far better than any other form of herbs.

Basil: Two of the newer cultivars of basil are 'Purple Ruffles' and 'Green Ruffles'. These have thick and (you guessed it) ruffled leaves like the potato chips of the same name. They also have a wonderful flavor and fragrance and last almost forever if cut and set in a vase of fresh water.

Dill: Fresh dill foliage is excellent with potato salad and the seeds are essential in pickles. But you can also use dill with chicken, fish, squash, carrots, and even in bread. One great new cultivar is 'Dukat', which yields a larger harvest of leaves than ordinary dill. Plant some seeds every few weeks throughout the gardening season so you can have some on hand at all times.

Parsley: Parsley is rich in vitamins and has a mild flavor that enhances almost any food. Those who love curly parsley will be excited about new 'Pagoda', which is triple curled forming extra frilly leaves.

Sweet Marjoram: The aromatic flavor of sweet marjoram complements chicken, fish, and most vegetables.

Summer Savory: This is an herb that has as much pizzazz as a spice. It's excellent in dishes that feature peas and beans.

KOHLRABI

Modern cultivars of kohlrabi stay mild and crisp, producing a delicious, juicy crunch when eaten with dips or salad greens. (It can also be eaten with just a sprinkle of salt.) Choose from green- or purple-skinned cultivars.

'Grand Duke': This award winner swells up to 4 inches across without losing tenderness. It only takes about 45 days from sowing to harvest, and can be picked earlier if desired.

'Purple Danube': Brighten up your yard with this beautiful, red-purple bulb. It's ready to pick in just 40 days. To eat the bulb, however, it's necessary to peel off the lovely skin and reveal the crisp, creamy flesh underneath.

LETTUCE

Leaf lettuce has been around for centuries but never before has there been so many colors and textures. Simply edging a garden in a frilly, red lettuce is eye appealing. Blending it with other greens turns an ordinary salad into a gourmet experience—a feat often employed by fine restaurants.

'Selma Lollo': Here's an outstanding lettuce cultivar with frilly, pink leaves in open rosettes that can reach up to 12 inches across. It takes about 45 days to reach full size, but you can harvest it earlier.

'Red Sails': This award winner produces tender, red-tipped leaves that grow large in about 45 days. It's slow to bolt to seed (making the leaves bitter) and can stay in good condition even if the weather turns unseasonably warm.

'Vulcan': Candy-apple red blazes atop a green background on this lettuce. It is ready to pick about 50 days after sowing.

PEAS

You'll never taste a better pea than one fresh from the garden. That's because peas begin to lose sweetness and flavor the moment they're harvested. When ultra fresh, you may have to resist the urge to eat them all raw; but remember, they're also delicious lightly steamed or sautéed. The most exciting development in peas is the snap pea—eaten pod and all. The tender pod is just as sweet as the peas inside, and the harvest size is triple that of ordinary shelling peas.

'Sugar Snap': This is the classic snap pea that started the edible, podded pea craze and remains one of America's favorites. Sweet, crunchy pea pods grow on 6-foot-long vines about 70 days after sowing. Harvest when the peas are swollen but the pod is still green and shiny. The peas are less sweet when they're full size.

'Sugar Ann': This is another award winner with short vines to 30 inches tall and early peas arriving two weeks before its parent, 'Sugar Snap'.

'Sugar Daddy': This snap pea develops no strings in the pods, which saves preparation time. (Other snap peas require removal of the tough strings. Break off the ends of the pods and peel down along the pod sutures.) Vines get up to 30 inches tall and begin bearing peas about 65 days after planting.

PEPPERS

Sweet peppers now come in many more sizes, shapes, and colors than ever before—a great opportunity to make beautiful stuffed or roasted peppers and pepper salads. Let the peppers ripen on the plant until they're sweet and fruity for an extra treat. You won't be able to resist eating them all by themselves! Try the following cultivars.

'Lilac' or 'Lilac Belle': This pepper is shaped like a traditional bell pepper but has a lilac-colored skin and white flesh. Its flavor is best once it ripens to red. The first lilac peppers are ready to pluck about 70 days after planting seedlings.

'Purple Beauty': This is a darker purple pepper that otherwise is similar to 'Lilac'.

'Lemon Belle': This is a lemon yellow–colored counterpart to 'Purple Beauty'.

'Gypsy': This award winner stands apart from the other peppers because it grows so incredibly well. It produces wedge-shaped fruit, greenish when first ready to pick and orange-red when fruity ripe. Harvest begins early, about 62 days after planting.

POTATOES

Potatoes have long been billed as pretty ordinary stuff, but the range of exciting new kinds of potatoes is rapidly expanding. Some of the best new cultivars have waxy flesh that holds up great in potato salads and needs little butter. Others have beautiful pink or purple skins which look as great as they taste

'Caribe': This newly rediscovered potato has glossy, purple skin with pure white flesh and a mild flavor quite unlike baking potatoes. It's an early crop that you can start during late spring or midsummer.

'Yellow Finn': Here's a great, golden-colored, waxy-fleshed potato that matures a little later than 'Caribe'.

PUMPKINS

Pumpkins have been around for a very long time and are a traditional part of the autumn season. But you can grow a

'Lemon Belle' (below) and 'Lilac Belle' (above) peppers.

different kind of pumpkin that's tasty and has Halloween shock value. It's 'Lumina', a ghostly white-skinned pumpkin. It gets to be about 10 inches wide in 85 days and is good for either carving into a ghostly character or baking into pies.

RADISHES

For extra fun with radishes, grow the multicolored assortment called 'Easter Egg Blend II'. It takes just 28 days for the seeds to sprout and turn into perfect globes of red, purple, pink, violet, and white. They'll liven up any salad or dip tray and are especially fun for kids to pull up.

STRAWBERRIES

Here's a real change of pace—a beautiful, pink-flowered strawberry for the garden edging. 'Pink Panda' is a hardy perennial that will grow year after year throughout most of the United States (except in tropical areas). It gets to be about 8 inches tall and spreads to form a ground cover, while continuously bearing large, pink flowers and small, red strawberries.

SUMMER SQUASH

Try something different from ordinary summer squash—round zucchini alternatives that are great for stuffing or salads.

'Gourmet Globe': About 45 days after planting, this cultivar produces the first of many, green-striped, ball-shaped squash. The squash are tender when small and great for eating fresh or lightly sautéing. Or let them grow 5 or 6 inches wide to slice open, scoop out the seeds, stuff with sausage or cheese, and bake.

'Kuta': This cultivar produces oblong squash that is good to harvest when young for salads, when midsize for stuffing, and when large to keep as a hard-shelled winter squash. It takes about 48 days to begin producing squash.

TOMATOES

Homegrown tomatoes allowed to ripen on the vine have an unbeatable flavor. Some contemporary tomatoes combine strong disease resistance with great taste appeal. They are well worth a try in this garden.

'Sweet 100': This tomato is so sweet that kids can't stop eating it. Little do they know that it has a higher vitamin C concentration than most tomatoes, so it's as good for them as it tastes. The tomatoes are ready to pick about 65 days after planting seedlings.

'Celebrity': This award winner produces good-tasting, medium-sized tomatoes beginning about 70 days after planting. The plants are resistant to nematodes and a number of diseases so they keep producing reliably even after the weather turns bad.

THE RECIPES

Try these great vegetables in the following combinations.

Salad

REGAL RAINBOW SALAD

This brightly colored salad embraces rich, sweet flavors that need little adornment. (Wait to harvest the vegetables until the recipe directs.)

1/2 cup young 'Regal Salad' beans, julienned

1/2 cup 'Sweet 100' cherry tomatoes, halved

1/2 cup 'Artist' carrots, slivered

1/4 cup red onion, chopped

1 cup cucumber, peeled and coarsely chopped

1/4 cup white wine vinegar

1/4 cup olive oil

2 tablespoons fresh sweet basil, chopped

Combine vinegar, oil, and basil in a ceramic, stainless steel, or plastic bowl. Set aside. Harvest, wash, and prepare vegetables. Combine in a salad bowl and drizzle with the vinegar, oil, and basil. Serve immediately.

YIELD: Serves 4

Side Dish

SAUTÉED 'GOURMET GLOBE' SQUASH WITH MARJORAM

2 4-inch-wide 'Gourmet Globe' squash

2 tablespoons margarine

2 teaspoons sweet marjoram leaves and buds, chopped

salt to taste

Melt margarine in large skillet over medium heat while cutting squash into 1/2-inch-wide slices. Add squash to skillet and sauté until almost tender, about 5 minutes. Flip and cook on the other side and sprinkle with sweet marjoram and salt to taste. Warm for 5 minutes and serve immediately.

YIELD: Serves 4

CULINARY GARDENS

Main Courses

SNAPPY PEAS AND NOODLES

2 cups sugar snap peas, stringed

1 small 'Gourmet Globe' squash, cubed

1 tablespoon margarine

5 ounces thick-sliced low-fat ham, cut into short strips

1-1/2 tablespoons fresh dill, chopped

1-1/2 teaspoons fresh chives, chopped

4 cups linguini, cooked

Cut peas in half across the width. Melt margarine in skillet, add peas and squash and sauté for 3 minutes until lightly cooked but still crisp. Stir in ham and heat 2 more minutes. Add dill and chives, stirring well. Serve over noodles.

YIELD: Serves 4

HAM AND CHEESE EGGPLANT

2 large 'Neon' eggplants

1 egg

1 cup bread crumbs

1/4 pound ham, sliced

1/4 pound brie cheese, sliced

Preheat oven to 350°F. Beat egg in a broad bowl and put bread crumbs in a second bowl; set aside. Remove stem and bottom of eggplant and cut eggplants lengthwise into 1/2-inch-thick slices. Immediately dip cut slices into egg and then coat with bread crumbs. Set on oiled baking sheet and bake for 20 minutes, or until tender but firm.

Remove to a microwave-proof dish. Top with a slice of ham and a slice of cheese. Microwave for 20 seconds or until cheese begins to melt.

YIELD: Serves 4

Sauce

CREAMY DILL SAUCE

—

Recipe courtesy of Millie Adams

2 tablespoons butter or margarine

2 tablespoons flour

1/4 teaspoon salt

1 cup milk

1/4 cup sour cream

2 tablespoons snipped fresh dill

Melt butter in a small saucepan. Blend in flour and salt. Stir well. Gradually add milk, stirring till thickened and bubbly. Add sour cream and dill; heat through and serve.

This sauce is excellent over fish—such as salmon, halibut, and ocean perch—and over vegetables—such as steamed fresh cauliflower, baby brussels sprouts, spinach, or broccoflower.

YIELD: Makes 1-1/4 cups

Fine-textured dill with medium-textured parsley make an interesting composition in the garden.

5
SMALL GARDEN OF BABY VEGETABLES

Tender baby vegetables are a special treat to eat and surprisingly easy to grow. Baby vegetables are ready to harvest earlier than most full-sized vegetables. Use them right away while they're snapping fresh to savor their fine flavor and tender texture at its best. Baby lettuce melts in your mouth. Baby carrots have a sweet crisp crunch that appeals to everyone, even kids. Baby vegetables are fun to serve whole—many are naturally bite-sized. They can also be sliced up for quick cooking.

A GREAT GARDEN DESIGN

Many miniature vegetables and fruits grow on compact plants which makes them easy to fit into small yards. This Small Garden of Baby Vegetables takes this concept one step further with a space-saving shape that fits snugly into a corner of any yard.

Grow baby vegetables in a sunny corner of your yard. (Longwood Gardens)

Baby Vegetables Garden Design

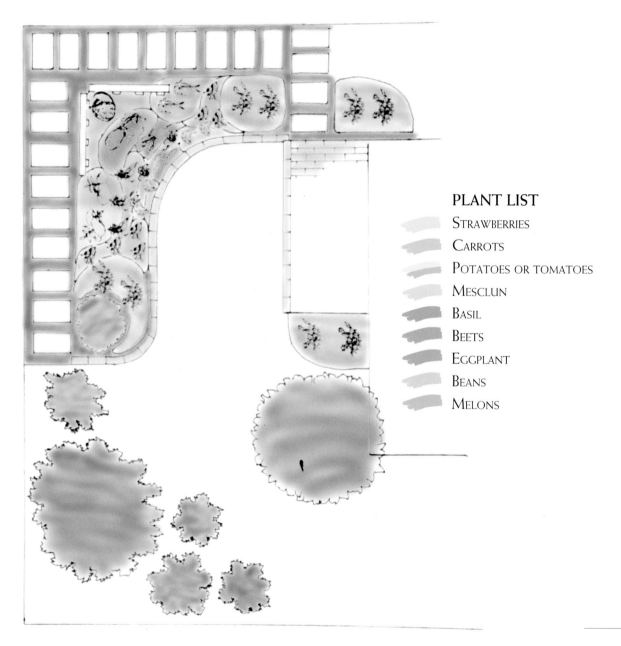

PLANT LIST

- STRAWBERRIES
- CARROTS
- POTATOES OR TOMATOES
- MESCLUN
- BASIL
- BEETS
- EGGPLANT
- BEANS
- MELONS

INSTALLING A BRICK EDGING

A classy way to separate your garden from your lawn is to install a brick edging. This looks especially neat if your patio, walks, or garden walls are also made of brick. The top of the brick should be higher than the surrounding soil but low enough so that you can mow over it. The most durable brick edgings are usually those set in cement, but in cold climates cement may shift and crack during winter. To reduce the likelihood of this occurring, add an extra layer of coarse sand or fine stone chips to the bottom of the edging trench.

Refer to the garden plan and outline the curving edge of your bed with a garden hose. Following that outline, dig a flat-bottomed trench—slightly wider than the length of the bricks and about 4 inches deeper than the brick height. Use wooden or metal edging to line the side of the trench that faces the lawn. Fill the trench with a 4-inch-deep layer of cement. Once the cement is thoroughly dry, mix up another batch of cement and apply it to the bottom and side of your bricks. Lay the bricks side by side on the cement base, squeezing and tapping them close enough together to fill any openings between the bricks with cement. Use a construction level to make certain the bricks are of even height.

When finished and dry, the bricks become an elegant edging as well as a troublesaver that helps keep lawn grass from invading the garden.

Brick edgings not only add personality, but they also keep weeds at bay.

It is a curving bed (about 5 feet wide by 15 feet long) nestled between the lawn and the edge of the property and neatly edged in brick to define its own territory. A vine-clad trellis sits snugly in the back corner, providing a high point easily visible from the house and a perfect place for growing minimelons. Taller vegetables such as the baby eggplants, potatoes, currant tomatoes, and beans cluster toward the rear of the garden. Shorter vegetables—mesclun (assorted baby greens), strawberries, bush basil, and miniature lettuce—take over the foreground of the garden. There is room to extend the garden for flowers, if you wish, sweeping them farther out around the perimeter of the yard.

In coming years, you can alternate where you plant each crop—for example, planting beans where you previously planted eggplants, potatoes, or tomatoes, and vice versa. Also switch the planting sites between the basil and lettuce and try different combinations of mesclun for variety in your salads and trouble-free rotation.

This garden calls for setting vegetables in space-saving, interplanted clusters instead of stiff rows. The beans, potatoes, and eggplants will form new moon-shaped plantings. The alpine strawberries sweep in arching double rows. The basil and lettuce form neat, single rows running parallel to the brick edging. The mesclun, carrots, and beets will share a central oval. Altogether, they will interweave like a tapestry of different hues of green with sparkles of red, yellow, and purple.

YOUR BABY FAVORITES

Some of these crops are true miniatures. Others have nearly full-sized stature but bear heavy trusses of baby vegetables.

BASIL, BUSH

This charming basil forms neat, emerald mounds that look like little pillows. It has soft, aromatic stems clustered with tiny leaves, which can serve as charming garnishes and even better flavorings and herbal vinegars. There's no better reason to shear frequently throughout the summer than to release its aroma and carry a bounty of young sprigs indoors for pesto or tomato sauce. The plants, meanwhile, quickly resprout and fill out more thickly than before. You can choose from several varieties—all reaching about 10 inches high. 'Greek Mini', 'Spicy Bush', and 'Dwarf Bush Fine Leaf' are among the best.

BABY BEANS

Try miniature snap beans or French filet beans for fun and flavorful eating. Baby beans need only a little steaming or sautéing and can be added at the last minute to nearly cooked casseroles or stir-fries. The trick to harvesting gourmet-quality beans is to look over your bean plants daily

'Greek Mini' bush basil has soft stems that can be used for cooking along with the leaves.

and pick young pods promptly, just as the seeds start to swell. The pod quickly loses its succulence after this point. Filet beans, however, become tough early and should be harvested before the seeds swell at all.

'Astrelle': This filet bean is ready once the little pods reach 3 inches long. Harvest begins about 60 days after sowing.

'Dandy': Dark green pods, produced in abundance and harvested when 4 inches long, are ready to begin picking about 55 days after sowing.

'Mini Yellow' and 'Mini Green': These Park Seed exclusives form tender baby beans at their peak when they are 4 inches long. They begin bearing suitable pods about 52 days after sowing.

BABY BEETS

These beets become sweet at a small size. Pick them promptly when they reach about 1 inch in diameter, then use them raw in salads or steam them whole until tender. Baby beets also are great for pickling or canning. Try these cultivars.

'German Baby': This is a sweet, small, dark red beet ready about 45 days after sowing.

'Little Ball': This beet rapidly grows to 3 inches across but swells little beyond that point. You can harvest them as soon as they reach about 1-1/2 inches wide, or 45 or 50 days after sowing.

'Spinel Baby Beet': This one takes a little longer to mature, about 60 days, but the wait is worthwhile. It's a favorite in many European gourmet restaurants.

BABY CARROTS

Little baby carrots are sweet and tender, seldom needing peeling. Just trim off both ends and eat them fresh, steamed, or baked. Or sauté them lightly in butter and sprinkle with brown sugar. They're also good for canning or pickling. Not every carrot cultivar has the potential to be a baby carrot.

The best baby carrots are bred to develop bright color and sweet flavor when young. They also tend to grow well in shallow soil where longer carrots cannot thrive.

'Thumbelina': These award-winning, short and round carrots grow up to 1-1/2 inches wide and tolerate slightly heavy soils, where few other carrots dare to grow. The beginning of the harvest season can range from 50 to 75 days after sowing.

'Minicor' ('Baby Nantes'): This is a slender alternative to 'Thumbelina' that develops its orange color and robust carrot flavor earlier than larger carrots. Harvest when they reach about 3 inches long, 50 to 65 days after sowing.

'Sucram': This carrot gets to be 3 or 4 inches long approximately 60 to 70 days after sowing and is very sweet.

BABY EGGPLANT

Baby eggplant—slim or round miniatures produced abundantly on moderate-sized plants—can go where no full-sized eggplant dares: into pickles, stuffed for appetizers, or baked whole. Or slice them in half, brush them with a little garlic oil, and toast them on the grill. Many begin producing earlier than larger eggplants and can continue to be productive all summer long. Here are some cultivars to watch for.

'No. 226': This is a productive plant that grows well even under less-than-ideal circumstances. The eggplants are ready for harvest when they reach 3 inches in diameter, beginning about 55 days after planting.

'Japanese Purple Pickling': These little eggplants—fabulous for pickling in a spicy vinegar brine—are ready to pick just 75 days from planting.

'Bambino': These plants are miniatures, just like the fruit. Plants reach only 12 inches high but bear dozens of round eggplants about the size of a ping-pong ball 45 days after planting. Keep harvesting, and they'll keep on producing.

'Slim Jim': Here's a different look in baby eggplants. The fruit, held dangling in clusters, turns lavender or purple when very small and can be harvested as baby vegetables. The plant, also small, is good for growing in containers. Harvest begins 65 to 80 days after planting the seedlings.

BABY LETTUCE

These are perfect, miniature replicas of full-sized lettuce. They tend to have soft, buttery heads suitable for serving whole, one head per salad plate, to enjoy the pretty rosette shape. They also can be sliced in half for two servings. Be certain to wash the entire head well, gently working any grit out from between the outer leaves. Rinse from the top, letting fresh water work down to the core of the lettuce. Shake the water out with a salad spinner and chill. Now the baby lettuce is ready to drizzle with your favorite salad dressing and serve. The tender leaves of baby lettuce also are great to break off and blend with other baby greens.

Baby lettuce quickly reaches its prime and needs prompt harvesting. If allowed to linger too long, it will send up a flowering stalk and grow bitter. After harvesting, plant more lettuce seed or seedlings to harvest in the next month or two.

'Little Gem': In about 50 days, this lettuce grows into upright, romainelike heads that reach 5 inches across—perfect for a single salad plate.

'Diamond Gem': This relative of 'Little Gem' matures a little earlier.

'Tom Thumb': This old-fashioned heirloom produces soft 4- to 6-inch wide heads of buttery, light green leaves, ready 50 to 70 days after sowing.

'Italian Red Parella': Little leafy rosettes up to 7 inches across change from green to red at the top and can be harvested abut 50 days after sowing.

BABY MELONS

Melons are ordinarily rambling plants that don't fit well into smaller gardens. But you can let the long vines grow up on a trellis without using up much space. Secure new melons to the trellis with a nylon hose sling for support as they swell. Pint-sized baby melons ripen before their larger counterparts, perfect for northern climates or gardeners who hate to wait. Eat your melons mouth-watering ripe, right off the vine. Freeze any extra to whirl in the food processor and enjoy in iced fruit drinks.

'Sugar Baby': This classic watermelon grows up to 8 inches wide and has an especially sweet flavor. It is ready to harvest about 70 to 85 days after planting.

'Garden Baby': This is a mini-watermelon that grows on vines that are half the length of other watermelons and produces 6-inch-wide melons about 75 days after planting.

'Yellow Baby': This award-winning yellow watermelon produces fruit in just 75 days. It's almost seedless and puts all its energy into great flavor. It can take some cool weather, unlike many watermelons, so is good for cold or high altitude climates.

'Earlidew' Honeydew: This is a half-pint honeydew that gets to be about 6 inches wide beginning as early as 80 days after planting. Although honeydews tend to be temperamental, this cultivar keeps on growing despite less-than-desirable weather.

MESCLUN

This term, coined in northern Italy and southern France, is becoming a gourmet buzzword used to describe salads made with assorted baby greens. Although it sounds exotic, gardeners everywhere have been making this kind of mixture for centuries. Grow any blend of salad greens that you like. Cut them young and toss them in a salad bowl. The variety of textures, colors, and flavors will make this easy-to-prepare salad naturally elegant.

Greens suitable for mesclun include lettuce, arugula, and cress, which all thrive in cool weather. Others, such as fennel, parsley, and sorrel, are suitable for harvesting during cool or warm weather. You can plant a tossed salad mixture of seeds in a single bed. Or plant individual crops together in clusters which usually end up easier to tend. Cut the leaves when they are 4 inches high or large enough to make a mouthful. Pluck individual leaves, plant by plant, for one salad at a time or shear the entire bed back close to the ground for a week of salads. Let the bed resprout or turn it under and plant a different kind of mesclun.

Arugula: Notched-leaf arugula (also called roquette) has a pungent mustard-garlic flavor.

Chervil: This parsleylike plant has finely cut leaves and a mild flavor, adding a delicate touch to mesclun.

Chicory: Leafy relatives of radicchio and Belgian endive have a mild, bitter flavor enjoyed in Europe.

Fennel: This anise-flavored plant has feathery leaves of bronze or green.

Lettuce: A great variety of leaf lettuce provides mild yet colorful additions to the blend.

Parsley: The rich green curly or flat leaves of parsley are a nutritious companion for other greens.

Sorrel: A perennial with lemon-flavored leaves, sorrel can add depth to mesclun flavoring.

Swiss chard: Related to beets, chard bears sweet-flavored foliage with scarlet or white midribs.

MINIATURE POTATOES

Some unique potatoes grow into slender, fingerlike shapes that are best suited for potato salad or cooking with baby beets and carrots. Their odd and unusual shapes are a pleasant surprise for hungry diners. But even ordinary potatoes can be harvested when very young by unearthing them just as the vines begin to flower. These babies—also called new potatoes—are delicate, thin-skinned, and widely esteemed.

'Rose Fin Apple': Here's a medium-sized potato that can be harvested while it's young. It has pretty, slightly pink skin and waxy yellow flesh that needs little butter. The tubers are scab resistant and, when mature, will store well.

'Russian Banana': These small, elongated tubers have both yellow skin and flesh.

ALPINE STRAWBERRIES

These perennial strawberries form a low mound of emerald foliage—without the spidery baby plants sprouting on runners that emerge from ordinary strawberries—which makes them perfect as a neat edging. They also produce white flowers and small, red fruit all summer long. The fruit is less juicy with more concentrated flavor than regular strawberries. One good cultivar is 'Ruegen Improved', available at nurseries or from seed. Once planted and thriving, more seedlings may spring up from fallen berries. Move young seedlings to new locations with a shovel.

CURRANT TOMATOES

Pea-sized tomatoes appear in waterfall-like sprays on full-sized tomato plants. They are delightful, colorful jewels in salads, stir-fries, casseroles, or side dishes. You can choose from red or yellow varieties, or grow one of each.

Plant currant tomatoes in combination with your lady-finger potatoes or grow the potatoes and tomatoes in alternating years. Because they are related plants and share similar diseases, switch the growing location each season to get off to a clean, fresh start. Here are some cultivars to look for.

'Red Currant' ('Raisin Tomato'): Unlike some currant tomatoes, this one hangs onto its pea-sized fruit until you pick it.

'Yellow Currant' ('Gold Currant'): Less common than 'Red Currant', this tomato is worth finding due to its superior flavor.

THE RECIPES

Here are some fun ideas for using the baby vegetables and fruits you harvest.

Salads

RAINBOW SHREDDED BABY BEET SALAD

3/4 cup baby beets, 1-inch diameter
3/4 cup baby carrots, sliced thin
1/3 cup tart apple, peeled, cored, and diced
1/4 cup fresh lemon juice
1/3 cup safflower oil

Peel beets with a potato peeler, then slice and cut into slivers. In ceramic mixing bowl or casserole dish, blend slivered beets and sliced carrots. Cover with lemon juice and oil mixture. Dice apple and add immediately, stirring until the apple pieces become pink. Chill for at least 1 hour. Serve cold.

YIELD: Serves 2

SMALL GARDEN OF BABY VEGETABLES

BABY BEAN SALAD

2 cups baby beans, ends removed

1/2 cup red onions, chopped

1/2 cup cooked, low-fat turkey bacon, chopped

1 teaspoon summer savory, minced

1 teaspoon rice wine vinegar

2 teaspoons toasted peanut oil

Before preparing beans, chop onions and mince summer savory. Stir in vinegar and oil, then set aside. Steam baby beans for 5 minutes or until tender-crisp. Transfer to a ceramic bowl. Stir in the onion mixture and crumbled bacon. Serve warm as a side dish.

YIELD: Serves 4

MESCLUN SALAD

2 cups assorted mesclun greens

1/3 cup salad dressing, or to taste

2 bush basil sprigs

Wash greens well, trimming off tough stems. Spin in salad spinner to remove excess moisture. Toss in salad bowl with dressing. Garnish with basil sprigs. Serve immediately.

YIELD: Serves 2

ALMOND NEW POTATO SALAD

Recipe courtesy of Millie Adams

1 cup sliced almonds, toasted and divided

1/4 cup olive oil

1/4 cup mayonnaise

2 tablespoons lime juice

1 teaspoon salt

1/4 teaspoon white pepper, freshly ground

1/4 teaspoon sugar

1/4 teaspoon cumin

1-1/2 pounds small, red new potatoes, steamed and sliced

1/2 cup green onions, sliced

1/2 cup red bell pepper, julienned

1/2 cup celery, diced

2 tablespoons fresh chives, chopped

1 tablespoon fresh cilantro, chopped

Combine mayonnaise and the next five ingredients. Gradually beat in 1/4 cup olive oil. Gently toss mayonnaise mixture with potatoes, vegetables, and herbs. Chill at least 2 hours. Just before serving, carefully stir 3/4 cup almonds into salad; sprinkle remaining almonds on top.

YIELD: Serves 6–8

MINIMELONS WITH STRAWBERRIES

2 miniature melons

2 cups alpine or other strawberries

sugar to taste

Slice melons in half and remove seeds. Cover with plastic wrap and chill for 1 hour. Wash and trim strawberries. Using a food processor, blend into a saucelike consistency and add sugar to taste. Pour over melons and serve immediately.

YIELD: Serves 4

Side Dishes

BABY CARROT AND POTATO BAKE

20 baby potatoes, sliced thick

20 baby carrots, ends removed and halved lengthwise

3/4 cup reduced-fat Swiss cheese

3/4 cup chicken broth

Preheat oven to 325°F. Place potato slices in the bottom of a medium-sized baking dish. Cover with carrots. Pour on chicken broth and top with cheese. Bake for 45 minutes or until potatoes are tender, liquid is reduced, and cheese is toasted on the top.

YIELD: Serves 4

SMOTHERED BABY EGGPLANT

6 to 8 'Bambino' baby eggplant

1/2 cup bread crumbs

1 egg, beaten

6 ripe tomatoes

1 green pepper, sliced

1 avocado, sliced

2 tablespoons fresh basil, chopped

1/2 cup mozzarella cheese, shredded

Preheat oven to 350°F. Dip tomatoes in boiling water briefly, until skin cracks. Let tomatoes cool and and peel off skin. Place peeled tomatoes in a large saucepan and cook with the lid off on medium heat until a chunky sauce forms. Add pepper slices to cooking tomatoes and simmer 15 minutes.

Slice baby eggplant in half. Dip cut side first in egg and then in bread crumbs. Set, skin side down, in oiled 2-liter baking dish. Bake at 350°F for 20 minutes or until just tender.

Mix basil in tomato sauce and pour tomato sauce over baked eggplant. Add sliced avocado and top with mozzarella cheese. Bake 30 minutes. Serve immediately.

YIELD: Serves 6

Salad Dressings

BUSH BASIL VINEGAR

3 sprigs bush basil

1 pint red wine vinegar

Place basil sprigs in vinegar, either pushing them into the bottle the vinegar is presently in, or rebottling into a pint canning jar, covering the top with plastic before sealing. (The plastic prevents the vinegar from reacting with a metal lid.) Let the vinegar sit in a warm place for 3 weeks. Label and strain out basil, if you wish. Store in a cool, dark location.

BASIL SALAD DRESSING

3/4 cup bush basil, finely minced

1/4 cup red wine vinegar or bush basil vinegar

1/2 teaspoon prepared mustard

3/4 cup oil

1/3 teaspoon salt

dash of white pepper

Wash and dry basil. Mince and add immediately to vinegar in a glass or ceramic bottle. Add other ingredients and shake well. Top with a nonmetal lid (or line metal lids with plastic) and let sit overnight in the refrigerator before serving. Shake well before serving.

YIELD: Serves 6–8

VARIATION: Substitute 1/4 teaspoon spicy brown mustard for the prepared mustard.

Sauce

STRAWBERRY BUTTER

1/2 cup pineapple juice

10 tart apples

2 cups alpine strawberries

1/4 cup honey

Peel and core apples. Slice thinly and place in slow cooker or Crock-Pot with pineapple juice. Cook with the lid on for several hours until soft. Mash with a potato masher and add strawberries and honey. Cook for 4 to 6 more hours, with the lid off until the butter becomes thick enough to spread. Store finished butter in the refrigerator or freezer. Serve on toast, sandwiches, bagels, waffles, or pancakes.

VARIATION: For a smoother butter, puree in food processor.

6
CREATIVE CONTAINER GARDEN

Anyone who has ever grown a houseplant successfully is the perfect candidate for growing food in containers. Containers accommodate a sense of wild freedom, letting you rise above practical limitations. Struggles with rock hard or swampy soil, wilt or rot diseases, or greedy tree roots will vanish with a potted garden. In shady yards, you can make the most of any and all sunny spots by setting containers in those precious places where the sun lingers longest. Containers can also make gardening less strenuous if you work with lightweight growing mixes and plastic pots. Set the pots on elevated benches to avoid bending and stooping that can strain your back.

Lettuce and viola flowers make a dynamic pair for spring gardens.

Creative Container Garden Design

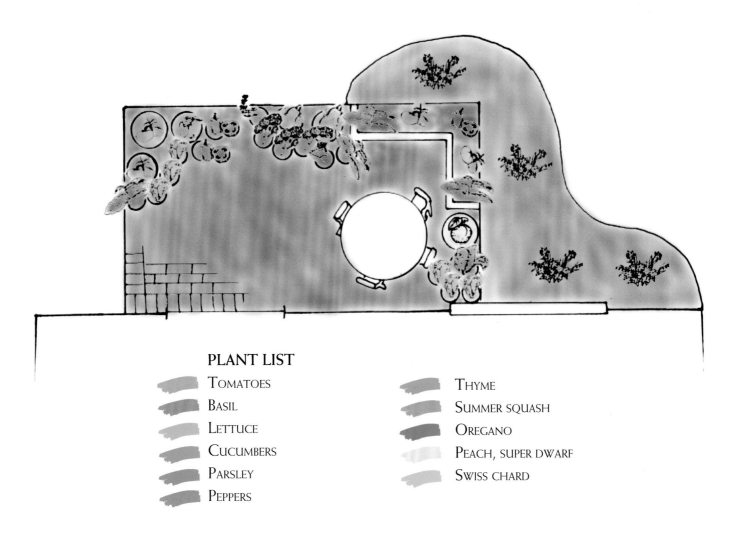

PLANT LIST

- Tomatoes
- Basil
- Lettuce
- Cucumbers
- Parsley
- Peppers

- Thyme
- Summer squash
- Oregano
- Peach, super dwarf
- Swiss chard

Containers of vegetables, herbs, and fruit become more than simply a potted garden; they become outdoor art created for a fraction of what a garden sculpture might cost. An attractive container full of cascading red strawberries, crimson Swiss chard, and a ruffle of parsley is a living, growing masterpiece.

Could it get any better than this? You bet. Contemporary plant breeders are in a frenzy, producing plant after plant suitable for growing in pots. Many new offerings—for example, tomatoes that grow in hanging baskets—are compact plants that have small but tasty fruit and provide early yields. Other good options for containers include hundreds of cultivars of small vegetables, such as lettuce, spinach, arugula, mini carrots, and radishes, which have modest root space requirements. Another must for containers are the visually attractive plants such as 'Pretty in Purple' peppers or super dwarf peach trees—colorful stars born for the spotlight.

A GREAT GARDEN DESIGN

When gardening in containers, design options are endless. You can play with the beauty of a variety of plants, a diversity of containers, and an abundance of different arrangements—even in different parts of the yard. Move smaller pots around to take advantage of their beauty when in flower or bearing fruit. Or change the color scheme and textural contrasts to fit your mood or entertainment schedule.

Just to get a feel for all of the options, make a trial run before planting anything. Get a wheelbarrow full of pots. Amass them in a sunny corner of your patio or porch. Set the tallest pot in the back corner, farthest from your usual vantage point. Cluster medium-height pots in front of it and arrange sweeps of smaller pots in front of them. Now, like in a well-designed perennial border, you'll be able to see all of the plants growing at once, without having your view obstructed by taller plants.

GREAT GALLOPING CONTAINERS!

Some great places to set conainers in any yard include the following:

Either side of a gate

Both sides of a doorway or stoop

The center of a round garden

On a table

On an old tree stump

In repeated groupings in a flower border

Beside a bench

Hanging from an arbor

On a pedestal

Beneath your window

Another option is to build a large planter to cluster smaller plants in. Because of its size alone, a large planter creates a strong, bold presence in the container garden. It will also be easier to maintain because it won't dry out as quickly as individual smaller pots would.

The most attractive container gardens are created with an eye to symmetry. Imagine you are making a container garden for your patio. Envision an invisible line dividing the patio in half—right down the center. Consider how the different planting schemes flow on each side of the dividing line and how they relate to each other. Try to balance the pot bulk on either side of the line so the arrangement won't look lopsided. You could use a symmetrical arrangement with a trio of three large pots on each side, for example. Or go informally asymmetrical—balance a large cluster of small pots on one side with a smaller group of large pots on the other. To take this a step further, incorporate the nearby landscape features. You could cluster pots in an open area on the patio to balance landscape features such as a small tree or barbecue pit on the other side of the patio.

CONTAINER SYNERGY

From a practical perspective, grouped pots are easier to tend. They are close at hand so you don't have to chase all over the yard when it's time to water. And there is also the power of synergy—grouping plants together helps them all grow better. Together, plants emit an invisible cloud of transpirated moisture that limits leaf moisture loss on a wind-free day. The canopy of foliage helps to shade the pots, providing relief from summer heat.

The most uniform container garden is achieved by planting in pots of similar make and design. This focuses attention on the beauty of the plants and the surroundings rather than on the containers. In contrast, a real assortment of different pots—each unique—can be distracting and uncomfortable. It's easy to avoid this problem by investing in bulk terra-cotta or plastic pots (prices tend to be lower when buying in quantity) to group together in a sunny corner. Set ornamental or unique containers in a prominent place by the front door or next to the picnic table so the container can be appreciated up close and separate from the crowd.

Terra-cotta pots suggest an earthy look.

Given a spacious pot, all of the plants detailed under Your Container Favorites will look good in a container. Leaf lettuce is lovely—basil is lush—tomatoes are lively. Expand on this beginning by combining several plants together in one oversized pot. Blend herbs with colorful foliage, annuals with bright flowers, and vegetables with complementary flower or fruit color. Silver variegated thyme looks great with white pansies and white-stemmed Swiss chard. Together they create a sparkling white potpourri and an interesting contrast to creeping thyme, upright chard, and rounded pansies. Another exciting blend features contrasting colors such as 'Pretty in Purple' peppers with a ground cover of yellow pansies.

Assign unique containers their own spaces.

HINTS FOR HEALTHY CONTAINER CULTURE

When container gardening, relinquish only modest control to Mother Nature. You are the boss! Give yourself a pat on the back and then get to work. Choose a container, then provide the soil, water, and fertilizer. (The only thing you don't do is grow!) Make the job as easy as possible. Get to know how different containers and soil blends work, then match them up with plants that like what they have to offer.

POTS

Pots enclose plant roots and enhance your patio. But they also do much more. They determine how quickly moisture evaporates from the soil and how much air moves in to replace it. They affect soil temperatures—dark-colored pots absorb more warmth, while light-colored pots reflect sunlight and heat. Insulated pots, such as thick wooden tubs or stone urns, tend to experience less extreme temperature variations from day to night, summer to winter, than do thin plastic or metal containers. This benefits the long-lived roots of strawberries or dwarf fruit trees as well as short-lived crops that have an aversion to very warm or cold temperatures. Beyond this, each type of pot has its own special virtues.

Light-colored pots tend to stay cooler in summer.

Terra-cotta or clay pots are blessed with a rich, rusty brown color and an earthy look that is compatible in most garden settings. When used for several years, clay pots become even softer looking, almost pink, sometimes frosted with silver salts or green algae. (A little salt frosting is okay, but a lot can be damaging to plant roots and requires soaking off in fresh water.)

Clay pots come in a variety of shapes and sizes, most of which are round. These include standard flowerpots, broad and wide bulb pans, tall and narrow contemporary pots, and decorative square, rectangular, or round pots with molding, latticework, or other decorative elements. They can be hand thrown (like fine pottery) or machine molded (and alike as identical twins). All are suitable for gourmet gardening, as long as they are the right size for the crop.

Unbeknownst to anyone but a pot specialist is how durable different kinds of clay pots are. More expensive clay pots—those made with a higher percentage of clay and fewer fillers and fired under high heat—are less likely to break and, because they last longer, are worth the initial extra cost. Inexpensive and cheaply made clay pots—which might be recycled from a gift plant or bought at a discount store—may last an entire gardening season (which makes them satisfactory)—or they may not (which creates a problem).

All clay pots have similar physical characteristics—their walls are porous, allowing air to move in and out, providing oxygen to plant roots, and helping the soil stay cooler on a hot day. But free airflow also encourages the soil inside to dry out relatively quickly. This means that during the summer terra-cotta pots (especially the smaller ones) will dry out quickly and need continual attention paid to watering.

In the winter, clay pots need to come indoors so they won't crack in freezing weather. Indoors, the pots are handy for growing lettuce, rosemary, or basil, and their porosity is a benefit. It helps prevent generous waterings from swamping the soil—a quick way to lose your indoor edibles.

Synthetics: Plastic pots are lighter than clay which makes them easier to move around but a little more prone to tipping over once a top-heavy plant is inside. You can use inexpensive nursery containers, which are innocuous but get the job done. Or you can buy more expensive, decorative plastic pots. Plastics are not porous, so they won't dry out as fast as clay. But small pots will still require plenty of watering in the heat of summer. If left out in frosty winter weather, plastics may fade or get brittle and chip from the exposure. In hot weather, they can heat up more rapidly than terra-cotta, stressing cool-weather-loving plants such as lettuce.

Some people feel that plastic pots, especially brightly colored ones, cheapen an otherwise elegant container garden.

This may be true of a conservative or formal garden. But in a contemporary setting, they can be particulary dynamic. If you hesitate to use plastic but want to benefit from its physical characteristics, look for plastics made to resemble terra-cotta pots to all but the closest inspection.

Metal, Stone, and Wood: When you want a truly beautiful pot, splurge on one made from these classic materials.

Metal—bronze, aluminum, and steel—can be formed into the usual shapes or adorned with intricate designs. Wire basket frames can be lined with sheet moss or coconut fiber liners, filled with planting mix, and planted. Metal containers that are not prone to rust or are treated to prevent corrosion can stand outside all winter. But they do not insulate plant roots from winter cold and are best used for annuals, not overwintering perennials.

Stone—available in a variety of lovely colors and blends of different sparkling minerals—can be hand hewn into rough containers that are full of character. Stone is heavy, so find a special place for a stone container and then leave it be. If you can't afford the real thing, try concrete containers, many of which are now made to look very similar to stone.

Wooden containers—such as large tubs or half barrels for large plants and smaller decorative planters or window boxes of redwood or cedar—also come in a variety of warm, brown colors that please the eye. Avoid pressure-treated wood for edible crops (there is some question about whether the rot-preventing chemicals leach into the soil and are picked up by plants) unless it is completely sealed with a weather-proofing product. Good alternatives are redwood or cedar which are naturally rot resistant.

Wood can be used to fashion a variety of different planters—permanent or semipermanent containers large enough to hold a small garden. A good size for a planter is 2 feet wide and deep and 4 or more feet long. This allows roots plenty of room and holds a larger reservoir of water than smaller pots, providing extra flexibility for a gourmet garden.

Other containers: Just for fun, be imaginative and recycle other containers from around the house to set in a prominent place like a floral centerpiece. Use an old-fashioned umbrella stand to hold dill, peppers, or other tall plants. Put it beside your front door where everyone can see it. Grow a short pea vine in an old high-top tennis shoe set on your picnic table. Plant lettuce in an old children's beach bucket or toy truck bed and position it beside the swing set.

The sky's the limit. If you can put enough soil in something, it will be suitable for growing plants—at least temporarily. If possible, use a drill to bore drainage holes in the bottom of the container so extra moisture can escape. Line containers made of fabric, fibers, fine woods, or rust-prone

A basket lined with plastic makes an ornamental pot.

metals with a waterproof plastic liner so the soil and moisture won't damage them.

A SIZE PRIMER

Most gourmet plants prefer spacious pots in order to reach maturity and thrive. In nature, roots continue to grow for the lifetime of the plant, tunneling through the soil to find new sources of moisture and nutrients. In a pot, part of growing success depends on allowing those roots to continue to expand as long as possible, especially while the plant itself is most actively growing. Most potted plants will, eventually, run out of rooting space. But, by that time the plant should be strong and established, ready to go about its business as long as you tend to yours—watering and fertilizing.

The moral of this story is to start a potted culinary garden in sufficiently large pots, as suggested below. To estimate pot sizes for other vegetable or herb crops, use a pot that is about as wide as the leafy top of a mature plant (excluding vines from this equation). When a plant has overgrown its pot—if roots run out the bottom or the plant stops growing and its roots pack every inch of soil—transplant it into a larger pot.

POT DIAMETER SUGGESTIONS

Basil: 6 to 18 inches, depending on size of plant
Cucumbers, bush: 12 to 18 inches
Lettuce, leaf: 6 to 12 inches
Oregano: 12 inches
Parsley: 8 to 12 inches
Peaches, genetic dwarf: 24-inches-wide, 18-inches-deep
Peppers: 12 to 18 inches
Squash, summer, bush: 18 to 24 inches
Strawberries, day-neutral: 12 inches
Swiss chard: 6 to 8 inches
Thyme: 12 inches
Tomatoes, compact or patio: 12 to 18 inches

POTTING BLENDS

Container gardening demands less set-up time than gardening in an outdoor bed. You can prepare the growing mix when it is convenient (without concern for whether it is raining or not). You can make an ideal potting blend by pouring ingredients out of bags into a large basin instead of mixing wheelbarrow loads of compost into a garden bed with a rotary tiller.

There is no need to work with real soil at all (it can get hard, soggy, and harbor disease). Now there are improved growing mixes that are peat-based and stay light and fluffy, allowing excess moisture to drain off freely. Preblended peat mixes contain peat moss with some perlite (a mineral puffed to resemble plastic foam), vermiculite (another mineral heat-expanded to form small, layered chunks), charcoal, or composted bark.

Although called a variety of names—grower's mix, professional mix, or soilless mix—they are easy to identify on a garden center shelf. Peat mixes are lightweight and more expensive than potting soil but can be purchased relatively economically in bulk 2.5-cubic-foot bags. Another option is to make your own peat mix. Here are some popular formulas:

- 1 part ground peat moss with 1 part vermiculite or perlite or …
- 2 parts ground peat moss with 1 part vermiculite and 1 part perlite.
- To enrich the above mixes for heavy-feeding vegetables or flowers, blend 2 parts of the peat-based mix with 1 part finished compost.
- For herbs such as lavender and rosemary that need sharp drainage, try 2 parts peat moss with 1 part coarse sand and 1 part compost.

Blend the ingredients well with a rake in a wheelbarrow or on a tarp. Add a dash of ground limestone and a sprinkle of slow-releasing, granular fertilizer to get plants off to a good start.

After a month or so, the nutrients from the compost and fertilizer added to the peat mix will be depleted. Be prepared to fertilize as needed. Fruiting plants such as tomatoes are heavy feeders that can be given balanced fertilizers (with nutrient ratios such as 5-5-5 displayed on the package label). Apply water-soluble fertilizers once every couple weeks or use granular fertilizers once a month. Light feeders such as thyme may only need to be fertilized once or twice during the growing season.

WATERING

When the weather gets hot and dry, watering can be a challenge. Even the biggest, most succulent, and productive plant can be knocked flat if the potting soil dries out. The damage is difficult to correct because sphagnum peat moss resists rewetting. When sphagnum peat dries, it shrinks into a tight mass, leaving openings between the peat and the pot walls. If water is poured over the dry peat, it will be shed (like water on a duck's back), running down the inside of the pot and out the drainage holes below. The best way to rewet dry peat—and hopefully save the plant growing in it—is to set the pot in a basin of warm water so it can soak it up gradually.

It is much better to let thirsty tomatoes, lettuce, and peppers enjoy a regular supply of moisture—a condition called evenly moist soil. Herbs and peach trees do better when allowed to dry out ever so slightly between waterings. Stick your finger down in the potting mix, checking subsoil dryness daily. If the top couple inches are dry, it's time to water again. Soak the soil thoroughly, letting a hose trickle into larger containers to be sure moisture gets down to the bottom. Remove water-catching saucers below the pots so extra moisture can run freely out the bottom, carrying away excess salts and preventing waterlogging.

If you don't have time to deal with watering every day—or twice a day in really hot weather—make provisions for some help.

Invest in a simple automatic watering system set on timers to turn it on automatically. You can buy these systems through gardening catalogs or irrigation specialists.

Buy self-watering pots, which when dry can pull water in from reservoirs below or beside them.

Make your own self-watering pots. Place a strip of nylon hose, socks, felt, or rope in the bottom of the pot, with one end sticking out the drainage hole. Set the pot over a bowl or bucket of water, with the makeshift wick dangling in the water, and it will be able to pull up extra moisture. You can also buy similar systems, made with plastic tubing and clip-on moisture reservoirs.

Minimize evaporation by mulching the surface of the pot with a half inch of compost, an inch of bark mulch, or for herbs such as rosemary that need an airy soil, with a half inch of coarse sand or fine rock chips.

Add water-retaining polymer crystals to the potting mix before planting. These swell into a water-filled gel that can be tapped by plant roots, supplementing moisture in the potting mix.

STAKING

Potted plants such as tomatoes and cucumbers will sprawl unless you provide them with a support to climb. One easy, homemade method is to space four bamboo stakes around the perimeter of the pot, sliding the bottom of the stake deep in the pot. Wrap twine around the stakes to make a cage that will hold the plant inside up. A more decorative option is a lattice trellis that cucumbers will climb but that you'll have to tie tomato vines to. Use soft strips of nylon hose to secure the tomato vines loosely, without damaging them. Set the trellis toward the center of a sturdy clay pot, so the pot will be less likely to come unbalanced as the vines grow.

YOUR CONTAINER FAVORITES

Look for compact plants especially suited to life in a pot.

CUCUMBERS

The crisp texture and fresh aroma of a cucumber picked right off the vine is something you'll never find in an older, store-bought cucumber. Grow your own for pickling—an art in which freshness pays big dividends—or try delicious slicing cucumbers for salads, snacks, garnishes, or sandwiches. When growing cucumbers in pots, you have a decorating choice: let the compact vines of these cultivars twine down around the pots or hold them up on a trellis.

'Bush Pickle': This plant will grow to 36 inches across, producing delicate, little pickling cucumbers in as few as 45 days from planting.

'Salad Bush': Here is an award winner that produces 8-inch-long, dark glossy green slicers on 2-foot-long vines 57 days after planting. It resists many common cucumber diseases, too.

'Bush Champion': If you want an even bigger cucumber, check this cultivar out. The cucumbers get up to 11 inches long. If harvested often, beginning about 55 days after planting, it can keep producing for up to 3 months.

HERBS

One thriving pot of each herb can provide enough sprigs to cook with all season long. Your homegrown herbs will have a wonderful flavor absent from processed herbal products. Most herbs grow easily in containers and make handsome displays. Consider trying some of the following.

Basil: The sweet, clovelike aroma of basil is wonderful in almost any kind of dish, especially those using tomatoes or cheese. Some of the most attractive are the mound-shaped bush forms, purple-leaved basils, crinkled-leaf 'Green Ruffles', and many others.

Chives: Put a small chive seedling or division in a big pot and watch it spread. Whenever you need some fresh chives for your baked potatoes or dips, snip off a few leaves. If you protect the pot during winter in cold climates, the perennial plant will come back to grow again next year.

Oregano: Oregano is renowned as a vigorous grower. Bushy Greek oregano, with spicy undertones unrivaled by other oreganos, will form a bushy mound of hairy, gray-green leaves, great for Italian dishes and more.

Parsley: Put a little curly parsley in some of your over-sized pots to pluck as needed and add a rich, green color and frilly texture to your container garden. Surround a tomato plant with parsley, or put a cluster of three parsley plants in each corner of a rectangular planter to give a orderly look to the whole container garden.

Thyme: This perennial herb comes in so many different varieties you could devote an entire container garden to them alone. Try citrus-scented lemon thyme, variegated silver thyme, or flavorful, narrow-leaved French thyme. If you protect the pot during winter in cold climates (partially burying it or surrounding it with insulating mulch), the perennial plant will grow again next year.

This super dwarf peach stands about 4 feet high.

CREATIVE CONTAINER GARDEN

PEACHES, GENETIC DWARF

Plant breeders have worked their magic with this new accomplishment: miniature peach trees that fit nicely into a patio tub and grow into easy-to-manage bushes bearing full-sized fruit. In warm climates, try cultivars that thrive with short winters; in cool climates, choose cultivars that need a long period of chilling before they begin to flower. Here are some possibilities.

Warm Climates

'Southern Rose': A red-blushed yellow fruit that is ready in August.

'Southern Flame': There's more red on this peach, for a glowing, warm appearance and delicious flavor. The fruit is ready for picking in late July.

Cool Climates

'Honey Babe': Great flavor develops in this orange-fleshed fruit with a brilliant blush. This precocious tree can produce fruit the first year it is planted and it ripens early, in mid-July. Where temperatures drop below 0°F, protect the potted tree during winter.

PEPPERS

These are decorative garden plants, some of which can rival the showiest flowers. Pick the most attractive of the lot to showcase in your container garden. You can choose from hot or sweet peppers—whatever your heart desires. Here are some options.

'Lipstick': This is a sweet pepper with 4-inch-long, top-shaped, red fruit, ready for picking in just over 50 days from seedling planting.

'Cherrytime': For a little variety, try this red-fruited sweet pepper. Unlike 'Lipstick', it has round fruit, up to 2 inches across. You can start picking green peppers in just 60 days, or leave the peppers on the plant to turn sweet and red.

'Pretty in Purple': Here's a magnificent looking plant that produces extra hot peppers. Grow it if you want to add a warm glow to your meals or if you just like to look at a pretty plant. The foliage is purple and more petite and rounded than other peppers. The peppers themselves begin life purple and then ripen to yellow, orange, or scarlet.

'Sweet Banana': This is a pepper without a gimmick—just great flavor. It's a full-season sweet pepper, taking more than 70 days to produce fruit—but what fruit! The peppers reach up to 6 inches long and are banana-shaped and light green ripening to yellow, orange, and red.

Spicy 'Aurora' pepper is hot in a pot!

SQUASH, SUMMER

Pretty, golden summer squash growing on compact bushes may be the most productive members of your container garden. The golden fruit and flowers are a visual treat so keep some close at hand in order to watch the flowers open and the fruit stretch out. Be vigilant and pluck the squash young, when tender, so the plant will produce more. To ensure a long harvest period, start a second plant several weeks after the first. Here are a variety of cultivars you might try.

'SweetPickle' pepper grows in baskets at the Chicago Botanic Garden.

'Sunburst': This award-winning, scalloped squash has brilliant yellow skin and a contrasting green blossom scar. It's highly productive, bearing fruit in just 52 days.

'Butterstick Hybrid': In 50 days, you could also be enjoying this bright golden, spear-shaped squash, similar to zucchini.

STRAWBERRIES

You can do amazing things with strawberries and containers. For this garden, concentrate on day-neutral types, which produce a big burst of berries in June, followed by several smaller harvests through summer and fall. Grow them in standard pots, or layer them vertically in strawberry towers (available in some nursery catalogs). The foliage is engaging and the ruby red fruits are colorful and delicious. Try to avoid eating every strawberry right off the vine if you want to try the recipe for Strawberry Sauce on page 73.

'Tristar': This is a classic day-neutral strawberry bearing solid, delicious red berries that are extra sweet. It resists a variety of common strawberry diseases.

'Tribute': This cultivar offers tart fruit displaying a softer red color. It grows well in cooler areas of the South and in the Pacific Northwest and is resistant to a variety of diseases.

'Brighton': For extra large berries, try this cultivar which thrives in warm, arid regions.

SWISS CHARD

This relative of the beet produces upright leaves, which can reach 2 feet high. Cultivars such as 'Ruby Red' or 'Rhubarb' are brightened by glowing ruby stems or leaves. They are sturdy growers that can hold up all summer if you harvest only the outer leaves and let the new inner leaves continue to expand. Be diligent with your watering and fertilizing to keep the new growth coming.

When small, chard leaves are sweet and mild—great for salads. If you let them get large, you can cut or tear the tender greenery off the midrib. Quickly steam or sauté the greens and use them like spinach. The large petioles and midribs are also edible although they require additional cooking to tenderize.

TOMATOES

You can enjoy the pleasures of homegrown tomatoes using a variety of different containers. Grow cascading basket cultivars dangling off pedestals or from a ceiling hook to relish the beauty of the ruby fruit from below. Or grow compact cultivars upward, trellising them into little bushes of juicy goodness. Here are some cultivar options.

'Tumbler Hybrid': Manageable fronds dangle from a hanging basket, holding sweet, red cherry tomatoes about the size of ping-pong balls. They may be ready to pick just 50 days from planting.

'Red Robin': Here's another dangling tomato for hanging baskets or containers. It reaches only 12 inches tall and produces fruit similar to 'Tumbler' after about 50 days.

CREATIVE CONTAINER GARDEN

'Oregon Spring': For extra early tomatoes, try this culti-var. The plant will set fruit, despite cool weather, and the fruit will ripen just 58 days from planting. The fruits are larger than the previous cultivars and seedless, combining good flavor with substance.

THE RECIPES

Impress your family and friends with dishes made with the yields of your own container garden plants.

'Micro-Tom', the world's smallest tomato plant, reaches only about 6 inches high and will grow nicely in a 4- or 6-inch pot.

Side Dishes

STIR-FRIED TOMATOES AND HERBS

30 small (cherry) tomatoes, whole
1 tablespoon olive oil
1 clove garlic, minced
1/2 cup or 1 small onion, minced
2 tablespoons fresh basil, chopped
1 tablespoon fresh oregano, chopped
salt and fresh ground pepper to taste

Sauté onion and garlic in oil in a large skillet for 3 minutes. Add tomatoes and herbs. Heat covered for 3 minutes, stirring once. When the tomatoes are warm but still firm, remove from heat. Season with salt and pepper and serve.

YIELD: Serves 4–6

CULINARY GARDENS

ONIONS AND GREEN PEPPERS

2 onions, cut into slices

2 banana peppers, sliced into rings

1 tablespoon sesame oil

Warm oil in a large skillet on medium heat. Sauté onions and peppers over medium heat for 10 minutes or until tender. Serve as a side dish or with sausage sandwiches.

YIELD: Serves 4

SWISS CHARD SALAD

2 to 3 cups tender Swiss chard leaves

1 medium carrot, grated

1/2 cup walnuts

1 tablespoon cider vinegar

2 tablespoons olive oil

Wash and chop chard leaves, removing any tough petioles. Microwave in covered casserole dish for 3 mintues on high. Toss with shredded carrots and walnuts. Dress with vinegar and oil and serve.

YIELD: Serves 4

DILLED SUMMER SQUASH

3 medium yellow squash, sliced

1-1/2 tablespoons peanut oil

1 teaspoon parsley, chopped

1 teaspoon thyme leaves, chopped

1-1/2 teaspoons salt

1 tablespoon dill, chopped

In a skillet, sauté squash in peanut oil. Brown lightly on both sides on medium-high heat. Reduce heat to low and add herbs and salt. Simmer for several minutes or until squash is tender.

YIELD: Serves 4

Sauce

STRAWBERRY SAUCE

2 cups strawberries

2 tablespoons corn syrup (or to taste)

Wash, trim, and cut strawberries in half. Put in food processor and puree strawberries. Taste for sweetness and add corn syrup as desired. Serve warm or chilled.

Pour this over ice cream or yogurt; smother it on eggrolls or spareribs.

YIELD: Serves 8

VARIATION: Puree strawberries with 1/2 cup (1 medium) ripe plum, peeled.

Summer squash can be especially prolific. Harvest when young for top quality and continuous productivity.

Careful clipping of herbal knots gives the impression of interwoven ribbons of varying colors.

Gardens of History

A wealth of gardening knowledge, garden plants, and recipes used by our ancestors can be enjoyed today—centuries later. Much of the credit for preserving our gardening past goes to heirloom seed savers—individuals and organizations who have kept older cultivars alive, generation after generation. One especially notable nonprofit group is the Seed Savers Exchange, 3076 North Winn Road, Decorah, IA 52101. They welcome new members and provide access to thousands of heirloom vegetables, herbs, and flowers.

Heirlooms hark back to a variety of times and places. American heirlooms from colonial days are arrayed in a Cottage Garden featured in the American Heirloom Garden (Chapter 7). Stepping back further, almost 500 years ago, an Elizabethan Knot Garden (Chapter 8) takes you to a time when herbs were the main source of decoration, medicine, and flavoring. A few centuries later in England and America, the Victorian era made its colorful stand. Bright edible flowers, blended with herbs and vegetables represent this period as illustrated in a Victorian Courtyard Garden (Chapter 9).

George Washington, plantsman as well as statesman, kept a large kitchen garden for feeding family and guests. The gardens are still tended at his estate, Mount Vernon. Some garden beds are outlined with low-growing boxwood hedges grown from plants most likely sent to Washington from Light Horse Harry Lee in 1786.

7
*A*MERICAN HEIRLOOM GARDEN

Purple tomatoes, white carrots, and black corn were among the diverse and delightful heirloom vegetables grown by our agricultural ancestors. These crops, as well as many other culinary treats, are returning to popularity as restaurants discover their unique qualities and magazines tout their outstanding visual features in glossy centerfolds.

Many heirloom crops possess exquisite flavor. Developed before commercial truck farms that cultivated only those food crops that could be harvested early, shipped, and stored easily, they simply offer great flavor. One good example is the 'Brandywine' tomato, an Amish heirloom from Chester County, Pennsylvania (1885). Its ripe tomatoes—big and beefy—embody an exquisite, rich, sweet flavor that shames most greenhouse tomatoes. But the plant doesn't fit the modern standards of an easy grower. The vines get to be long and are best kept in tall cages. 'Brandywine' also lacks disease resistance, so it can easily fail if wet weather brings on fungus or bacterial diseases.

In the 1760s, George Washington enclosed his kitchen garden in Mount Vernon with brick walls to deter deer.

American Heirloom Garden Design

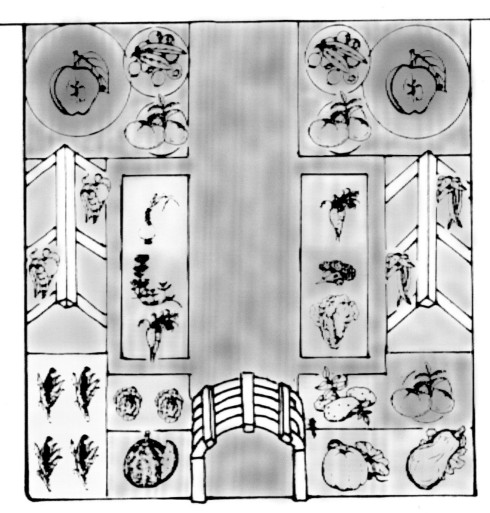

PLANT LIST

Corner Beds

APPLES

BLUEBERRIES

TOMATOES

POTATOES

SQUASH

PUMPKINS

WATERMELONS

CABBAGE

CORN

On Trellises

PEAS

BEANS

In Low Vegetable Beds

CARROTS

LETTUCE

ONIONS

PARSLEY

THYME

Other heirloom crops are unique and valuable as breeding stock for future generations of gourmet crops. 'Wolf River' apple trees, found in Wisconsin in 1875, produce huge apples that are yellow with a red blush and weigh a pound or more each. The apples are not quite as fine flavored as a good 'McIntosh', but the trees maintain a natural resistance to most common apple diseases and may be useful for breeding a new generation of easy-care apple trees.

In colonial America, more different kinds of crops were grown than we can imagine today. This is because many farmers or farming communities developed their own unique strains. Importing their seeds from Europe was too expensive to do every year, so instead, pioneer farmers saved seed from their best plants to sow the next year. Parent plants were those that thrived in the local soil and climate—tolerating clay in Cleveland and sand near the seaside. When inbred for generations, they developed into regional strains with their own unique adaptations. Hence, there arose pink celery, tomatoes covered with peach fuzz, and other great creations. This American Heirloom Garden is dedicated to the celebration of this diversity!

A GREAT GARDEN DESIGN

In colonial times, the kitchen gardens of wealthy statesmen such as Thomas Jefferson and George Washington were large and formal, producing enough food to feed armies of guests and farmhands. But more common folk, who had less land and fewer hands to tend it, often nestled a variety of edible plants in a modest cottage garden near their home. They grew an assortment of plants—hand-me-downs, family favorites, seeds shared with a neighbor, or cuttings handed around at town meetings. This garden reflects those early cottage gardens with places for neat rows of assorted small vegetables, symmetrical fruit plantings, and informal areas for tucking in whatever inspires you. There is room for organization and also flexibility.

STARTING SAVING SEED

Like the early pioneers, you, too, can save seeds from your garden. The trick is to end up with seeds that will grow to be as good as their parent plants. This means you will have to control what kind of pollen falls on the flower and forms the seed. Here are some tips.

Save seed from nonhybrid parent plants which tend to produce similar seedlings. (Hybrids allowed to go to seed produce a varied batch of offspring, few or none of which are superior to the parent plant.)

Easy crops to experiment with are those that naturally self-pollinate such as peas, beans, tomatoes, and peppers. Simply bag newly opened flowers with floating row cover fabric secured with a twist tie to the stem so that no outside pollen can get in. Harvest seeds of pure lineage when they are mature.

Isolate crops such as lettuce, radishes, sunflowers, or dill that can cross with other cultivars by planting different cultivars at different times or just growing one cultivar each year.

This garden, designed to be set on the sunny east, west, or south side of a house, is 20 feet square with a 4-foot-wide walk up the center. It is enclosed by a fence—a necessity in early America to keep out unwanted animals, and a benefit today to frame the garden and keep out uninvited kids and dogs. This is achieved using a rustic split rail fence which won't cast much shade.

Beside the house sits a foundation planting of dwarf apple trees and blueberry bushes—productive and attractive. Both plants flower in the spring, sparkle with colorful fruit in the summer or fall, and the blueberry foliage turns ruby in the fall, further expanding the color spectrum.

A trellis for spring peas and summer beans or cucumbers provides a high point to the rear of both sides of the garden. The foreground, beside the central walkway, is devoted to grid plantings of low vegetables such as carrots, lettuce, onions, and herbs such as dill and parsley. Perennial herbs such as sage, chives, and thyme can be nestled near the walk so they are not disturbed when the soil is reworked for new plantings. Taller vegetables such as broccoli, tomatoes, and corn flourish near the fence and share this space with spreading vines such as pumpkins, squash, sweet potatoes, and watermelon.

Perennial herbs such as chives can be grown at the edge of the garden such as in Mount Vernon.

YOUR COLONIAL FAVORITES

Some of the more common yet delightful heirlooms are called for in this garden. To be true to the spirit of cottage gardening, feel free to experiment with other heirloom foods, fitting them into the plan according to their height, spread, and whether they need trellising.

FOR TRELLISES

The following crops are heirlooms that will thrive on trellises at the perimeter of the garden. Peas are a cool-season crop and beans can cover the trellises during the warmth of summer.

SCARLET RUNNER BEANS

This native of South America reached North America before 1750. Colonists ate the tender, young pods like green beans or let the beans mature and dry to shell and store for winter meals. The plants can get to be tall—12 feet high—perfect for a tall trellis or even an arbor. They bear handsome red flowers—more distinctive than on an ordinary bean vine—but don't begin bearing until later, at least 70 days after sowing.

CUCUMBERS

Eaten primarily boiled or sautéed, early cucumbers must have been an acquired taste. But one early heirloom is unique and well worth growing. 'Lemon' (an 1894 introduction with aliases such as 'Lemon Apple', 'Crystal Apple', and 'Lemon

above: Scarlet runner beans blend well with hyacinth beans (Dolichos lablab), another vining legume enjoyed by pioneers.

right: Hyacinth beans are frisky vines from northern Africa that thrive in warm climates and can grow as tall as 20 feet. The plant displays bright purple flowers in showy spikes and produces pea-shaped pods with seeds that can be eaten like lima beans.

CULINARY GARDENS

Crystal') forms small, round cucumbers covered with soft, prickly spines and firm white flesh. When slightly overripe, the skin turns yellow resembling a lemon. Cucumbers are ready to be picked from 60 to 70 days after sowing.

PEAS

After the middle 1600s, people began growing sweet peas instead of the starchy storage peas that were dried and used for split pea soup. Thomas Jefferson ate his sweet peas boiled with shredded lettuce and topped with chopped mint and cream. Most early sweet peas grew on long vines—compact dwarfs so common today did not appear until the mid-1800s. Although they require trellising for support, full-sized pea vines are more productive than dwarfs.

'Alderman' (also called 'Tall Telephone'): Vines to 6 feet long hold 5-inch-long pods containing up to 10 wrinkled peas each. They are ready to pick about 75 days after sowing. This late-1800s pea is still widely grown and readily available because it is so productive.

'Patriot': Compact vines to 24 inches tall have 4-inch-long pods that are remarkable for being easy to shell. Less productive than 'Alderman', 'Patriot' produces its first pods only 65 days from sowing and can be grown on a shorter trellis or even on twiggy shrub branches stuck in the ground several inches away from a row of peas.

FOR LOW GRIDS

Set these crops in the allotted low-grid area, providing a square of open growing space around each plant. Use the following planner as a guide.

Carrots: 4 square inches per plant
Chives: 18 square inches per plant
Dill: 4 square inches per plant
Leaf lettuce: 10 square inches per plant
Pot marigolds: 8 square inches per plant
Onions: 6 square inches per plant

Parsley: 6 square inches per plant
Sage: 12 square inches per plant
Thyme: 24 square inches per plant

CARROTS

Originally used only as animal food, carrots had to be bred to be sweet and tender before American pioneers welcomed them into their own homes. They chose from large-rooted, storage carrots (which could be kept in the root cellar all winter), or more tender, table carrots. These were mostly boiled, often drizzled with butter or mixed with sweet cream to serve.

'Oxheart': This variety dates back to 1884 and is valued for its tolerance of heavy soils. (Most carrots need light, sandy soil to thrive.) The roots are extra plump and reach about 6 inches long about 75 days after sowing. They also store well in the refrigerator for weeks.

CHIVES

These onion-flavored greens are useful and undemanding—good qualifications for any cottage garden. The clumps are easy to divide and share among friends, and they develop into long lasting perennials that can flourish for decades.

HERBS

Dill: Used since the time of the ancient Roman Empire, dill has maintained a place in gardens throughout the Western world. This lovely, lanky herb is easily grown from seed scattered on warm, loose soil in a sunny location. Its finely cut leaves blend wonderfully with assorted vegetables and the seeds provide a flavoring for pickles.

Parsley: Packed with nutrition, this herb makes a frilly green border and a pleasant addition to many dishes. It has been grown since the time of ancient Greeks who ate it on bread for breakfast.

Sage: Silver-leaved sage enhances poultry stuffings and pork chops with its bold flavor. It may also have been used by colonists in medicinal teas to soothe everyday ailments.

Thyme: Perennial thyme grows well in much of the United States and is easy to divide and share with friends—the sign of a great cottage garden plant. Early American colonists may have used thyme as an antiseptic as well as for cooking.

LETTUCE

Pioneers had a choice of head-forming lettuce, which they enjoyed cooked as well as raw, or fast-growing leaf lettuce, a great spring and fall green. Iceberg lettuce, however, was not an option, not arriving on the scene until about 1900.

'Tennis Ball': Loose leaf heads of tender, light green leaves look just as they did in 1805 growing at Thomas Jefferson's Monticello.

'Black Seeded Simpson', a classic leaf lettuce from 1850, is ready to harvest just 45 days after sowing. Be sure to pick it promptly. The outer leaves are dark green with a crispy, light, inner heart.

POT MARIGOLDS

These perky, yellow- and orange-flowered annuals arise from seed scattered on open ground and thrive in cool, mild weather. Early Americans used the edible flowers, which have a mild, pungent flavor, for coloring golden sauces and flavoring puddings, stews, salads, and teas. Modern cooks may sprinkle the flowers on salads or float them on soups and use them as garnishes or seasonings for herbal vinegar.

ONIONS

Onions, grown in spring and summer in northern climates or fall and winter in southern climates, were ideal for colonial gardens. Pungent, northern onions could be stored for months

Pot marigolds offer bright colors and interesting flavors to a cottage garden.

in a cellar. They added bold flavor to bland, boiled dishes but were not always viewed as healthful.

ONION ALERT

Robert Bruist (*The Family Kitchen Gardener*. New York: C. M. Saxton, 1851) describes onions as indispensable in cooking and nutritious but warns that if too many are eaten, onions become unwholesome and indigestible: "Used in its crude state, it often remains in the stomach 48 hours before being dissolved by the gastric juice, and in this state has been known to produce spasms."

'Red Wethersfield' (also called 'Hamburger' and 'Large Red Weathersfield'): This is a northern onion suitable for spring planting and summer harvesting that was developed around 1800 and remains popular today. It's available from seed or onion sets and grows into a large, globe-shaped bulb with rich purple-red skin and moderately good keeping qualities.

'Tree Onion' (also called 'Egyptian Onion', 'Walking Onion', 'Everlasting Onion'): These onions produce clusters of small bulbs on the top of a long, round stem. As summer progresses, the stem yellows and folds to the ground, allowing the bulbs to root and multiply. The bulblets were generously shared by cottage gardeners and can be used in cooking if you have the patience to peel them. The greens are a great substitute for scallions.

TALL OR SPREADING CROPS

Grow these crops near the front of the garden where they have a little extra room to spread.

CABBAGE

Cabbages grown in colonial times were often firm, late-maturing types suitable for keeping a month or more in a root cellar (and also in a refrigerator). Cabbage could be kept even longer once pickled as sauerkraut.

With a blue green hue to its leaves, cabbage plays a prominent role in a gardener's color symphony.

WHOLESOME CABBAGE

William Kenrick (*New American Orchardist.* 5th ed. Boston: Otis, Broaders, and Co., 1842) shared his views on using cabbage:

When boiled, it forms a wholesome and agreeable food. In making sour krout, the heads of cabbage, after being chopped fine, are strewed in layers in a barrel, and a handful of salt, mixed with a few caraway seeds, are strewed between each layer, til the barrel is filled. A heavyweight is now placed on the mass and as soon as the fermentation, which soon commences, has subsided, the weight is removed and the barrel is headed. A fine article for the sea stores of ships sailing on distant voyages—a powerful antiscorbutic, and highly relished by all who become accustomed to it when boiled with beef.

'Early Jersey Wakefield': This crop, introduced in 1840, produces cone-shaped heads 64 days after transplanting seedlings. An early cabbage, it will not store more than several weeks to a month in the refrigerator. It is resistant to frost and to a disease called cabbage yellows.

'Late Flat Dutch': This flat-headed cabbage takes about 100 days from planting to maturity. It was brought to America by German immigrants who enjoyed a wide variety of cabbage cultivars in their native homeland.

SWEET CORN

In the mid-1800s, starchy Indian corn used for drying, grinding, or popping was superseded by sweet corn which was eaten (like modern sweet corn) after boiling or steaming or made into corn pudding, creamed corn, succotash, and other dishes.

'Golden Bantam': This is one of the first golden sweet corns which previously had been available only in white-kernel forms. 'Golden Bantam' was introduced by W. Atlee Burpee in 1902. About 80 days after sowing, it produces small ears, about 6 inches long. Newer forms of 'Golden Bantam' ripen earlier and have larger ears and more tender kernels.

'Stowell's Evergreen': This is one of the earliest sweet corns, refined by Nathan Stowell of New Jersey in 1848. It produces 8-inch-long ears of white kernels about 90 days after sowing.

POTATOES

Foods such as the potato that could store well during long winters were a lifesaver for early American colonists. Potatoes journeyed from their place of origin in South America to Europe and back to the Americas via Irish immigrants in the early 1700s. They were roasted on a slow fire, mashed into a pudding, or fried into potato pancakes.

'Lady Finger': This is a small, slender, German potato that grows 1 inch wide and up to 5 inches long. When it reached America in the early 1800s, its golden, waxy flesh was a big hit. It is wonderful fried or mixed in potato salad.

'Russet Burbank': This classic baker, introduced in the mid-1800s, has large tubers with russeted skin and white flesh. It produces big yields but takes a long time—120 to 140 days from planting.

PUMPKINS

These impressive fruits, famous for their large, orange, good-eating globes, were grown originally by Native Americans. High-yielding pumpkins, which could store for months in a cool, dry place, became a staple that sustained many colonists through the winter.

'Connecticut Field': This variety was grown by Native Americans prior to the 1700s and remains popular today as a source of jack-o'-lanterns. Pumpkins, which can reach 20 pounds, begin to mature 110 days after plant-

Pumpkin and large winter squash were dried for emergency rations, made into pies, or boiled and eaten like a vegetable.

ing. Any that are not used for celebrating Halloween are great for pies.

'New England Pie' (also called 'Small Sugar' or 'Sugar Pumpkin'): This small, pre-1860, culinary pumpkin has firm but stringless, sweet flesh that makes wonderful pies. The pumpkins, which reach 8 pounds, begin to mature 100 days after planting.

TOMATOES

This vegetable was late to be accepted into American cuisine. Colonists were suspicious of tomatoes' poisonous leaves and toxic nightshade relatives. Not until the 1830s to the 1850s did people finally accept the tomato fruit to be good eating. Then it became revered for catsup, pickling, stewing, and other forms of cooking uses.

'Red Pear': This variety was grown before 1850. It has a lovely, unusual pear shape with thick flesh and a small seed cavity.

'Yellow Pear': This bright yellow brother to 'Red Pear' was available in the United States as early as 1805, making it one of the earliest cultivated tomatoes in this country. About 75 days after planting seedlings, it begins to produce small fruit about 1-1/2 inches long. It was used primarily for preserving or pickling but also can be eaten fresh especially when blended with 'Red Pear' tomatoes.

WATERMELON

These juicy fruits are a naturally sweet treat, once grown primarily in the southern states but now available for growing even in northern climates. One of the most beautiful heirloom cultivars is 'Moon and Stars', which displays yellow speckles on its leaves and golden stars and larger moons on the melon rind. The pink-fleshed melons can reach 25 pounds. This variety was grown in Amish

For lush foliage and great flavor, grow 'Moon and Stars'.

communities before 1910 and has been reintroduced as modified versions with either yellow flesh or extra long melons. Harvest begins about 95 to 100 days after sowing seeds.

FRUIT

Two pairs of blueberry bushes and apple trees add a sweet dimension to the garden. Growing two different cultivars of each crop—carefully selected to flower si-multaneously and cross-pollinate, is essential for fruit production.

APPLES

Some contemporary apple cultivars incorporate a disease resistance that makes them much easier to grow than the older varieties. So, although there are many wonderful heirloom apples with rich histories, this garden plan calls for the disease-resistant newcomers. Check nursery catalogs for the best disease-resistant cultivars including those listed below and newcomers with improved features. Take advantage of dwarf trees that will fit comfortably into the American Heirloom Garden.

'Freedom': This red apple ripens in mid-season and has slightly tart fruit that is ideal for cooking. It cross-pollinates well with 'Liberty' and is hardy to -45°F.

'Jonafree': A red Jonathan-type fruit with crisp, golden flesh ripens in mid-season and resists many diseases. It may, however, be troubled by occasional mildew.

'Liberty': This red-blushed apple ripens in mid-season and resists scab, fire blight, mildew, and cedar apple rust—all common diseases of apples.

A HINT FROM HISTORY

P. Barry (*The Fruit Gardener*. Detroit: Kerr, Doughty, and Lapham, 1853) described the apple's increasing availability in colonial America: "At one time apples were grown chiefly for cider; now they are considered indispensable articles of food. The finer fruits, that were formerly considered as luxuries only for the tables of the wealthy, are beginning to take their place among the ordinary supplies of every man's table ... ."

'MacFree': An updated McIntosh-type apple with tangy flesh, red skin, and disease resistance ripens in mid-season.

'Prima': This early-ripening apple features a red blush on yellow skin with white, slightly tart flesh. It resists several diseases.

BLUEBERRIES

Blueberries, a native American crop, were harvested from wild meadows and open woodlands by the earliest colonists. Later cultivation produced a wide variety of cultivars. Choose two cultivars that will grow well in your climate and that are compatible cross-pollinators; your Cooperative Extension Service can help you make wise selections.

THE RECIPES

Enjoy some old-fashioned flavors that are still delightful today.

Johnny Appleseed would agree that an apple tree is a natural in a colonial garden.

Salads

DILLED POTATO SALAD

3 cups 'Lady Finger' or similar yellow fleshed potatoes, boiled, peeled,
   and sliced

1/2 cup carrots, shredded

3/4 cup peas, shelled and lightly cooked

1 cup mayonnaise

2 teaspoons vinegar

2 teaspoons prepared mustard

2 teaspoons dill leaves, chopped

1/4 cup 'Tree Onion' leaves or other scallions, chopped

Cube potatoes and set in large bowl with peas and carrots. In small bowl, blend mayonnaise, vinegar, mustard, dill, and scallions. Add to potato mixture and stir to coat. Chill before serving.

YIELD: Serves 6

LEMON CUCUMBER SALAD

3 cups 'Lemon' cucumbers, peeled and sliced

2 cups 'Red' and 'Yellow Pear' tomatoes, quartered

1/2 cup red onions, separated into rings, thin sliced

1/8 cup herbal vinegar

1/4 cup olive oil

4 to 8 lettuce leaves, whole

In medium-sized bowl, gently combine cucumber slices, onion rings, and quartered tomatoes. Whisk together vinegar and oil in separate bowl and drizzle over salad. Serve on lettuce leaves without chilling.

YIELD: Serves 4

Soup

PUMPKIN SOUP

1/2 small pumpkin (4 cups)

2 cups chicken broth

1 cup onion, chopped

1 cup half-and-half

1/2 cup dried tomatoes, crumbled

Slice pumpkin into strips and cut off rind. Cut into 1-inch-wide cubes. Simmer pumpkin in chicken stock with onion until tender. Puree. Add half-and-half and warm without boiling, stirring occasionally. Pour into bowls and float crumbled dried tomatoes on top.

YIELD: Serves 6

Side Dishes

STEWED CUCUMBERS

This colonial favorite is taken from R. Bradley's *The Country Housewife and Lady's Director*, 6th ed. (London: D. Brown, Publisher, 1736):

Take a dozen large green Cucumbers, that are not too full of seed; pare them, and slice them; then take two large Onions, and shred them indifferently small. Put these in a Sauce-Pan and set them over the Fire to stew, with as much salt as you think convenient; stir them now and then, till they are tender, and then pour them into a cullender [colander] to drain from the water, and are as dry as possible you can make them. After this, burn [heat] some butter in a Frying-Pan; and when it is very hot, put in your Cucumbers and stir them continually till they are brown; then put to them about a Gill of Claret; and when that is well mix'd with them, serve them hot, under roast mutton or lamb . . . .

OLD-FASHIONED BAKED BEANS

Fresh beans add a delightful texture to this classic dish.

1 cup fresh shelling beans
3 slices turkey bacon
1/4 cup onion, chopped
2 tablespoons catsup
2 tablespoons dark molasses
1 teaspoon prepared mustard

Shell and boil the beans gently in a little water for 5 minutes or until just tender. Drain and set aside. Cut bacon into bite-sized pieces and cook with chopped onions in medium saucepan until onions are tender. Drain off excess fat, if any. Add beans, catsup, molasses, and mustard to pan. Simmer for 10 minutes, stirring often until well blended.

YIELD: Serves 4

VARIATION: Try different kinds of beans for variety.

Mild sweet cabbage, fresh from the garden, can be shredded, lightly steamed, and tossed with rice vinegar and oil.

Sauce

OLD-FASHIONED APPLESAUCE

2–3 quarts apples, peeled, sliced, and cored
1/2 cup apple cider
honey and cinnamon to taste

In a slow cooker, add apples and cider. Cover and cook on high for 1 hour or until soft. Stir apples and mash with potato masher. Remove cover and cook for 2 or 3 more hours, stirring occasionally. When sauce reaches desired consistency, add honey and cinnamon to taste. Freeze extra in freezer bags or containers.

YIELD: Serves 16–24

Desserts

BLUEBERRY PIE

9-inch pie crust
4 cups fresh blueberries
1/2 lemon
2-1/2 teaspoons cornstarch
1/4 cup whole wheat flour
3/4 cup sugar

Preheat oven to 350°F. Wash berries, drain, and put in a large mixing bowl. Add sugar and lemon and mix well. Add flour and cornstarch, stirring in gently. Pour into pie crust and bake for 35 to 45 minutes, or until crust is golden.

YIELD: Serves 6

HONEY-DRIED APPLES

Eat these delicious, flavor-packed apples as snacks or with yogurt or ice cream.

1/2 cup honey
1 teaspoon cinnamon
1/2 lemon
6 medium apples

Peel, core, and slice apples. Blend honey, lemon, and cinnamon in a small nonmetallic bowl. Dip slices in honey lemon and dry in dehydrator at 135°F until leathery and no longer sticky.

YIELD: Serves 6

PIONEER APPLE PIE

This pie lets the great flavor of homegrown apples shine through.

9-inch graham cracker pie crust
5 cups apples, peeled, cored, sliced thick
1/4 cup honey
1/4 cup white sugar
1/2 tablespoon fennel flowers, chopped
1-1/2 tablespoons cornstarch
Topping:
2 tablespoons margarine
4 tablespoons flour
3 tablespoons sugar

Preheat oven to 450°F. In ceramic bowl, blend sliced apples, honey, sugar, cornstarch, and fennel flowers until well mixed. Fill pie crust with mixture. Prepare topping and crumble on top of pie.

Cover with foil and bake for 10 minutes. Remove foil and lower temperature to 350°F. Bake for 45 more minutes, or until apples are tender and topping is lightly browned.

YIELD: Serves 6

8
ℓLIZABETHAN KNOT GARDEN

The sixteenth-century Elizabethan era is remembered for the reign of England's Queen Elizabeth and for the knot garden—a unique and dynamic style of gardening that developed while England enjoyed isolation from the rest of Europe. Knot gardens, like embroidery, interweave plants with varying foliage colors and textures into simple or elaborate patterns. Herbs such as blue-green, needle-leaved rosemary, silver, leather-leaved sage, and petite, green-leaved thyme, were carefully sheared into ribbons that appear to weave amongst the other herbs. Contemporary knot gardens may be composed of annual herbs and flowers such as purple and green leaf basil and golden or orange marigolds, which require little or no trimming.

A GREAT GARDEN DESIGN
This Elizabethan Knot Garden, designed by Alexander Apanius, revives the past and creates a visual symphony. A big garden—30 by 38 feet—will yield an abundance of

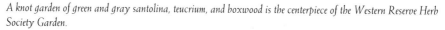

A knot garden of green and gray santolina, teucrium, and boxwood is the centerpiece of the Western Reserve Herb Society Garden.

Elizabethan Knot Garden Design

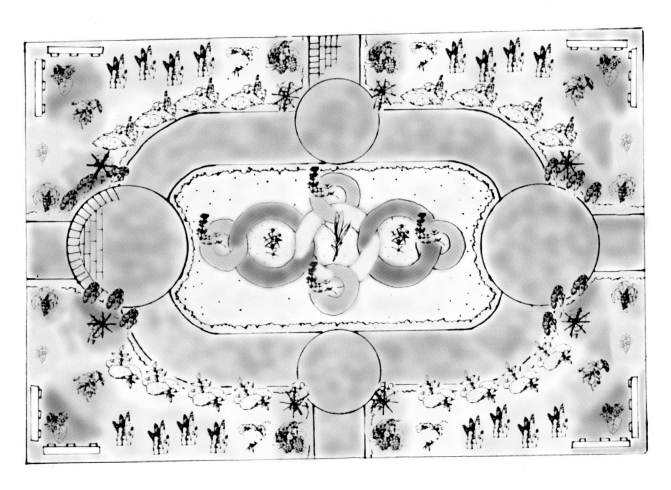

PLANT LIST

Angelica	Potatoes
Asparagus	Raspberries
Blackberries	Rosemary
Brussels sprouts	Rutabaga
Lovage	Sage
Parsley	Thyme
Peas on sapling teepee	

herbs as well as plenty of vegetables and berries from the surrounding beds. It features a central oval sporting a timeless knot garden of classic rosemary, sage, and thyme. The knot foliage is set off by a background of light-colored, crushed limestone or white granite, which highlights the interplay of greenery. You could situate this knot garden on the sunny south side of a house or in any dramatic location in the yard.

Surrounding the garden is a brick pathway, with a running board pattern of staggered lengthwise bricks, and a roll-lock edging of bricks sunk lengthwise to hold everything in place. The path is lined in white or light blue lobelia—the only nonedible plant in the design—which earns its keep by softening the transitions from knot to brick and gently cascading over the walk.

The walks divide four corner gardens devoted to decorative clusters of Elizabethan vegetables, herbs, and berries. The most distinctive resident is towering angelica, which bears huge heads of small, white flowers over broad, compound, licorice-scented stems. Asparagus grows in ferny clumps near the perimeter of the garden. Blackberries rise in bristly clumps at each corner and raspberries mark either side of two entryways. Parsley lines the entryways with frilly green foliage while peas climb on sapling teepees to welcome visitors to the garden. The plantings are matched in each bed, lending the whole garden a balance and unity that would have comforted Elizabethan gardeners.

To adapt this garden for smaller yards, cut the length down to 16-1/2 feet. The garden now will include two corner beds with a half-circle knot garden. Reorganize the interwoven circles of the knot to form a pleasing composition within the allotted space.

YOUR ELIZABETHAN FAVORITES

These crops were favorites more than 400 years ago and many remain valuable today—real classics. The one histori-

---

PLANTING KNOT GARDENS

Knot gardens require precise planting so they will retain neat geometric shapes. One way to ensure precision is to premeasure and mark planting areas before putting any plants in the ground.

For even circles, put a stake in the middle of each circle and attach a rope half the diameter of the intended circle. Move the rope around the stake, marking the perimeter of the loop with ground limestone. Space plants a foot apart; they will mature to blend with their neighbors and form one continuous line. Trim with grass or hedge shears at least once a month to maintain a well-defined ribbon of color. Use the clippings right away or preserve them for later.

To form square or rectangular lines with herbs, stretch two ropes through the center of the bed between alternate corners of the garden—where they cross is the center of the bed. Create straight planting lines under the crossing ropes or measure from the center and edges of the bed to create other symmetrical geometric shapes.

---

cal stretch is the inclusion of potatoes in this garden. They probably were not known in England at that time. But once introduced by early American explorers, potatoes quickly became part of the British culture and cuisine.

ANGELICA

This licorice-flavored plant will grow to be a masterpiece in your garden the second year after planting. When flowering, it can reach 6 feet high stretching out huge, compound leaves and tiny, white flowers in mammoth umbrella-shaped clusters. Angelica was reputed to have magical and medicinal powers in ancient times and was expected to repel evil as well as the plague. It also has been used to flavor alcoholic drinks. Young angelica stems can be stewed with sugar or sliced into pie with rhubarb. You can also candy stem slices and use them to garnish cupcakes, frosted cookies, and other fancy pastries.

ASPARAGUS

Slender, spear-shaped stalks arise in mid-spring, providing tender fare and sweet flavor quickly lost after harvest. Asparagus has been enjoyed since the time of the ancient Roman Empire. Green, white, and purple forms became popular in England in the early 1500s. Today it is eaten crunchy and raw right out in the garden, or lightly steamed until just tender and drizzled with butter. Creamy sauces were popular in Elizabethan times, as they are today. You can also slice asparagus and add it to stir-fries, casseroles, and other mixed dishes.

BLACKBERRIES

These are the thorny-stemmed counterparts to the thornless blackberries used in the Victorian Courtyard Garden. They are freestanding and yield large crops of fat, sweet berries. Blend blackberries with raspberries and other fruit in fruit salads, put them on cereal or ice cream, mix them into yogurt, and freeze the extras for later. The best cultivars of blackberries to plant will vary according to your climate. Ask your local Cooperative Extension Service for specific recommendations.

BRUSSELS SPROUTS

These minicabbage heads cling to tall, leafy stems—an unusual and remarkable sight. Julius Caesar may be the person who introduced this plant into England. In 1700s England, they had not yet received the brussels and were just called sprouts. At that time, they were cooked until thoroughly soggy—a habit modern chefs strive to avoid.

LOVAGE

This old-fashioned perennial herb sprouts big heads of small golden flowers on stems up to 6 feet tall. The oversized leaves look like flat-leaved parsley or celery but have a bold celery flavor and taste. Ancient Anglo-Saxons used lovage to make an herbal diuretic and a magical potion to cure jaundice and typhoid fever. Today, lovage makes a fine celery leaf substitute and the dried seeds can stand in for celery seed spice.

PARSLEY

This herb, chock full of vitamins and minerals, adds mild flavor to many dishes, and a sprig eaten raw is said to freshen breath. Ancient Romans used it to make a tea for treating rheumatism and spread it throughout Europe on their world conquests. Extra parsley is easy to dry or freeze for later.

PEAS

Dried peas were a sustenance item used in Elizabethan porridge, a kettle of which was left stewing

'Rubine', a lovely, old-fashioned brussels sprouts plant, blends handsome blue foliage with purplish sprouts. A mature plant can survive until temperatures drop below about 20°F, so you can harvest it through much of fall and winter in some areas.

Lovage foliage harvested in spring is at its best.

on most hearths day and night to the chagrin of folks who hated leftovers. Today, high-quality, dried field peas are inexpensive to buy so this garden focuses instead on good, sweet garden peas—later arrivals that are wonderful for vegetables, salads, and side dishes. Any tall, vined pea will grow luxuriously on a teepee of saplings.

'Multistar': This pea has vines that reach 4 to 6 feet high and bears twin pods 3 inches long. It is a late pea, cropping 70 days from sowing, but offers high yields, tolerates powdery mildew, and resists wilt.

POTATOES

Once they reached England, these tubers quickly gained popularity over other, skimpier root crops such as skirret and turnips. They were sliced into stews or eaten with cream or butter, much like today. A favorite dish paired them with bacon or ham. Moderate-sized cultivars such as 'Dark Red Norland' or heirloom 'Early Rose' roughly approximate what was available to early gardeners, although you can substitute any potato you enjoy.

Wait until black raspberries are swollen and completely black before harvesting.

RASPBERRIES

Tender raspberries are so delicate that only homegrowers can savor them fully ripe and at their best—a secret that Elizabethan gardeners surely shared. Pluck the berries off the cane and drop them in your mouth for a treat. Or collect a bowlfull to use for desserts, baked goods, purees, or fruit salads. Good raspberry cultivars vary according to climate and even soil type. Ask your local Cooperative Extension Service agent for the name of one that thrives in your area.

ROSEMARY

This perennial herb symbolizes remembrance—an appropriate attribute of this historical garden. Elizabethan herbalists are believed to have used rosemary to protect themselves against evil. It has strongly fragrant, needlelike leaves cherished with meats and in tomato casseroles. Pulverize the dried needles in a food

Rosemary cascades gracefully over a brick wall.

processor or blender before adding them to dishes for easy eating. Or, remove rosemary sprigs after cooking but before serving.

For this knot garden, you can use prostrate forms that naturally stay low. Many forms of rosemary are hardy to about 20°F. Slightly hardier choices are 'Arp' or 'Hill Hardy'. Where winters are colder than 20°F, you'll either have to bring your rosemary indoors or grow hardy winter savory instead.

Winter savory (used as an edging here) exhibits both fine leaves and great flavor, making it a suitable substitute for rosemary in northern gardens. (Western Reserve Herb Society Garden)

RUTABAGAS

This was an Elizabethan staple before the arrival of potatoes. It resembles a large turnip with sweet and mild flesh. Rutabagas are little known today but worth a try. They are tasty mashed and mixed with potatoes or drizzled with butter and minced thyme. They can also be cubed and added to soups or stews.

'Purple Top' rutabaga closely resembles early purple shouldered rutabagas. Eighty to 120 days after sowing, the root can reach 6 inches in diameter and is prime for harvesting. The cut-leaf foliage rises to 20 inches high.

'York': This modern counterpart produces purple-topped roots in just 95 days. Better yet, it is resistant to clubroot disease, which can stop the growth of rutabagas and any related crops in infected soil.

PRESERVING EXTRA HERBS

For even the most ardent cook, this garden may produce more herbs than can be used fresh. Extra herbs can be frozen as is (see Chapter 3). They can also be made into herb pastes, concentrating the flavor in an easy-to-use form. Blend 2 cups of herb leaves with 1/4 to 1/2 cup of oil in a food processor until smooth. Freeze the resulting paste in ice cube trays, transfer to freezer bags, and keep frozen until needed. The paste is great for using on breads, pastas, for blending into pesto, drizzling on potatoes, or dropping into soups or stews.

Another option is to dry surplus herbs. Although heat processing releases some of the volatile flavorings, dried herbs are more concentrated than fresh and can still retain a great deal of flavor. Dry individual leafy sprigs on an open rack—a nylon mesh tray or piece of cheesecloth in a warm location with low humidity. Another good place is near an air conditioner which can cool and dry them quickly. A dehydrator is an even better option, especially in humid climates. Buy a brand that has a low setting for herbs. They can dry overnight and be ready to strip off the stems and store in airtight jars for future use.

SAGE

Silver-leaved garden sage, a perennial herb and all-purpose medicinal tea from antiquity, has bold-flavored leathery leaves—a must in turkey dressing and a bonus with pork chops. The dried sprigs add shimmering gleams to dried flower arrangements or wreaths.

THYME

Ladies would give a sprig of thyme to their favorite knight for protection in battle. Thyme was also important in medicine and cooking. There are dozens of types of thyme, bearing different colors of leaves and flowers with subtle to dramatic differences in aroma and flavor. Browse through your local garden center or nursery and find the type you enjoy most. Then buy enough of that one cultivar to use in the entire knot. You can harvest that thyme to use with meats, vegetables, vinegars, teas, soups, and more.

THE RECIPES

Some of these recipes are modern; others are from an eighteenth-century British cookbook.

Side Dishes

ASPARAGUS IN CREAM

This recipe comes from R. Bradley (*The Country Housewife and Lady's Director*, 6th ed. London: D. Brown Publisher, 1736):

Break the tops of your Asparagus in small Pieces, then blanch them a little in boiling Water, or parboil them, after which put them in a Stew-Pan or Frying-Pan with Butter or Hogs-Lard and let them remain a little while over a brisk Fire, taking care that they are not too greasy, but well drain'd; then put them in a clean Stew-Pan with some milk and cream, a gentle seasoning of salt and spice, with a small bunch of Sweet Herbs; and just when they are enough, add to them the yolks of 2 to 3 eggs beaten, with a little cream to bind your sauce.

PICKLED SPROUTS

2 cups firm brussels sprouts, fresh picked

1/4 cup white wine vinegar

2 tablespoons fresh thyme leaves, chopped

1/4 cup olive oil

Wash sprouts well and trim off base. Boil for 5 minutes or until slightly tender. Transfer to microwavable casserole dish and set aside. In small bowl, mix vinegar, oil, and chopped thyme. Pour over brussels sprouts and mix well. Refrigerate for 4 hours or overnight.

To serve, stir well and microwave on high for 2 minutes or until warm throughout. Serve immediately.

YIELD: Serves 4

Main Courses

BREAKFAST POTATOES

Early English potatoes were served with milk and sugar or with bacon.

4 medium-sized red skin potatoes, washed

1 medium onion, peeled and thinly sliced

6–8 slices turkey bacon, cut in half

2 tablespoons olive oil

salt and freshly ground pepper to taste

Add oil to a large skillet and warm on medium heat. Cut potatoes into quarter-inch slices and add to the oil. Brown lightly on one side, turn over, and reduce heat to low. Top with onion slices and bacon halves. Cover and cook for about 15 minutes, stirring often to prevent sticking. When the potatoes are tender and the onion is soft, remove from heat and sprinkle with salt and pepper to taste. Serve immediately.

YIELD: Serves 4

AUTUMN STEW

1 onion, chopped

1 clove garlic, peeled and sliced

3 medium carrots, sliced into coins

1 rutabaga, peeled and cubed

2 cups chicken breast, cooked and cubed

2 cans chicken broth

1/2 teaspoon black pepper

1 teaspoon rosemary

1 teaspoon parsley

1/2 cup peas

In large pot, simmer chicken in chicken broth. Add onion, garlic, carrots, and rutabaga while simmering and cook for 30 minutes or until root crops are tender. Add peas, pepper, rosemary, and parsley and simmer another 5 minutes.

Note: This is good served with noodles or dumplings.

YIELD: Serves 8

Seasoning

SALT-FREE HERB MIX

Use this blend to add zest to any dish without using a single grain of salt.

1/4 cup dried thyme

1/4 cup dried parsley

1/8 cup dried lovage

1 tablespoon dried rosemary, ground

Blend herbs in a food processor and pulse to chop the herbs into flakes. Sprinkle on food as needed. Store in a sealed jar in the refrigerator.

Dessert

ROSEMARY SHORTBREAD

Recipe courtesy of Lori Zaim

These sweet and savory cookies are the perfect complement to a cup of afternoon tea.

8 tablespoons butter
1/4 cup powdered sugar
1-1/2 cups all-purpose flour
1/4 teaspoon baking powder
1 tablespoon fresh rosemary leaves, chopped
small rosemary sprigs for garnish

Preheat oven to 350°F. Butter a 9-inch-round cake pan. Cream the butter and sugar until smooth. Work in the flour, baking powder, and rosemary into a soft dough.

With floured hands, press dough evenly into the cake pan. Score the dough into 8 pie-shaped wedges using a fork dipped in flour. Press the edges with the flat side of the fork to form a decorative border. Press one small rosemary sprig onto each wedge.

Bake until golden, about 25 minutes. Let cool in the pan for 10 minutes. Carefully invert the shortbread onto a cooling rack. Cut about halfway through the score marks.

YIELD: 8 cookies

Beverage

SAGE TEA

From R. Bradley (*The Country Housewife and Lady's Director*, 6th ed. London: D. Brown, Publisher, 1736):

Pour on your boiling water, and when it has been half a minute upon the sage-leaves, pour it off and fling away the Leaves; for if you pour more water on them, you must expect your Tea of a dark Color and ill tasted.

9
VICTORIAN COURTYARD GARDEN

The Victorian era, the early to mid-1800s, was an exciting time in horticultural history. Victorian gardens experienced a new kind of artistic freedom. Designers broke away from the stiff formality of earlier eras and introduced the use of a large, more random array of bright flowers. This gaiety was enhanced even further by the development of greenhouses—formerly a luxury limited to the upper class. Now they were available to the rising middle class, recently empowered by the industrial revolution and anxious to grow new tropicals from South America, Africa, and other exciting warm climates.

In celebration of the festivity of the Victorian era, this cheerful courtyard garden is brimming with edible flowers

A courtyard garden at L'Auberge Provençale in White Post, Virginia, provides herbs and edible flowers for the gourmet restaurant.

Victorian Courtyard Garden Design

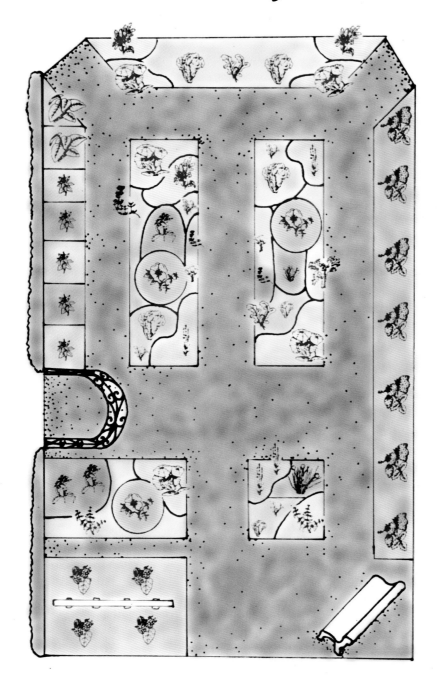

PLANT LIST

THORNLESS BLACKBERRIES

LAVENDER

JUNE-BEARING STRAWBERRIES

LEMON THYME

WOOLLY THYME

ENGLISH THYME

ROSES

NASTURTIUMS

CHIVES

BEE BALM

SCENTED GERANIUMS

ASSORTED GREENS

LEMON BALM

ASSORTED MINT

SAFFRON

and herbs. Beautiful and colorful, this gourmet garden wears the disguise of flowers. Bright plants interweave amid square and rectangular beds separated by bluestone walks. The edible flowers and aromatic foliage yield gourmet harvests the likes of which you may never find in a grocery store. This is an adventure—a journey into the past and future—beyond what most people would normally experience.

THE COURTYARD AT L'AUBERGE PROVENÇALE

This Victorian garden was inspired by a courtyard herb and flower garden at L'Auberge Provençale, a French country inn and restaurant in White Post, Virginia. "It is essential for us to have fresh herbs and edible flowers and well worth growing our own," says owner Alain Borel.

The garden rests between several guest cottages and a yew hedge that forms a courtyard. When entering this secluded area, you must walk beneath an arbor covered with flowering clematis, then down several steps to discover what lies beyond. Surrounded by the green of farmland and spreading country lawns, the courtyard garden gleams with purple bee balm, orange, pink, and golden-flowered nasturtium, and silver, green, and woolly white herbs. The fragrance of herbs and flowers—released when temperatures push into the 90s and retained within the courtyard walls—hints at the culinary pleasures that await behind this colorful display.

A GREAT GARDEN DESIGN

A courtyard is a special space—enclosed and secret with an aura all its own. It is easy to create near the front door of an L-shaped house, or, perhaps, between the house and a garage or walled pool. It also could be situated in more open surroundings using fencing and hedges. Taller walls should be reserved for the north and west sides. To the east, enclose the garden with a low-growing hedge of landscape roses such as 'The Fairy', barberries such as *Berberis thunbergii* 'Sparkle', or evergreen yews such as *Taxus x media* 'Chadwickii'. Leave the garden open to the south.

This Victorian Courtyard Garden (30 by 45 feet) is crossed by bluestone walks, a durable stone of subtle color ideal for garden use. The walks vary from 3 to 7 feet wide and give the garden a tailored look, a pleasant contrast to the informal planting pattern within the beds. A bench, on the southern end of the garden, provides a place to relax and enjoy all the flowers. A small ornamental tree such as a crabapple or redbud could be planted nearby for shade.

For privacy, sitting areas are walled with tall ornamental grasses.

Many of the plants in this garden—including bee balm, thyme, strawberries, blackberries, and self-sowing chives—are enthusiastic ramblers, spreading about the soil forming large and informal clumps. Their big sweeps of color are showy, but they will need occasional dividing for rejuvenation and size control. The beds are edged by brightly colored nasturtiums, silver lavender, golden-leaved lemon thyme, green English thyme, and silvery woolly thyme. Amid the ground-hugging woolly thyme, saffron crocus emerges to provide color and a spice harvest in fall.

The garden pulses with pleasant color rhythm, due to repeated plantings of roses, lavender, nasturtiums, and thyme located throughout. Mints—notorious spreaders—are caged in individual planting squares in their own isolated beds to prevent excessive intermingling. Strawberries freely explore the westernmost bed. In the background of the garden, blackberries quietly climb a trellis, producing plump berries of exquisite quality.

YOUR VICTORIAN FAVORITES

The following edible flowers and herbs make up this Victorian garden.

BEE BALM

Full, shaggy heads of purple, red, or pink, spice-scented flowers and foliage exuding citrus undertones are the trademark of perennial bee balm. Bee balm is a North American native, discovered by the Spanish doctor, Nicholas Monardes, who is honored in the plant's botanical name, *Monarda didyma.*

Bee balm grows to a height of 30 to 36 inches and spreads on runners to form broad clumps. Use the aromatic foliage or flowers in herbal teas, cookies, potpourri, and punch. Bee balm, unfortunately, is susceptible to powdery mildew, which is difficult to control, especially when trying to avoid spraying edible plants with toxic fungicides. To minimize the problem, use only naturally mildew resistant cultivars such as red-flowered 'Gardenview Scarlet', pink-flowered 'Marshall's Delight', and lavender-flowered 'Violet Queen'.

Bee balm accompanies clary sage.

BLACKBERRIES

Vine-ripened blackberries—sweet and plump—are a delicious treat. What makes these berries even better is that they grow on thornless stems so they're extra easy to pick. Blackberries are delicious eaten fresh or frozen for later. You can sprinkle them on cereal or yogurt, blend them into unique soups, or vinegars, or dry them to add to herbal teas. Ask your local Cooperative Extension Service which thornless cultivars are best suited to your climate. In southern areas, heat tolerant 'Black Satin' may be ideal. In northern areas, a hardy cultivar such as 'Illini Hardy' or 'Darrow' will do better.

CHIVES

Once a Chinese antidote for poisoning, chives are valued for their bold onion flavor and aroma that enlivens any recipe calling for scallions or the like. In addition, chives cut a handsome figure. Their upright, foot-high clumps of round tubular leaves and purple balls of flowers are as showy as any ornamental perennial. Use the edible flowers in salads, to float atop soups, or to color and season herbal vinegars.

A BLACKBERRY TRELLIS

Thornless blackberries have limber canes that grow best supported on a trellis. When held upright, sun and fresh air can reach the entire plant, creating a healthier environment than if allowed to flop or grow into a tangled mat. Trellises also facilitate the trimming, organization, and harvest of blackberries—a labor-saving exercise for you.

A traditional blackberry trellis is simply an upright fence, with three rows of horizontal wires set at 2-, 4-, and 6-foot heights. Blackberry canes are tied to the wires with strips of nylon hose or other soft, flexible supports.

Another upright trellis employs double strands of wire, caging the blackberry canes to hold them up without the need for hand tying. For this trellis, set three sturdy 4-by-4 timbers in a row across the center of the blackberry bed—one at each end and the last in the center. The posts should be sunk 1 foot deep and rise at least 5 feet high. Run strands of wire on either side of the posts at 2 and 4 feet high. As new canes grow, sandwich them between the wires to hold them upright.

A high-tech, V-shaped trellis can be made using three sturdy, 6-foot-long, 4-by-4 timbers, set similarly to the previous trellis. But the supporting wires are connected to cross boards that allow them to angle out as they rise to form a V-shape. Tie new canes to one side of the V and year-old canes to the other. Once the year-old canes fruit, cut them back (they won't produce again) and tie new canes to the recently vacated side.

A three-wire trellis.

GERANIUMS, SCENTED

The most delicious aromas waft from the leaves of these geraniums—relatives of the bedding geranium. They flaunt finely cut or full and round foliage with coconut, ginger, apple, lime, mint, rose, strawberry, and other scents—great for adding fragrance to herbal teas or scented sachets. A sampling of cultivars includes the following.

'Apricot': Rose flowers appear on an upright plant with fruity apricot undertones to the foliage.

'Dr. Livingstone': Pink flowers hover over finely divided foliage radiating a strong lemon scent.

'Rober's Lemon Rose': Pretty pink flowers are an extra bonus. This plant is usually grown for its large divided leaves that exude an extra strong rose fragrance that is delicately discernible in cakes and cookies.

'Lemon': Purple flowers and small, notched leaves emitting lemon fragrance set this cultivar apart.

'Snowflake' scented geranium shows off its lush variegated foliage.

GREENS, ASSORTED UNUSUAL

Greens can be as lovely as they are flavorful and beneficial for you. Lettuce leaves, for example, come in varied shades of rich emerald, ruby, pink, or bronze. Other delicious salad greens include arugula (with a warm mustard flavor), chicory (mildly bitter and very European), radicchio (with red or green heads resembling a miniature cabbage), chard (with a sweet, mild flavor and white, golden orange, or red petioles), or cress (tiny and peppery). Plant assorted greens in early spring and replant immediately after harvesting, substituting heat-tolerant lettuce or chard during summer.

LAVENDER

Silver-leaved lavender—with spikes of blue or purple flowers and slender silver leaves—is perfectly at home in scented potpourri or sachets but also excellent sprinkled lightly into culinary dishes for an innovative taste. For culinary use, harvest the flowers while in bud, removing the entire flowering stem.

English lavender (*Lavandula angustifolia*): This hardy lavender grows even in cold climates, down to about -10°F. The species reaches 24 inches high but compact cultivars such as 'Munstead' stay in a 12-inch-high mound.

LEMON BALM

Lemon balm, which grows to about 3 feet tall, has pungent, lemon-scented, scalloped leaves and was once used medicinally to encourage digestion and circulation. The abundant foliage is at its best when fresh, so pinch off stem tips freely and use lemon balm often. Drop the sprigs in iced tea, herbal sun tea, punches, or use as a garnish for fruit salad. Take care to cut off all of the small, white flowers so the plant cannot set seed and spread aggressively throughout the garden.

MINT

Mint, with smooth or hairy opposite leaves, square stems, and spikes of small pink, white, or lavender flowers, is quite versatile around the house. Peppermint sprigs, for example, steep into a stomach-calming tea and complement peas, vinegars, chocolates, and lamb. Mint grows and spreads enthusiastically, so in this garden it is isolated in its own bed. Cut and use sprigs often and divide as needed to rejuvenate.

Spearmint emits a cool mint flavor from a vigorous plant.

Like scented geraniums, there are many varieties of mint including some with classic mint aromas and others asserting more fruity essences.

Peppermint (*M. x piperita*): Clean peppermint scent on purple-flowered plants.

Apple mint (*M. suaveolens*): Round, fuzzy leaves bear a distinct apple scent with white or light purple flowers.

Pineapple mint (*M. suaveolens* 'Variegata'): A singularly attractive upright plant with white-marked leaves and pineapple fragrance.

Orange mint (*Mentha citrata*): Strong citrus scent with dark green leaves.

NASTURTIUMS

This festive annual flower from South America is edible right down to the leaf, flower, and seed. The orange, red, yellow, salmon, or mahogany flowers and the shield-shaped leaves hold a peppery flavor. Use them in salads, as a garnish, or to float on cold soups. Nasturtium flowers create a tantalizing, golden-colored vinegar, touched with hints of nasturtium pepperiness. The foliage is great for chopping and mixing with lettuce. The pickled seeds taste like capers. Nasturtiums come in bush or bedding forms or as vining trailers.

'Alaska' nasturtium is noted for its cream-marked leaves and warm-colored flowers on plants reaching 10 inches high.

'White Meidiland' rose, shown here with asters, grows only two feet high.

'Semi-Tall Double Gleam Mix': This award winner boasts fragrant double flowers on trailing vines up to 3 feet long, supplying more petals for your space.

ROSES

The rose, with its white, pink, red, or yellow flowers, is the queen of a Victorian garden—gorgeous yet useful. The petals and buds can lend a mild flavor and aroma to herbal teas, beverages, and baked goods. The dried flowers are wonderful in scented potpourri and sachets. Disease resistant modern shrub roses—compact enough for small gardens—do not require spraying so are suitable for use in the kitchen.

'Scarlet Meidiland': This 3-foot-high rose features arching stems that cascade gracefully. The small but pretty flowers are a bright scarlet.

'The Fairy': Many small, light pink flowers grow on a mounding plant that reaches about 3 feet high and spreads only slightly wider. It bears small, light pink flowers in abundance throughout the growing season.

SAFFRON (*Crocus sativus*)

This autumn-blooming crocus produces lavender flowers—just like a spring bloomer—but the golden flower centers contain the pungent spice saffron. Grow as many of these as you can and use tweezers to pluck out the spice inside. Dry and store saffron in an airtight glass jar and use its golden color and warm flavor for pasta, rice, and cream sauces.

(*Caution:* Do not confuse saffron with autumn crocus [*Colchicum autumnale*] which has similar looking flowers but is poisonous.)

STRAWBERRIES

Cultivate a bed of classic, June-bearing strawberries to enjoy fresh, puree into sauces, sprinkle on yogurt and ice cream, or dry for herbal teas and snacks.

June-bearing strawberries, unlike day-neutral or everbearing, bear one crop per season—but that one crop provides big, luscious berries that are easy to freeze for later. The charming, three-parted leaves, white spring flowers, red berries in June, and ruby foliage in fall render strawberries as attractive as they are delicious. In warm climates, stick with heat-tolerant cultivars such as 'Apollo' or 'Chandler'. In cool climates, try cultivars such as 'Earliglow' and 'Surecrop'. Ask your Cooperative Extension Service agent for other recommendations.

THYME

This low-growing perennial, a symbol of courage to ancient Greeks, provides interesting foliage for the foreground of any bed. Use thyme in herbal teas, roasts, casseroles, herbal vinegars, even herbal breads and cakes. The small but aromatic leaves come in shades of green, gold, and gray. The flowers—pink, purple, or white—cover the plant in late spring or early summer.

Golden lemon thyme (*T.* x *citriodorus*): Gold-marked leaves on low plants impart a distinct lemon-thyme aroma and flavor. The flowers are pale purple.

English (*Thymus vulgaris*): These plants form solid green mats about 12 inches high and have a robust thyme flavor. The flowers are white or purple.

THE RECIPES

You'll have fun experimenting with edible flowers and flavorful herbs. All the flowers and herbs used in this garden are healthy and nutritious. If you intend to cook with another kind of flower, check it out carefully to be certain it's safe to eat. Special thanks goes to the International Herb Association and Western Reserve Herb Society, who allowed reproduction of their recipes. The Herb Society recipes were taken from their cookbook, *Cooking with Herb Scents*, 1991. This 311-page cookbook is available for $16.95 plus $2 shipping and handling by sending a check to the Western Reserve Herb Society, 11030 East Boulevard, Cleveland, OH 44106.

Woolly thyme exhibits furry, silvery leaves on 1-inch-high plants with a mild thyme fragrance.

Side Dishes

SAFFRON RICE

Recipe courtesy of Lori Zaim

1/4 cup shallot, minced

1 tablespoon olive oil

1 cup converted rice

1/4 teaspoon saffron threads, crumbled

2 cups chicken broth

2 tablespoons dried currants

1/4 cup parsley leaves, minced

1/4 cup pine nuts

Toast the pine nuts in a dry skillet over medium heat, stirring constantly until lightly browned; about 5 minutes. Heat the oil in a saucepan over moderately low heat. Add the shallots and stir until they are softened; about 5 minutes. Add the rice and saffron and cook, stirring for 1 minute.

Add the chicken broth and the currants, bring to a boil. Cover and reduce the heat to low. Cook for 20 minutes. Fluff the rice with a fork and let stand covered, off the heat, for 5 mintues. Stir in the parsley and the toasted pine nuts. Season with salt to taste.

YIELD: Serves 4

GLAZED LEMON TEA BREAD

Recipe courtesy of Millie Adams

3/4 cup milk

1 tablespoon fresh lemon balm, chopped

1 tablespoon fresh lemon thyme**, chopped

1/2 cup (1 stick) butter or margarine

1/2 cup sour cream

1 cup sugar

2 large eggs

2 cups all-purpose flour

1-1/2 teaspoons baking powder

1/4 teaspoon salt

1 tablespoon grated lemon rind (about 2 lemons)

Lemon Glaze (see below)

Grease a 9-by-5-inch loaf pan. Line it with waxed paper. Grease the waxed paper, then flour the pan. Combine the first 3 ingredients in a saucepan; bring to a boil. Remove from heat, cover, and let stand 5 minutes. Cool.

Beat butter at medium speed with an electric mixer until creamy; gradually add sugar, beating well. Add sour cream; beat in eggs, one at a time. Slowly blend in milk mixture. Combine flour, baking powder, and salt. Blend in flour mixture and lemon rind. Mix just until all ingredients are moistened; do not overbeat. Pour batter into prepared loaf pan.

Bake at 325°F for 50–60 minutes, or until cake tester comes out clean. Cool in pan on a wire rack 10 minutes; remove from pan. Cool completely. Poke holes one inch apart in top of loaf with wooden skewer, being careful not to pierce through to the bottom. Slowly pour glaze over bread. Allow gaze to harden at least 15 minutes before serving.

Lemon Glaze: Mix 2 tablespoons fresh lemon juice with 1 cup sifted powdered sugar until smooth.

**You may substitute 1 tablespoon chopped thyme or 1 teaspoon dried thyme for the lemon thyme.

YIELD: 1 loaf

Sauces

LAVENDER SYRUP

Recipe courtesy of Western Reserve Herb Society

1 cup fresh lavender blossoms and stems, packed

2 cups sugar

2 cups water

1/3 cup blueberry syrup (commercial brand or homemade)

Wash lavender and pat dry. Cut the stems into small pieces. Place ingredients in a saucepan and bring just to a boil. Remove from heat immediately. Stir until sugar is dissolved. Cool to room temperature and let steep for several hours before straining into a glass jar. Refrigerate until ready to use.

VICTORIAN COURTYARD GARDEN

LACED WITH LAVENDER PUNCH

Recipe courtesy of Western Reserve Herb Society

This is a special champagne punch that's perfect for a June party. Fresh lavender is required for the syrup, which may be made several days before serving.

2 cups lavender syrup
2 bottles dry champagne, chilled
1 quart club soda, chilled

Combine ingredients in a punch bowl. Serve over ice. May be decorated with fresh flowers.

Seasonings

NASTURTIUM OR CHIVE BLOSSOM VINEGAR

---

6 nasturtium flowers or chive blossoms
1 pint white wine vinegar

Gently wash flowers with cold water, using care to remove any debris from inside as well as outside the flower. Slide flowers down the neck of the vinegar bottle and recap. Set in a warm dark place for two weeks, or until vinegar picks up the peppery nasturtium flavor and the flower color. Store in the existing bottle or sieve out flowers and put in a decorative glass bottle or jar with a nonmetallic lid. Store in a cool, dark place.

NASTURTIUM BUTTER

Recipe courtesy of Lori Zaim

4 nasturtium flowers
1/4 pound unsalted butter, softened

Place the flowers around the sides of a 4-ounce glass custard cup. Place the softened butter into the cup being careful not to displace the flowers. Chill and serve with homemade bread or rolls.

Desserts

CANDIED FLOWERS

———

This imitates a practice from medieval times, used to add beauty and flavor to otherwise modest fare.

edible flowers, washed and dried
egg white, beaten
powdered sugar

Brush flowers gently with egg white. Dip in powdered sugar and set on wax paper to dry. Transfer dried flowers to a freezer container and store in the freezer until needed. Use to decorate cupcakes, cookies, cakes, and other desserts.

LAVENDER SHORTBREAD COOKIES

———

Recipe courtesy of Lori Zaim

These cookies are a perfect accompaniment to a cup of afternoon tea.

6 tablespoons softened butter
5 tablespoons powdered sugar
1 cup all-purpose flour
1/4 teaspoon baking powder
1/4 teaspoon salt
1 teaspoon organic lavender buds

Cream the butter and sugar until light and fluffy. In another bowl, stir together the flour, baking powder, salt, and lavender. Beat the two mixtures together just until combined. Knead the dough on a lightly floured surface until it holds together—about 10 times.

Press the dough evenly into a buttered 9-inch-round cake pan. Score the dough into 8 wedges with the tines of a fork. Press the edges down with the flat side of the tines.

Bake at 350°F for about 25 minutes, until lightly browned. Cool in the pan for 10 minutes. Remove and cut into wedges. Let cool.

YIELD: 8 cookies

ROSE PETAL ICE CREAM

Recipe courtesy of Lori Zaim

The subtle flavor of this ice cream has made it a family favorite. Serve it topped with fresh berries.

2 untreated roses
1 cup half-and-half
1 cup whipping cream
1/2 cup sugar
2 egg yolks

Add the rose petals, half-and-half, cream, and sugar to a heavy saucepan. Heat to just under the boiling point. Remove from the heat, cover, and let sit for 10 minutes.

In a small bowl, beat the egg yolks. Add a small amount of the cream mixture to the eggs and mix thoroughly. Continue to add small amounts of cream to the egg mixture until it is warm. Return the egg mixture to the pan and cook over medium heat, stirring constantly until it is thick enough to coat a spoon.

Strain the mixture into a bowl and cool in the refrigerator. Freeze according to your ice cream maker's instructions.

YIELD: about 2-1/2 cups

Beverages

PINEAPPLE BALM PUNCH

Recipe courtesy of International Herb Association

1 quart pineapple juice
1 quart peach nectar
2 quarts bee balm tea
2 quarts cranberry juice
2 quarts ginger ale
2 oranges, sliced

To make bee balm tea, pour 8 cups of rapidly boiling water over 1/2 cup bee balm flowers or flowers and leaves. Cover and steep until cool, about an hour. Strain and discard flowers. Chill if not using immediately.

Combine all ingredients except ginger ale to chill. Set aside 2 quarts of the liquid to freeze in ice cube trays or freezer containers.

To serve: Place frozen juice in punch bowl. Pour juice and ginger ale over frozen ingredients. Garnish with fruit and flowers.

YIELD: about 50 servings

ROSE GERANIUM FRUIT FIZZ

Recipe courtesy of Western Reserve Herb Society

2 cups fresh rose geranium leaves, washed

4 cups cold water

In a saucepan, add leaves to water. Bring just to a boil, but do not allow to boil. Remove from heat and let cool. Strain into a large glass jar. Discard leaves.

Add:

1 cup sugar

8 cups cranberry-apple juice

4 cups orange juice

2-liter bottle lemon-lime soda (such as 7-Up™)

Serve over ice.

YIELD: 15–20 servings

Rose geraniums add a delightful aroma to cold drinks.

Gardens Around the World

Much of the fun of eating out in restaurants comes from sampling cuisine from different parts of the world. You can do the same kind of experimenting with great European or Mexican foods by growing one of the following gardens.

Italian food never tasted better than when made with fresh, homegrown herbs and tomatoes from a formal Italian Villa Garden (Chapter 10).

Journey to France where a romantic garden of herbs, leeks, baby peas, and courgettes form the foundation for gourmet cooking. It all can be found in the Cook's Garden of Fine French Favorites (Chapter 11).

A Geometric Garden from Great Britain (Chapter 12) is the perfect solution for cool-climate gardens. It blends berry bushes, cabbages, and more in a handsome, round garden.

Mexican cuisine—ripe with hot chili peppers—is never better than when made from homegrown novelties. See what opportunities await in the Mexican Sun Garden (Chapter 13).

The Montague Inn's culinary garden was the inspiration for the Geometric Garden from Great Britain.

10
*Í*TALIAN VILLA GARDEN

A garden of Italian specialties features robust culinary crops such as rich, red tomatoes, full-flavored herbs, zesty peppers, onions, garlic, mild, delicious, true Italian beans, zucchini, and spaghetti squash. Italy's gardening history harks back to Roman times when a great gardening legacy was conceived. Many food crops from the east and north met at Roman crossroads and were embraced as medicinals, foods, or simply oddities worth cultivating. Their use was documented by Roman herbalists and scholars in classic herbals that are still referred to today, hundreds of years later. Later Italian gardeners and cooks were noteworthy for being the first to use broccoli, eggplants, and tomatoes—which today are all classic Italian fare.

A GREAT GARDEN DESIGN

Italian landscape architecture has long focused on symmetrical formal gardens, as depicted in this villa garden. The ability to create precise, balanced gardens of perfect proportion and order instilled early mankind with a feeling of control over natural elements, which could be frighteningly violent and unpredictable. The Romans were among the

Basil and garlic chives.

Italian Villa Garden Design

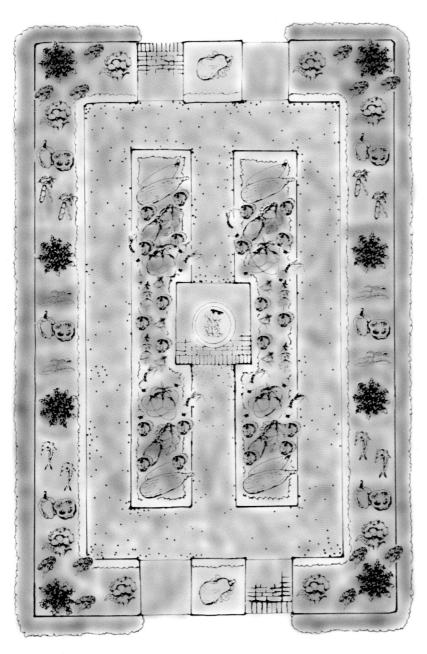

PLANT LIST

- Broccoli
- Parsley
- Peppers
- Italian beans
- Basil
- Radicchio or broccoli raab
- Eggplant
- Tomato
- Onions
- Garlic
- Marjoram
- Oregano
- Zucchini
- Spaghetti squash
- Fennel

first to develop intricate irrigation systems, and their early gardens often featured fountains and pools.

The Italian Villa Garden, designed by Alexander Apanius, is 36 feet long by 24 feet wide, and surrounded by an evergreen hedge or wall. Hedges, ideal at 18 to 24 inches high, are composed of fragrant, silver lavender or dark green dwarf boxwood. Another alternative is to build a low stone wall 18 inches high. Keeping the edging low defines boundaries for the garden without blocking the view of the surrounding countryside (which in Italy might be olive orchards or the seashore) or limiting the amount of sunlight that reaches the garden.

True to Roman standards, the garden centers around a water feature such as a fountain or pool of your choice (or alternatively, an upright urn of fennel). Browse for suitable water features at garden centers, sculpture galleries, or florist shops.

The Italian food crops grow in four elongated garden beds, divided by bright walkways of washed river gravel. Make the gravel walks 2 to 3 inches deep and hold them in place with 1-by-6 inch, rot-resistant boards. Formal entryways and the center point of the garden are paved with cobbles and secured with a roll-lock edging, lending an aura of antiquity.

Along the perimeter of the garden, tall, narrow, upright 'Skyrocket' junipers simulate pillars once found in Roman formal gardens and atriums. The junipers also give the garden a groomed look year-round, providing focal greenery even in winter. In the center beds, sculptural tomato hoops furnish a decorative showcase for these beautiful and colorful vegetables.

Peppers, broccoli, beans, and basil fill the outer beds. Zucchini, with its broad, bushy leaves, adds a lush, tropical look to the ends of the inner beds; while radicchio, garlic and onions, tomatoes on their decorative hoops, and assorted herbs fill the central portions.

CREATIVE TOMATO SUPPORTS

Tomato supports can be a design aspect of the Italian garden. Break free from ordinary tomato cages and stakes—seek out handsome metal trellises and other unique supports.

The designer's favorite is a combination of two wrought iron hoops, used in the Western Reserve Herb Society Garden in Cleveland, Ohio. Antiques from a member's garden were added to the original plan for elegance. These hoops provide enough support to hold up compact tomatoes such as 'Celebrity', but taller tomatoes with a tendency to flop may have to be tied to the top of the rings with strips of nylon stockings or soft plant tape. Similar globes can occasionally be found in mail-order catalogs.

Garden catalogs offer other interesting options—trellises, simple ladderlike structures, grid trellises, or ornately decorated arbors made for ornamental vines can also hold tomato vines. Smaller tomato plants can be upheld with wire topiary forms, shaped like globes, pyramids, spirals, or a series of hoops.

Spaghetti squash—a delicious pasta substitute—intertwines amid the entryways.

This is a large and impressive garden, but it's also adaptable to downsizing and setting in a smaller space. The size is easy to reduce by eliminating repeated portions of plants such as one group of juniper, basil, pepper, and beans.

YOUR ITALIAN FAVORITES

Great Italian cooking gets even better with choice ingredients from the garden.

'Lemon' and 'Opal' basil.

BASIL

Basil, which probably originated in India, was an early arrival in Italy and an essential ingredient in early Roman pharmacopoeias. It later served as a loyal companion for tomato sauces of all kinds. There are dozens of different cultivars of basil available but several originated in Italy and are perfect for this garden.

'Genova Profumatissima' (perfume basil): This basil reaches about 18 inches tall with long leaves that release an intense and memorable flavor.

'Fino Verde Compatto': A bush basil with small leaves on mounded plants up to 15 inches tall.

'Napoletano': This plant hails from the south of Italy and has broad, crinkled leaves with a sweet, mellow scent on stems about 18 inches high.

BEANS

Romano beans are heirloom Italian beans with a rich, buttery flavor and broad, flat pods that set them apart from ordinary snap beans. Harvest the pods when they are a little larger than domestic snap beans and slightly swollen with seeds. You can also harvest the mature beans to shuck out of the pod.

'Romano': This is an old-fashioned pole bean with stringless pods and plenty of them. It takes 60 to 70 days from planting to harvest.

'Roma II': This bush version needs no staking and is ready to harvest about 55 days after planting.

BROCCOLI RAAB

This unique Italian favorite is actually a turnip, grown for its new shoots and tender flower buds which have a bold, spicy, broccolilike flavor. They can be eaten raw in salads or cooked like spinach. The plants mature quickly, 40 to 60 days after sowing. They grow best in cool weather and are harvested in midwinter in Italy.

Lavender-white eggplants add visual diversity.

EGGPLANT

Eggplant is native to Thailand but blends so well with tomatoes that it has become an Italian specialty. Italians were the first Europeans to embrace eggplants, which like tomatoes are members of the poisonous nightshade family and were viewed with suspicion by much of Europe. Fortunately, the fruit is nutritious and savory—grilled, roasted, fried, or baked. To grill, cut eggplants into slices, marinade in a garlic vinaigrette, and grill until tender. They are even better when smothered with tomato sauce and other goodies. To prevent browning after cutting eggplant, dip the exposed surface in lemon juice.

'Violetta Lunga': This 8-inch-long eggplant has dark purple skin on a teardrop-shaped fruit. It is ready to harvest about 75 days after transplanting.

'Violette di Firenze': Here's a lovely, white-striped, lavender eggplant that is as lovely to look at as it is good to eat. It is ready to begin harvesting about 75 days from transplanting.

'Rosa Bianca': Another Italian heirloom with lavender and white skin that is shaped like a teardrop and has bitter-free flesh. Harvest 75 days after transplanting.

'Vittoria Hybrid': This eggplant bears long, slender, dark purple–skinned fruit that are ready a week earlier than many other cultivars. The plants are resistant to tobacco mosaic virus.

'Lista de Gandia': Consider this slender purple and white fruit that grows well in southern gardens. Seedlings are a little slow to get started, taking at least 75 days to begin bearing, but once large, they tolerate some drought and produce well despite heat.

FLORENCE FENNEL

This unusual, anise-flavored vegetable produces a layered bulb of swollen leaf bases that you can cook like a

Florence fennel.

vegetable, bake, or use to season other foods. In ancient Rome, fennel was believed to improve eyesight and was associated with flattery. Florence fennel has become a tradition in Italian cuisine and is also good to use raw with crudités or as a replacement for celery in many recipes. Blend it in a salad with apples, raisins, honey, mustard, and vinegar and oil.

'Zefa Fino': Some Florence fennel cultivars can bolt if planted in spring, but this one tends to hold well into summer.

GARLIC

Several forms of garlic have been given Italian names because of their fine flavor and suitability for Italian cuisine. 'Italian' has a full, pungent flavor and keeps well during winter in a cool location. 'Italian Purple' has purple-blushed skin with a mild, full flavor. Both types should be planted in fall to harvest the following summer. Several of the best bulbs can be saved to replant, separating the individual cloves and sowing them like seeds.

MARJORAM, SWEET

Sweet marjoram, with its silvery leaves and round, fragrant flower buds, yields a robust, warm flavor that harmonizes with tomatoes, beef, and chicken. It is a tender perennial, grown as an annual in the north or dug up and brought indoors to preserve through the winter.

ONIONS

Many different onions thrive in this garden. Among them is an Italian heirloom called the Italian button onion or 'Borettana'. Suitable for growing in northern areas with long summer days, this onion takes 120 days to mature but only reaches up to 2 inches in diameter. Rather than sliced, these onions are usually served whole—cooked, pickled, or skewered on kabobs.

OREGANO

Few Italian dishes are complete without oregano—a standard in spaghetti sauce, pizza sauce, and more. There are

Italian parsley and sweet basil.

many types of oregano but the classic for Italian dishes is Greek oregano, which has a spicy aroma.

PARSLEY

Italian parsley, also called 'Italian Single Leaf' and 'Italian Dark Green Plain Leaf', has flat leaves growing up to 18 inches tall and retaining a richer flavor than curly leaf parsley. If planted in spring, you can harvest the foliage throughout the growing season and even into winter if the weather is mild. You can also pluck it the following spring and early summer, until the plant begins to send up a flowering stalk and the foliage becomes scrawny and bitter.

ITALIAN PEPPERS

Many fine cultivars of sweet peppers are available in Italy. Long, slender bulls horn-shaped peppers are Italian classics, but the broader bell peppers also are available. Full-flavored, ripe peppers, allowed to turn golden or red-ripe, are delicious sliced and sautéed in olive oil. Or brush them with oil and toast on the grill. Sauté them with onions, garlic, tomatoes, and cheeses, and serve with pasta or fresh bread for an easy but exquisite light lunch. Or slice them fresh into a pasta salad.

'Corno di Toro': This is the classic bull's horn pepper—an heirloom cultivar about 8 inches long that ripens to red or golden. Many seed companies sell the two colors mixed in one seed packet. The peppers are ready to harvest about 70 to 80 days from transplanting.

'Italia': This is an early bull's horn type, ready just 55 days from transplanting. It bears sweet, flavorful crimson fruit.

'Marconi': This Italian heirloom, like the bull's horn, is available in red and gold but grows up to 12 inches long with broader, three-lobed shoulders.

'Quadrato D'Oro': This golden bell pepper was developed specifically for Italian and French market gardens and comes complete with some disease resistance.

RADICCHIO

This is a type of head-forming chicory with slightly bitter, crisp leaves, the most eye-catching of which are colored ruby and white. Mix it with lettuce for extra flavor in salads. Many cultivars hail from Italy and from there have spread to other parts of the world. Older forms of radicchio may need to be cut back to force production of the esteemed head. Newer cultivars need no extra coaxing.

'Rossa di Verona': Plant in early summer for harvest in cool, mild fall weather. Remove foliage in early fall and the head will emerge soon after. Harvest can begin from 65 to 85 days after planting.

'Guilio': A modern form of the previous cultivar, this one produces heads without forcing. You can sow plants in late spring and harvest them 60 to 100 days later in summer.

SPAGHETTI SQUASH

Grow your own pasta with spaghetti squash. It is mild and slightly sweet, with a pleasant taste that enhances tomato dishes. Spaghetti squash is not as heavy as ordinary pasta, good for those who are watching their calories. Mature winter squash can keep in a cool basement for several months.

'Pasta Hybrid': 85 days from sowing, you'll be harvesting this ivory spaghetti squash. This hybrid offers high yields from compact and early-producing vines.

'Spaghetti Squash': The generic form of spaghetti squash promises up to 5 fruits, 5 pounds each, in 88 days.

'Vegetable Spaghetti': This one takes 100 days to produce fruit up to 3 pounds each.

'Hasta La Pasta Hybrid': Just 73 days from sowing to harvest, this cultivar offers 8-inch-long and 5-inch-wide squash on compact vines.

TOMATOES

Rich and thick Italian tomatoes are perfect for making sauces or dried tomatoes. If you need either extra fast, spoon out the seedy center and cook down or dry the meaty walls. Italian tomatoes are also good for slicing into almost any casserole, stir-fry, soup, or stew. But many lack a juicy center and are not as good when eaten fresh as a good cherry or beefsteak tomato. They are tasty grilled, however, brushed with vinaigrette.

'Roma': This is a popular paste tomato that grows well throughout most of the United States, aided by its resistance to wilt and other diseases. It also is unappealing to fruitworms. Harvest begins about 75 days after transplanting.

'Milano VF': This is an extra early hybrid, ready just 63 days after transplanting. It produces meaty tomatoes that are good for sauces, paste, drying, or canning.

'San Remo': This sweet fruit is larger than the others, which makes for easier peeling. They are borne on indeterminate plants, so have an extended harvest season and high yield.

'Viva Italia Hybrid': This newer paste tomato is outstanding for its disease resistance and ability to set small but flavorful fruit even in hot weather.

'Hungarian Italian Paste': This tomato produces its pear-shaped fruit about 80 days after transplanting. The fruit is small but flavorful and attractively arranged in clusters.

'Italian Gold Hybrid': This golden-orange paste tomato is ready to pick 70 days after transplanting.

ZUCCHINI

These productive members of the squash family produce mild flavored, cylindrical fruit, blending well with just about anything. Pick them when they are young, tender, and solid through to the core, then marinade in a garlic, thyme, bay leaf, and red wine vinegar. Medium-sized zucchini can be sliced and steamed or sautéed with Italian sausage, onions, peppers, and tomatoes. Baby zucchini can be steamed whole and served with butter and melted cheese.

To make the most of a single zucchini plant, harvest often to catch the young fruit and to encourage new squash to form.

'Cocozelle Bush': A classic, old-fashioned variety has slim, striped fruits ready just 45 days from sowing.

'Seneca Hybrid': This dark green squash tolerates slightly cool weather and can be harvested 42 days after sowing.

'Florentino': Here is a new hybrid similar to Italian cocozelles that bears robust, ridged fruit on a semibush plant.

THE RECIPES

Here are some new ways to use Italian produce.

CULINARY GARDENS

Side Dish

HERBED SPAGHETTI SQUASH

1 large spaghetti squash

1 tablespoon each fresh sweet marjoram, thyme, and parsley leaves, chopped

4 tablespoons margarine

Parmesan cheese to taste

Preheat oven to 350°F. Cut squash in half and scoop out seeds. Set cut side down on a cookie sheet and bake for 50 minutes or until tender. Remove from oven and set aside.

Melt margarine in a small skillet on low heat. Add herbs and heat for 2 minutes. Remove from heat.

Turn squash over and remove insides with a fork. They should flake into noodlelike strands. Transfer to a serving bowl. Pour herbed margarine over and sprinkle with cheese. Serve immediately.

YIELD: Serves 8

VARIATION: Instead of serving with herbed butter, try with tomato sauce.

Main Courses

SCAMPI PRIMAVERA

Recipe courtesy of Millie Adams

12 ounces spaghetti

1/2 cup olive oil

3 large cloves garlic, minced

1/2 teaspoon lemon peel, grated

2 carrots, cut in 2-inch julienne strips

1 medium zucchini, cut in 2-inch julienne strips

1 medium red pepper, cut in 2-inch julienne strips

1-1/2 pounds medium (50–60/lb.) shrimp, cleaned

2 tablespoons fresh lemon juice

3/4 teaspoon salt

1/8 teaspoon pepper

2 tablespoons fresh basil, torn

2 tablespoons Italian parsley, or cilantro, torn

Cook spaghetti according to package directions. Meanwhile, heat oil over medium heat in a large skillet or wok. Cook and stir garlic and lemon peel about 30 seconds. Add carrots and stir-fry about 2 minutes. Add the rest of the vegetables and shrimp; stir-fry until vegetables are tender-crisp and shrimp are pink, 4–8 minutes.

Season with lemon juice, salt, and pepper. Stir in basil and parsley. Spoon over drained pasta and toss well. Serve hot.

YIELD: Serves 6

ITALIAN VILLA GARDEN

FETTUCINE WITH PORK AND FENNEL SEED SAUCE

Recipe courtesy of Millie Adams

3 stalks celery, diced
1 medium onion, diced
2 tablespoons olive oil
1 pound ground pork
1 teaspoon fennel seeds
1/2 teaspoon salt
1/4 teaspoon pepper, freshly ground
3-1/2 cups chunky tomato puree
6-ounce can tomato paste
6-ounces of fettucine
1/2 cup Parmesan cheese, freshly shredded

In a large skillet, sauté celery in olive oil over medium heat until tender. Add onion, ground pork, fennel seeds, salt, and pepper. Cook until meat is thoroughly browned and pan juices evaporate. Stir frequently to prevent scorching.

Add tomato puree and paste; heat to boiling. Reduce heat to low. Cover and simmer 10 minutes. Meanwhile, prepare fettucine according to package directions. Drain fettucine. Serve meat sauce over fettucine; sprinkle with shredded cheese.

YIELD: Serves 6

LAYERED EGGPLANT

2 medium eggplant, sliced
1 medium onion, sliced
2 medium tomatoes, cut into wedges
1/4 pound salami, chopped
1 tablespoon Italian parsley, chopped
1 tablespoon Greek oregano, chopped
1/2 cup sharp cheddar cheese, shredded

Preheat oven to 325°F. Oil a 2-liter baking dish. Layer eggplant slices on the bottom. Top with a layer of onion slices, tomato wedges, and chopped salami. Sprinkle with parsley and oregano. Cover dish and bake for 20 minutes. Remove cover and top with cheddar cheese. Bake 15 more minutes or until cheese is melted.

YIELD: Serves 4

CULINARY GARDENS

ASSORTED VEGETABLE PIZZAS

1 tablespoon fresh basil, chopped

1 refrigerated pizza crust

4 teaspoons oregano, chopped

1 clove garlic, minced

6 ounces skim mozzarella cheese, grated

1 cup tomato sauce

2 to 3 cups assorted sliced vegetables such as mushrooms, peppers,
    onions, carrots, broccoli raab, radicchio, tomatoes, zucchini

Preheat oven to 450°F. Lightly steam crunchy vegetables such as carrots or broccoli raab. Spread crust on baking sheet according to package directions. Make pizza sauce by blending tomato sauce with herbs. Spread on crust, sprinkle with vegetables, and top with grated cheese. Bake on bottom rack of oven for 7 to 15 minutes, or until cheese is melted.

YIELD: Serves 4

EASY GARDEN PASTA

1 pound chicken, ground

2 medium onions, chopped

1 cup mushrooms, chopped

1 cup dried tomatoes

1/4 cup dilled white wine vinegar

1/4 cup water

1 tablespoon each of fresh basil, parsley, chopped

1 teaspoon fresh thyme, chopped

1-1/2 cups mozzarella cheese

1 cup black olives, sliced

1 package wheat lasagne noodles

Brown chicken with onions and mushrooms, and drain off extra fat. Microwave dried tomatoes in vinegar and water for 2 minutes on high. Blend tomato mixture into chicken and sauté on low heat 15 to 20 minutes, uncovered. Add herbs and keep warm.

Bring large pot of water to boil and cook whole wheat lasagna noodles for 7 minutes or just until tender. Use half of the noodles to cover the bottom of a large, oiled casserole dish. Add meat mixture, and half of the olives and cheese. Cover with rest of the noodles and top with remaining olives and cheese. Bake at 350°F for 30 minutes.

YIELD: Serves 4

Sauce

TOMATO SAUCE

6 large tomatoes

1 tablespoon olive oil

1/4 cup onion greens, chopped

1 teaspoon salt

1 tablespoon oregano, chopped

1 tablespoon basil, chopped

1/4 teaspoon black pepper, freshly ground

2 tablespoons red wine basil vinegar

Dip tomatoes in boiling water until skins crack. Remove and set aside to cool. Peel off skins and chop tomatoes coarsely. Simmer in a saucepan until slightly thick, about 20 minutes on medium heat. Stir frequently to prevent scalding. Add remaining ingredients and simmer for 5 minutes. Serve immediately.

The first, much-anticipated tomato of the season is likely to grow on a staked plant.

11
COOK'S GARDEN OF FINE FRENCH FAVORITES

France is famous for its elaborate cuisine and simple blends of French vegetables and herbs grown in decorative potagers or kitchen gardens. French cooking reached distinction in the seventeenth century, when haute cuisine originated to nourish King Louis XIV's lavish entertaining. More common folks of that time enjoyed French home cooking (cuisine bourgeoisie), which blended fresh, pure, and delicious regional foods. You can do both types of cooking with the bounty from this garden. Great French filet and flageolet beans, flavorful endive, escarole, tarragon, chervil, sorrel, shallots, petits pois (baby peas), and other favorites will be yours for the picking.

Patterned flower gardens can be incorporated into a French kitchen garden.

Fine French Favorites Garden Design #1

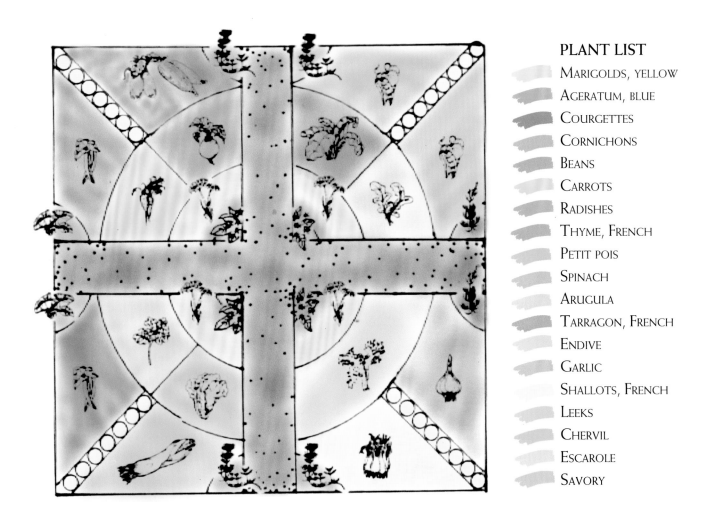

PLANT LIST

MARIGOLDS, YELLOW

AGERATUM, BLUE

COURGETTES

CORNICHONS

BEANS

CARROTS

RADISHES

THYME, FRENCH

PETIT POIS

SPINACH

ARUGULA

TARRAGON, FRENCH

ENDIVE

GARLIC

SHALLOTS, FRENCH

LEEKS

CHERVIL

ESCAROLE

SAVORY

A GREAT GARDEN DESIGN

French gardening developed into a romantic art beginning with sixteenth-century Renaissance flower parterres (patterned plantings created to look as if they were embroidered in the earth and set off against a background of colored sand or rock). Gardens were often strictly symmetrical employing mirror image beds. Vegetable gardens sometimes nestled beside flower gardens and were planted to look just as enticing and controlled as their floral counterparts.

In this spirit, this Cook's Garden of Fine French Favorites (twenty-two-and-a-half feet square) consists of four square planting beds divided by crossing walkways. The center of each bed is encircled with blue ageratums and yellow marigolds and bordered by salad vegetables. Main crops such as French beans, leeks, shallots, garlic, petits pois, and courgettes spread out in the main planting areas. They are easily tended from narrow access paths. Fragrant herbs and French sorrel stand beside garden entrances.

In spring, salad crops and petit pois garnish the garden with greenery. In summer, courgettes and French beans, plus new plantings of salad crops and peas for fall harvest are in place. Garlic and shallots have a schedule of their own. Plant them in fall and harvest in late summer, then replant cloves from the biggest bulbs for next year. In subsequent years, alternate planting locations by moving crops clockwise into the next garden area. This prevents a buildup of pests and diseases and varies nutrient requirements to maintain a healthy soil and garden.

ROMANCE OF ART

One way to add romance to a garden is to include garden art. In a classic French garden, a bust or nude statue might be right at home. Historic gardens might feature a Roman sundial or Early American bee skep. A more naturalistic garden might display a bird in flight or a crouching panther. Contemporary gardens could add abstract wood, metal, or ceramic pieces, using curves or angles that sustain an excitement level appropriate for the surroundings.

Abstract garden art. (Minneapolis Museum of Art, Sculpture Garden)

To get inspired about garden art, check in local art galleries, some of which may cater to outdoor settings. Consult gardening supply catalogs, some of which may also sell garden decorations. If there is a botanical garden or arboretum in your area, see if they have exhibits by sculptors or garden artists. They may also be able to recommend a local artisan. Another good resource is an art institute or academy for talented, new artists.

Rustic garden art. (Rodale Institute)

Fine French Favorites Garden Design #2

If you have only a small amount of sunny yard space, you can still enjoy fine French produce and herbs. This small, four-square garden, half the size of the previous garden, depicts a French potager with formal elegance and a simple parterre of yellow marigolds and blue ageratum. For a more romantic effect, cover the entryways with arbors topped with flowering vines.

YOUR FRENCH FAVORITES

A wonderful way to enjoy French cuisine is by using delicious, homegrown French vegetables and seasonings. Here are some classics to include.

ARUGULA

This leafy green from southern Europe has a bold, mustard-garlic flavor that adds gusto to salads or stir-fries. Once considered an aphrodisiac, it is now used much like spinach. A quick-growing green, it can be sown repeatedly in spring or late summer for harvest during cool seasons. It is ready to pick about 35 days later. Pick leaves when small or sprinkle a few flowers in salads.

BEANS

In France, shelled beans are called haricots or flageolet beans and green beans are called haricots vert. Shelling beans, including broad beans used in the Geometric Garden from Great Britain (see Chapter 12), have long been an integral part of French cuisine. Not until the twentieth century did green beans gain favor and become widely available in France.

Haricots vert may be boiled until tender but crisp and blended with vinaigrette and herbs, sautéed in olive oil with garlic, simmered in cream, or topped with meat stock. Popular French filet beans have narrower pods than ordinary green snap beans. They must be harvested when young and tender—less than the diameter of a pencil. Harvest daily before the strings form because filet beans quickly become overmature.

'Triomphe de Farcy': This is a French favorite that matures early, as soon as 50 days after sowing the seed.

'Vernandon': This newer cultivar stands out for its resistance to bean virus and anthracnose.

Shelled flageolet beans may be enjoyed fresh when sweet and tender, or dried and then soaked and boiled. They provide a delicious alternative to snap beans. Allowed to mature until the beans reach full size and the pods become fibrous, they can be plucked from the pod and enjoyed fresh. Or let them dry in the pod—outdoors during dry weather or indoors in a dry room or dehydrator. Store dried beans in a jar in the cupboard until needed.

Haricots can be added to vegetable soups, sautéed in butter with onions, boiled and drenched with cream or tomato sauce, or served in cassoulets layered with pork, lamb, or other meats.

'Chevrier Vert': A classic in France, these fresh beans are tender, buttery, and easy to remove from the shell. The beans are ready to harvest about 75 days from sowing seed.

CARROTS

This culinary basic is quite at home in French cooking. Carrots are cooked in cream, roasted, served with vinaigrette, pureed, souffléd, or gratinéed, cooked with roasts, or added to soups and stews.

'Nantes': These carrots can reach 7 inches long and 1-1/2 inches wide and are ready to harvest 60 to 70 days after sowing seed. A variety of new Nantes offspring that are shorter, broader, smoother skinned, or brighter colored are also available.

'Paris Market': This is an early-maturing, small, round carrot that grows well in shallow soils and is among the first to be harvested in the spring in France. Roots, which are sweet and dark orange, are ready as soon as 50 days after sowing seed.

CHERVIL

This delicately anise-flavored herb, native to Europe, is used like parsley in many French dishes. Cook it lightly, if at all, to enjoy its subtle flavor. Chervil shines in omelets, herbal butters, or chicken soups. The fresh leaves make a lovely garnish. They won't hold their flavor if dried but are fine if frozen for later. A classic herbal combination called "fines herbes" combines chervil, parsley, chives, and tarragon. A quick-maturing annual, chervil grows well in the cool spring and fall seasons. You can also plant seeds in late summer to overwinter for spring use.

CORNICHONS

Tiny cucumbers, picked very young (about 1 inch long and the width of a little finger) are used to make sour baby pickles. They may be pickled in salt brine and canned or pickled in vinegar and refrigerated. Harvest daily to capture these cucumbers at the ideal stage.

COURGETTES

These summer squash—a standard in Italian cooking—have become important in French cuisine, too. They can be eaten raw, steamed, fried, flavored with cream or au gratin sauces, or made into fritters.

'Vert de Massy', a cornichon cucumber, boasts scab tolerance and is ready to harvest about 53 days after planting seedlings.

'Seneca Milano': This cultivar bears extra-early-maturing, dark green speckled fruits that can reach 12 inches long. Tiny, young fruit is served in fine French restaurants.

ENDIVE

French cuisine relies heavily on two forms of chicory: endive (chicorée frissée) with decorative, narrow, and curly leaves; and escarole (chicorée sauvage) with broader leaves. Both may have a slighty bitter flavor, kept mild by growing the plants during cool weather and providing them with plenty of moisture. The heart of the plant is creamy yellow. Endive can be blanched (made milder and lighter) by tying the outer leaves together to shade the interior a week before harvesting. An alternative is to cover the plant with an empty margarine tub (anchored with a rock) three days before harvesting. Endive plants can be spaced as close as 8 inches apart for natural blanching.

Terra-cotta blanching pots can be used to cover endive, asparagus, and other vegetables several days before harvest.

The French eat either kind of endive drizzled with a garlic or shallot vinaigrette, and often accompany it with bacon. Both may be blended into a salad, cut with plenty of lettuce for milder flavor. They may also be blanched and braised or cooked au gratin.

'Batavian': This is a classic escarole with large heads up to 15 inches wide and deep, white hearts. Harvest begins about 90 days after sowing.

'Tres Fine Maraichere': A small-headed endive with finely cut leaves, this one is ready for harvest 50 to 60 days after sowing. A single head makes a beautiful individual salad.

'Grosse Bouclée': Here is an endive from France with a naturally blanched heart and bolt resistance. Its heads are ready to harvest 70 to 90 days after sowing.

GARLIC

Many great recipes rely on garlic, which has played an important role in food, medicine, and more through history. Garlic cloves were fed to Roman laborers for strength. During medieval times, garlic was thought to provide protection from plague and devils. It was sometimes eaten as a paste made with almonds and bread crumbs or blended with parsley and sorrel to eat with fish.

Garlic cloves sprout from a bulb that develops underground much like a French shallot. The garlic is most nutritious if eaten raw and most pungent if finely minced. It can be used in pesto herb pastes and herbal vinegars and oils, or rubbed on a wooden salad bowl to season it. Garlic can be sautéed or roasted, alone or in combination with onions, other vegetables, meats, or potatoes.

LEEKS

These onion relatives have a mild onion flavor and creamy white stem bases that are cherished in French cuisine. Leeks may be blanched and drizzled with vinaigrette for a cold salad or served hot covered with cream sauces or butter.

They also may be added to roast meats, served beside baked fish, or added to soups.

Leeks have interesting blue green leaves that stand 12 to 18 inches high. They take a long time to mature, and can linger over winter in some climates. In cold climates, it may be best to grow the milder, smaller, and faster maturing cultivars during spring and summer.

Leeks' place in history is well established. Emperor Nero, like many ancient Romans, ate leeks to improve his singing voice.

PETITS POIS

These are baby peas, sweet and succulent, too delicious to smother in heavy sauces. For best flavor, harvest before the peas are full size and eat as soon as possible. For easy shelling, snap off the stem end and pull off the strings. Then squeeze the pod suture and it will pop open. Run your finger down the inside of the pod to release the peas. Try sautéing them for a minute in a little pat of butter, if you can keep from eating them all straight out of the pod. Or top them with a little chopped mint for an old-fashioned flavor.

'Petits Pois': These baby pods are only 2-1/2 inches long with 6 tiny, round peas each.

'Precovelle': These peas grow on compact vines and are ready for harvest in just 60 days. They resist fusarium wilt and top yellows.

'Petit Provençal': Another great French pea on 20-inch-tall vines is ready to pick 60 days from sowing.

RADISH, FRENCH

French radishes, including cultivars such as 'French Breakfast', are cylindrical instead of round and up to 4 inches long. They are extra quick to mature, being ready to harvest in as little as 20 days after sowing the seed. Many French radishes, such as 'D'Avignon' which is popular in the south of France, are red with a white tip. While some folks may enjoy a brisk, crunchy radish for breakfast, most are eaten in salads or as crudités with dip.

SHALLOTS, FRENCH

These mild, sweet relatives of the onion have been grown in France since before A.D. 1000. Shallot bulbs are a tradition in Bordeaux and Parisian cooking, used raw in salads and vegetable trays, cooked with fish or meat, and added to a variety of butter, wine, and cream sauces for seasoning.

SORREL, FRENCH

Another full-flavored green, this one is a member of the rhubarb family, grown in France since the 1300s. Sorrel has a pungent, lemony flavor. The triangular leaves are quick to wilt, thus making homegrown harvests superior to commercial sorrel. Add to that the fact that sorrel can grow like a weed—it easily yields large harvests with minimal effort. Sorrel can be eaten steamed like a vegetable. Or sauté it in butter until it melts into a lemony sauce for fish or potatoes. Sorrel can also be used in omelets or soups and tossed into salads. A perennial, it will grow from seed or divisions and return year after year for additional harvests.

SPINACH

This vitamin-rich, leafy vegetable originated in Persia but was brought to Europe during the Crusades. It was made into chopped spinach balls in the Middle Ages and used in sugary vegetable dishes in the 1600s. It is widely adaptable—used with eggs and meats, stuffings, salads, purees, and soufflés. Spinach is essential in Florentine dishes and salads. Spinach can be grown in spring and fall in cool climates or in winter in mild climates.

TARRAGON, FRENCH
This bushy perennial has linear leaves with a mild anise flavor called for in many French dishes. Tarragon freezes and dries well, so large harvests can be preserved for later. A small handful of sprigs added to a bottle of white wine or champagne vinegar creates a gourmet herbal vinegar. The French puree tarragon and add it to cream sauces to drizzle over vegetables, canapés, and broiled meats. It can also be added to meat stocks to accompany beef or fowl.

THYME, FRENCH
This perennial herb stands apart from other forms of thyme because of its narrow, almost needlelike, gray-tinted leaves. The flavor is refined and delightful. Thyme is good fresh, dried, or frozen and is often combined with chicken, fish, or lamb in French cuisine.

THE RECIPES
The following elegant dishes are not at all difficult to make.

Salads

SAUTÉED LEEK SALAD

4 leeks
1-1/2 tablespoons margarine
1 teaspoon tarragon, chopped

Cut leeks into 1/2-inch-wide slices. Melt margarine in medium skillet and sauté leeks on medium heat until tender, about 7 minutes. Sprinkle with chopped tarragon and let sit 5 minutes before serving.

YIELD: Serves 4

CULINARY GARDENS

ARUGULA SALAD WITH GRAPES, WALNUTS, AND ROQUEFORT

Recipe courtesy of Lori Zaim

1/4 cup balsamic vinegar

1 teaspoon Dijon mustard

3/4 cup olive oil, preferably extra virgin

1 bunch arugula

2 Belgian endives

1 bunch watercress

1/2 pound seedless red grapes

1/4 pound Roquefort cheese, crumbled

1/3 cup walnuts

salt and pepper to taste

Toast the walnuts for 7 minutes in a preheated 350°F oven. Discard the stems of the arugula. Wash in several changes of water and spin dry. Separate the leaves of Belgian endive. Wash the watercress, discarding stems; spin dry.

Divide the greens among 4 plates. Arrange the grapes, walnuts, and Roquefort on top. Drizzle with the desired amount of dressing.

Dressing: Combine vinegar, mustard, and salt and pepper to taste, then gradually whisk in the oil to emulsify.

YIELD: Serves 4

Soups

FRENCH ONION SOUP

2 medium onions, peeled and sliced

2 tablespoons margarine

2 tablespoons flour

2 cans beef broth

croutons and mozzarella cheese to taste

Melt margarine in a large skillet on low heat. Add onions and cook, covered, until translucent. Stir in flour and cook for 3 minutes until flour begins to brown.

Transfer to a large saucepan. Add beef broth. Bring to a boil, stirring to dissolve flour. Cover, reduce heat to low, and simmer for 30 minutes. Top with croutons and mozzarella cheese.

YIELD: Serves 4

FRENCH SORREL SOUP

1 cup sorrel leaves
2 tablespoons margarine
3 tablespoons whole wheat flour
1 medium onion, minced
4 teaspoons fresh tarragon leaves, chopped
2 cups chicken broth
1 cup plain, nonfat yogurt

Wash sorrel leaves well and remove leaf blades from the tough midribs. Discard midribs in compost pile. Melt margarine in saucepan while chopping sorrel leaf blades. Add onion and sorrel to saucepan. Sauté until sorrel melts. Add flour, tarragon, and chicken broth. Heat to boiling, stirring occasionally. Stir in yogurt and simmer for 3 minutes, stirring. Puree in blender or food processor and serve.

YIELD: Serves 6

Side Dishes

PETITS POIS

2 cups baby peas, shelled and steamed for 1 minute
1 tablespoon fennel leaves, chopped
1 red pepper
1 tablespoon olive oil
1/4 cup pecans, chopped
salt to taste

Roast red pepper under broiler, a minute or two on each side or until the skin is lightly charred. Set aside to cool. Boil peas in a little water for several minutes, until slightly tender. Peel charred skin off pepper and slice into thin strips, about 2 inches long. Blend in a medium-sized bowl with peas and fennel leaves . Mix in olive oil and pecans. Add salt to taste. Serve immediately.

YIELD: Serves 4–6

CARROTS WITH RAISINS

4 large carrots
1 tablespoon flour
1/2 cup raisins
1 cup hot water
1 tablespoon brown sugar
1 tablespoon margarine

Wash carrots and slice 1/4 inch thick. Heat margarine in medium-sized skillet. Add carrots and cook for 5 minutes, stirring several times, while mixing brown sugar into hot water. Sprinkle carrots with flour and cover with water and sugar. Simmer covered for 7 minutes. Add raisins. Cover and simmer until tender and the sauce is slightly thick, about 5 minutes.

YIELD: Serves 4

Main Course

TARRAGON CHICKEN SALAD

12 sprigs fresh French tarragon

3/4 cup mayonnaise

3 cups chicken breast, cubed

1-1/2 cups petit peas, cooked

3/4 cup pecans

Combine mayonnaise and tarragon, with tough stems removed, in food processor and blend until smooth. Refrigerate for at least 2 hours. Combine chicken, peas, pecans, and tarragon mayonnaise in a mixing bowl and blend well. Serve on fresh French bread.

YIELD: Serves 6

Seasonings

FINES HERBES

1 tablespoon fresh parsley, chopped

1 tablespoon chives, chopped

1 tablespoon tarragon, chopped

1 tablespoon chervil, chopped

Blend and use immediately in vegetable and fish dishes or omelets.

CHERVIL BUTTER

3 tablespoons fresh chervil leaves, removed from stem

2 sticks margarine

Wash and dry chervil leaves then mince finely. Let margarine soften then cream in chervil leaves. Refrigerate for at least 3 hours before serving on crusty French bread or broiled fish.

TARRAGON VINEGAR

———

6 sprigs tarragon

1 bottle white wine vinegar

Wash tarragon in cold water and dry well with a thick towel. Push tarragon into vinegar bottle, seal, and store in cupboard for two to three weeks. Use the vinegar as is or strain out the tarragon. Or transfer it to a decorative bottle.

A VARIETY OF VINEGARS

Herbal vinegars can be made using white wine vinegar, rice wine vinegar, red wine vinegar, distilled white vinegar, or even cider vinegar as a base. Each has its own virtues.

White wine vinegar, which can be pricy, has a pleasant mild aroma of its own which complements any herb and always produces pleasing results. The light color will change to golden when used with nasturtium blossoms, lavender when used with chive blossoms, and garnet when used with purple basil.

Rice wine vinegar is similar to white wine vinegar but has a sweeter flavor so it doesn't need to be mixed with as much oil in a vinaigrette. Lower acidity brands may be milder flavored revealing more herbal flavor than high acidity types.

Red wine vinegar varies in quality but all have a rich, ruby color. Cheap generic brands may be lacking much aroma, which is disappointing when used as is, but may allow herbal flavors to shine. Stronger flavored red wine vinegars demand combinations of bold-flavored herbs such as garlic, rosemary, and thyme.

Cider vinegar—an apple product with a strong, fruity smell and golden color—is useful only for strongly flavored herbs or herbs used in large quantities.

Balsamic vinegar, made from an expensive blend of white grapes aged for years in wooden casks, is dark red (almost black) with a strong, sweet wine smell. Alone, balsamic vinegar is delightful. But it has such an impressive smell and fragrance, it overwhelms herbs.

Distilled white vinegar is inexpensive, without much aroma, and clear, so it shows off the colors of chive flowers or purple basil. But it has a strong acid taste that herbs cannot mask.

12
$\mathscr{G}$EOMETRIC GARDEN FROM GREAT BRITAIN

Beautiful British flower gardens, filled with long-blooming delphiniums and wallflowers, radiate from glossy spreads in coffee-table books, providing inspiration for many gardening newcomers. British vegetable gardens, although perhaps not as flashy, can also be fun to try (assuming you adapt for the differences in climate). The cool summers typical of Britain limit the likelihood of growing heat-loving tomatoes and squash outside greenhouses—not a problem in most of the United States. Britain has an advantage over North American areas because they can grow onions, cabbages, and other cool-season vegetables during the winter. This offers them an extra season for gardening.

This British garden includes familiar cool-weather-loving crops such as cabbage, lettuce, onions, parsnips, and

This garden was inspired by the herb and vegetable garden at Montague Inn, a bed-and-breakfast located on elegant and spacious grounds of the cultural center of Saginaw, Michigan. The property backs up to Lake Linton where lawns are peppered with magnificent, mature walnut and oak trees along with sweeping beds of flowers. The Montague Inn garden features a great variety of culinary herbs with a few vegetables and edible flowers as well. Order arises from the tidy beds and neatly edged grass paths. During the summer, visitors may find large glass jars of Montague Inn's herbal vinegars out steeping in the sun. The vinegar is used for gourmet cooking at the Inn and is also bottled to sell to guests.

Geometric Garden Design

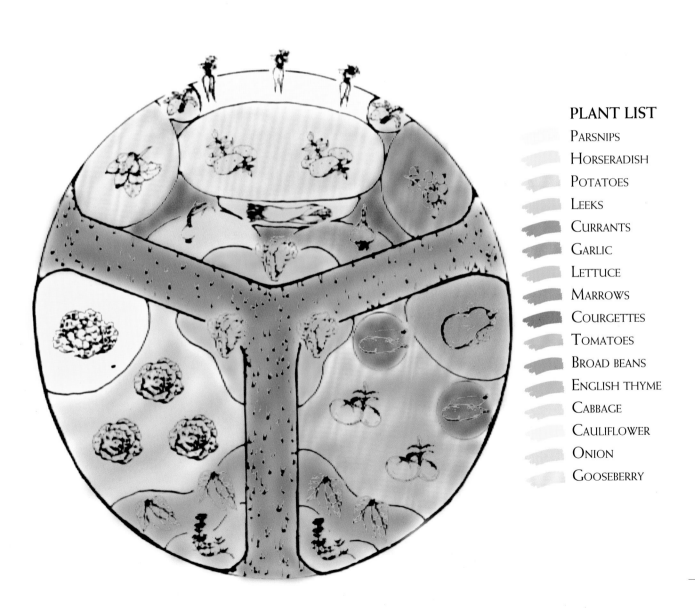

PLANT LIST

Parsnips

Horseradish

Potatoes

Leeks

Currants

Garlic

Lettuce

Marrows

Courgettes

Tomatoes

Broad beans

English thyme

Cabbage

Cauliflower

Onion

Gooseberry

cauliflowers, and also introduces broad beans—fat and buttery beans produced on upright plants. For summer, there are warm-loving tomatoes, courgettes, and marrows (the latter two are summer squash in disguise). Some of these crops include unique British varieties, well worth trying.

A GREAT GARDEN DESIGN

This round garden, measuring about 25 feet in diameter, is composed of three pie-shaped beds divided by grass walks. They come together in the center with a vortex of 'Tom Thumb' lettuce—neat, lime green, miniheads that almost melt in your mouth. Like island beds used for perennial flower planting, the plants build in height toward the center of the front beds creating interesting visual gradients.

The rear bed is straddled on each side by fruiting bushes, gooseberries and currants—easy-care fruits much appreci-

ated in England. They share the bed with underground crops such as horseradish, potatoes, onions, leeks, and garlic. Another bed is devoted primarily to cabbage and cauliflower. The third bed features fruiting plants such as tomatoes, courgettes, and marrows. Matched plantings of broad beans and English thyme mark the front entrance to the garden.

With the exception of perennials such as gooseberries, currants, horseradish, and English thyme, the annual crops can be rotated to keep the soil healthy. Switch beds every year, preparing loose, deep soil for root crops and rich, moist soil for cabbage and fruiting crops. Broad beans—capable of fixing their own nitrogen—will improve the soil whereever they are grown. Just leave their roots in the soil when the crop is done.

Broad beans sport vibrant white and black flowers.

ODE TO OPEN SPACES

A notable feature of the Montague Inn garden is that it is left open to the surroundings instead of enclosing it in walls or hedges. The idea of opening up the garden to become one with the surrounding landscape is eloquently described by William Kenrick in his *New American Orchardist*, 5th ed. (Boston: Otis, Broaders and Co., 1842).

The art of modern Gardening is to form a landscape most beautiful. Nature having drawn the outline, art must accomplish the rest; art itself being subservient or so far concealed, as that all may appear the work of nature alone. Walls and boundary fences should be demolished, or as far as possible concealed.

YOUR BRITISH FAVORITES

Amuse family and guests with sophisticated British cuisine right out of your own garden.

BROAD BEANS (Fava Beans)

These Old World beans are only distantly related to snap beans, their New World counterpart. With a whopping 25 percent protein content, broad beans have been grown and eaten from the time of earliest civilization. Unlike snap beans, broad beans thrive in cool weather and suffer in heat, growing best in mild spring, fall, or winter weather. They have pea-shaped flowers with black-based white petals that sprout on upright stalks, most reaching about 18 inches high but some rising to 4 feet high. The flowers mature into dangling pods that can grow surprisingly long. Broad beans are at their best if picked while the seeds are green and tender. Try them boiled and served with butter and bacon. Or allow the beans to mature fully and dry for storage in a sealed plastic bag or jar.

'Jumbo': This is a quick-growing, early-maturing broad bean. Just 70 days after sowing, it produces short pods containing three huge bean seeds each.

'Loreta': This American version of the British broad bean tolerates hot weather if summer arrives before the beans are ready to pick. It produces inch-long beans in 8-inch-long pods 75 days after sowing.

Savoy cabbages provide added texture to gourmet gardens.

'Imperial Green Longpod': An older classic, this cultivar produces pods 15 inches long with up to 9 seeds in each, 84 days after sowing.

CABBAGE

Britain's mild winter and long, cool spring allow for the growth of great cabbages, which became a staple in England during the time of the Roman Empire. Some Romans believed eating cabbage prevented drunkenness and healed sores and tumors. Choose from tender, early-maturing cabbages, which are good steamed or sliced for coleslaw, or later-maturing cabbages which—if they mature in fall—will keep for a month or more in a refrigerator or root cellar.

'Minicole Hybrid': This is a small-headed cultivar—a British Royal Horticultural Society Award Winner—planted in the fall to grow during a mild winter. The heads mature about 60 days after transplanting but can stay outside in cool weather for up to 4 months. Plant the seedlings 10 inches apart to derive maximum yield from a small space.

'Marvellon Hybrid': This is an extra-large-headed, mild-flavored cabbage that matures 60 to 65 days after transplanting.

CAULIFLOWER

The British answer to the temperamental whims of this delightful crop is to breed extra-durable and quick-maturing cauliflowers that can be planted whenever the weather is likely to be right. Be certain to pluck the creamy heads while tight and full of rounded curds.

'Elby Hybrid': This cultivar will produce large yields if planted in spring for summer harvest or planted in summer for fall harvest. It grows well across much of the United States and matures 70 days after transplanting.

Cauliflower appreciates a climate where the temperature lingers at about 60°F throughout the growing period. It also needs rich, moist soil and plenty of sun.

'Cargill Early Maturing': This small-headed cauliflower can be planted directly from seed in spring to harvest about 85 days later. Thin the seedlings to 6 inches apart.

COURGETTES

This is the British name for zucchini. Courgettes are best picked young—while firm and tender—which then encourages the plants to produce even more new fruits. Slice them into salads, or use them sautéed, baked, grilled, or microwaved, cooked with butter, or blended with cheese, sausage, or other vegetables. The options for this versatile vegetable are endless.

'Green Fingers': This is a new development in zucchini, a plant that produces more fruit-bearing female flowers than male flowers and can produce bigger harvests. The first fruits can be ready to pick just 40 days after sowing seed.

CURRANTS AND GOOSEBERRIES

These two fruiting bushes excel in cool climates and bear crop after crop of fruit with little maintenance. Berries picked before they are fully ripe are used for making jelly and wine. Currants, packed with vitamin C, can be dried like raisins and added to baked goods. Or let the berries ripen fully and eat them fresh. Usually a single bush is sufficient for producing a full harvest. In areas where these plants may be outlawed due to susceptibility to white pine blister rust, you could substitute two blueberry bushes for the currant and gooseberry bushes.

Currants: Choose from red, white, and black currants. Each has a very different flavor, so go to a nursery where you can sample the berries before buying. 'Consort' and 'Coronet' black currants are both rust resistant.

Gooseberries: With plump, transparent green or pink berries, gooseberries can add novelty to your cuisine. It's easiest to grow mildew-resistant types such as 'Pixwell' and 'Poorman' to avoid having to spray for fungus diseases. 'Pixwell' bears pink berries when ripe that are sweet and good for baking. The leaves change to purple in fall, giving an extra season of color. 'Poorman', which originated in Utah, has large berries that turn red when ripe.

GARLIC

Aromatic cloves of garlic are essential for garlic soup as well as for seasoning meats, tomato dishes, and vegetable stir-fries.

HORSERADISH

The fresh root of horseradish has a pungent flavor esteemed by lovers of spicy food. A native of eastern Europe, it is especially popular in northern European countries including Britain. Horseradish is wonderful with roast beef and in Bloody Marys. It is a perennial capable of spreading like a weed in preferred sites. To control its size, harvest the roots every fall, replanting a few healthy roots to produce next year's crop.

LETTUCE

'Tom Thumb' lettuce in America dates back to 1830 and was grown in England before that. Slice a head in half and drizzle it with dressing for two perfect salads. The seeds are widely available, and it's easy to sprinkle them directly on the ground in spring, summer, and fall for a succession of harvests. The leaves are ready to pick about 48 days after sowing.

Experimental winter gardeners may also want to try winter lettuces.

'Winter Density': This is a British vegetable developed specifically to grow during winter. It has firm, thick, upright heads that tolerate heat and especially cold. It matures about 58 days after sowing.

MARROWS

British marrows are summer squash allowed to grow big and beefy. In Old England, they were cooked down to a pulp, but it's better to pick them when small and firm and cook them lightly until just tender.

'White Bush Vegetable Marrow': Lovely, white fruit, harvested young at about 8 inches long, are a British favorite. These are ready to harvest about 75 days after sowing seed.

'Long Green Bush Vegetable Marrow': This is a zucchinilike fruit with dark skin highlighted by lighter stripes. It can grow to 16 inches long and 6 inches wide but is best harvested much smaller. Otherwise you have to pare away the skin, scrape out the seeds, and cook the flesh to make it palatable.

ONIONS

The lure of a blue ribbon coaxes many British gardeners to strive to grow the largest onions ever. This quest begins with naturally large cultivars such as 'Beacon', that can grow up to 6 pounds, if given fertile soil, plenty of sun, and a long, mild summer. A long-day onion, it has a handsome teardrop shape and good flavor to boot. It is ready for harvest 110 days after planting large seedlings.

PARSNIPS

Although you can find parsnips in a grocery store, they are not considered a staple in the United States. In the garden, they have been neglected as well. The reason may be because they take such a long time to reach maturity. But if you plant them in spring and harvest them after the weather turns cold in fall, the frost will make the roots extra sweet and worth the wait. In many climates, parsnips can remain in the ground, covered with mulch in cold climates, for harvest during winter or early spring. This way they don't have to take up space in the refrigerator. Parsnips are particularly delicious roasted in the oven, which tenderizes them and concentrates the flavor.

'Tender and True': This extra long parnip has been given an award of merit by the British Royal Horticultural Society. It is ready for harvest 102 days after sowing.

POTATOES

This native of South America became a staple in Ireland but in the 1840s was devastated by blight disease—widespread famine followed. Today in England, potatoes are still popular.

The starchy, white, baking-type potato is more common in England than the waxy, golden-fleshed potato-salad potato—although both are available in the United States.

French fries are called "chips" and used in the famous fast food, fish and chips. Potato chips are called "crisps."

'Duke of York': Although not widely available, this is a classic from Ronniger's (mail-order potato specialist listed in Appendix B) with creamy skin and fluffy, white flesh. It matures late.

'Irish Cobbler': This American-made potato was developed by an Irish shoemaker from New Jersey in the late 1800s. It has white skin and flesh, ripens early, is good for boiling and baking, but won't store long.

ENGLISH THYME

To add spice to cooking, grow this lovely, aromatic, perennial herb. Although a native of the Mediterranean, thyme was transported to Britain centuries ago and used by Anglo-Saxons as a charm. Its low-growing, woody stems slowly creep across the soil, rooting as they go. 'Broad Leaf English' boasts small, rounded leaves and vigorous growth. It prefers well-drained soil and plenty of sun.

TOMATOES

These can be a bit of a challenge to grow in parts of England where summers are cool and cloudy. But they are cherished enough to be cultivated under glass in greenhouses. Along with eating them fresh, tomatoes are also enjoyed baked and boiled in England and often found on the breakfast menu.

'Super Marmande': This is a large-fruited Provence tomato with an irregular shape, pink shoulders, and sweet juicy flavor. It begins fruiting 62 days after transplanting.

'Tigerella': This tomato parades attractive red and yellow stripes and a tangy sweet flavor. It has received an Award of Merit from the Royal Horticultural Society and begins to bear ripe fruit 59 days after transplanting.

THE RECIPES

Modern and authentic Old English recipes offer plenty of ideas for using garden produce.

Side Dishes

SAUTÉED CABBAGE

2 cups cabbage, cut into 1/2-inch-thick slices
1/2 onion, finely chopped
1 tablespoon margarine
1 teaspoon English thyme leaves, chopped
salt and pepper to taste

Melt margarine in skillet, add onion and sauté for 2 minutes or until soft. Add cabbage. Cover and cook on low for 5 minutes, stirring often. Stir in thyme, salt, and pepper and cook 5 minutes more. Serve immediately.

YIELD: Serves 4

GEOMETRIC GARDEN FROM GREAT BRITAIN

OVEN-ROASTED CARROTS AND PARSNIPS

6 large carrots, cut into 3-inch-long pieces
6 large parsnips, cut into 3-inch-long pieces
2 tablespoons roasted peanut oil
magarine, salt, and freshly ground pepper to taste

Preheat oven to 325°F. Wash both vegetables well and trim off tops and bottoms. Use oil to lightly coat the vegetables. Place, without letting them touch each other, in a roasting pan and roast for 45 minutes or until tender inside. Top with margarine, sprinkle with salt and pepper and serve.

YIELD: Serves 6

BAKED TOMATOES

This delicious dish is for adventuresome eaters.

2 tomatoes
2 teaspoons cider vinegar
2 teaspoons brown sugar
1 cinnamon stick, broken in half

Wash tomatoes and cut out a funnel-shaped center to about 1/2 inch from the bottom of the tomato. Leave skins on. Warm vinegar and mix in brown sugar until dissolved. Divide evenly into tomato hollows. Set 1/2 of a cinnamon stick into each hollow. Place on baking dish and bake 90 minutes at 300°F. Use two spoons to scoop soft tomatoes out into small serving bowls.

YIELD: Serves 2

Where the walk ends, delicious aromas and fragrances begin.

Main Courses

SAVORY POT ROAST

———

Recipe courtesy of Millie Adams

This pot roast is delicious served with horseradish sauce.

3-pound pot roast, top round or chuck roast of beef
1 tablespoon vegetable oil
1/4 cup soy sauce
1 cup decaffeinated coffee
1 teaspoon sugar
2 bay leaves, crumbled
1 large clove garlic
2 tablespoons fresh oregano, snipped
2 onions, divided and sliced
Optional: 1 cup each of broad beans (shelled), potatoes, and/or
   tomatoes

Brown meat in oil in heavy skillet. Meanwhile, mix soy sauce, coffee, sugar, bay leaves, garlic, oregano, and one onion in bowl. Pour soy mixture into large covered baking dish. Place browned meat on top of soy mixture. Top with second sliced onion. Surround with optional potatoes, if desired. Cover. Bake in 300°F oven for 2–2-1/2 hours. Baste meat hourly. If liquid boils away, add 1 cup coffee plus a liberal splash of soy sauce. Add optional beans and tomatoes in last 30 minutes of cooking. When done, slice thinly across the grain of the meat. Serve with pan juices.

YIELD: Serves 6–8

EASY COURGETTE BAKE

———

3 cups medium courgettes (zucchini), cubed
1 egg, beaten
1 can cream of mushroom soup
1-1/2 cups cashews
1-1/2 cups sharp cheddar cheese, grated

Preheat oven to 350°F. Blend zucchini and egg. Place in oiled 2-1/2–liter baking dish and bake for 15 minutes. Top with soup and sprinkle with cashews and cheese. Bake 30 minutes uncovered.

YIELD: Serves 4

Seasoning

LORI'S LOVELY HORSERADISH SAUCE

Recipe courtesy of Lori Zaim

This sauce is the perfect accompaniment to a roast beef or turkey sandwich.

1/2 cup mayonnaise
1 tablespoon horseradish, finely grated
1 tablespoon minced parsley
1 teaspoon lemon juice
1/2 teaspoon salt

Mix all ingredients. Add salt to taste. Refrigerate.
    Extra grated horseradish may be preserved by placing it in a glass jar and covering it with vinegar.

Beverage

BOLD BLOODY MARY

Recipe courtesy of Lori Zaim

1/3 cup vodka
1 cup chilled tomato juice
1-1/2 teaspoons horseradish, freshly grated
1 teaspoon sugar
1/2 teaspoon salt
1/8 teaspoon hot pepper sauce

Blend all ingredients with 3/4 cup crushed ice. Shake or stir well. Do not strain. Pour into 2 glasses with salted rims. Garnish with a leafy celery stalk.

YIELD: Serves 2

13
MEXICAN SUN GARDEN

Lovers of full-flavored Mexican food can satisfy their passion with a rich selection of chili peppers, herbs, and vegetables that are easy to grow and perfect for Mexican cuisine. This Mexican Sun Garden allows you to experiment with dozens of different chili peppers (from very hot to slightly sassy), herbs such as Mexican mint marigolds, salsa classics such as cilantro and tomatillos, as well as delicious tomatoes, aromatic onions, and native Mexican squash and beans.

Mexican gardening can be dated back to the ancient Mayan culture—a civilization who learned to utilize irrigation systems to grow lush gardens amid arid lands. The results were incredible. One early 1500s formal Mayan garden had tropical flowers, fruit trees, trellis-

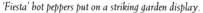

'Fiesta' hot peppers put on a striking garden display.

Mexican Sun Garden Design

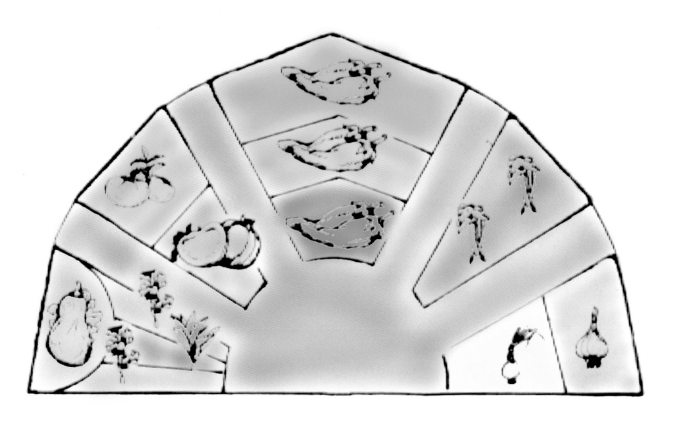

PLANT LIST

CHILIS (SUCH AS ANAHEIM, ANCHO, JALAPENO)	MEXICAN MINT MARIGOLD
TOMATOES	CILANTRO
TOMATILLOS	ONIONS
SQUASH	GARLIC
	BEANS

lined paths, and water-filled canals. Another walled garden had fountains, baths, caged songbirds, and abundant flowers. This great heritage and exciting cuisine combine to form a Mexican Sun Garden that's compatible with your yard.

A GREAT GARDEN DESIGN

This 25-foot-long by 15-foot-wide Mexican garden is designed for a small yard. The garden takes the shape of the sun—a symbol revered in ancient Mexico. Four paths divide five beds, allowing easy maintenance and creating the unique pattern of sun rays.

The largest bed is devoted to a variety of chili peppers, chosen according to your tastes. Other beds are devoted to herbs and squash, beans, tomatillos and tomatoes, and onions and garlic. In subsequent years, you can rotate crops—switching chilis, tomatoes, and tomatillos into the beds previously used for squash, herbs, beans, onions, and garlic.

In temperate climates with moderate rainfall, the beds can be raised with 4- to 6-inch-high wooden timbers or stone walls to encourage good water drainage. In arid climates, the entire garden can be lowered 6 inches or deeper to collect runoff rainfall and irrigation water. When growing heat-loving chili peppers and Mexican mint marigolds in cool climates, try setting them against the south side of a stone or brick wall. The sun will warm the wall which radiates heat throughout the day and also into the night creating a more tropical environment.

YOUR MEXICAN FAVORITES

Mexico, the southwestern United States, and South America are home to many indigenous crops essential in Mexican cuisine. A few plants from other lands, such as cilantro from southern Europe, also have been incorporated into Mexican cooking.

BEANS

High-protein beans, shelled from the pod, are a staple in Mexican diets. They are important in burritos, refried beans, bean dips, stews, casseroles, and more. Although many types of beans will do, you can grow classic Mexican beans for authentic flavor.

'Tepary': There are several forms of tepary beans—Mexican natives with light, dark, or speckled seed coats. These beans—well adapted to their native homelands—tolerate heat, drought, and alkaline soil. Relatives of the green bean, these plants differ in that they have short, twining stems and pods only about 3 inches long. Harvest the pods before they dry out completely and drop their seeds to the ground.

'Black Turtle': Mexican black beans have their own distinctive flavor and grow well in most parts of the United States. They are great in black bean soup, chili, burritos, refried beans, or even basic baked beans. In northern climates, look for early-maturing cultivars, ready for harvest in about 100 days.

CHILIS

These peppers, which grow wild in South America, have been cultivated for centuries for their spicy flavor. Chilis add zip to everything from tacos to tamales and are so relished by lovers of spicy foods that they have almost a cult following. Gardeners and cooks subscribe to magazines, clubs, and cooking academies that specialize in chili peppers, always looking for another wonderful way to use chilis. Chili peppers spread from South America to Mexico and then were taken to Europe by Spanish conquistadores, where they quickly spread throughout the Old World. In Mexico, chili peppers are important in chili con carne, chili rellenos, chili con queso, in mole sauces, dips, and much more. They can be dried and ground to sprinkle on dishes as seasoning or frozen for later use. Chilis are also roasted and used in salads or casseroles.

Chili peppers tend to grow spicier as they mature, especially if the weather is warm and sunny. The heat resides in the white placenta within the fruit which can be scraped out to moderate the burn for people with sensitive palates.

'Ancho' (the fresh pepper)/'Poblano' (the dried pepper): Anchos, which are mildly spicy, start out black green and mature to a reddish brown with a mild, fruity flavor. The triangular fruit is ideal for stuffing with rice, beans, and cheese. The plants get to be 36 inches high and may produce harvest-sized, green fruit about 85 days after transplanting though ripe fruit takes considerably longer.

'NuMex'/'Big Jim': These are great peppers for the Southwest, thriving in an extended, warm growing season. Long, slender, moderately hot peppers are produced in abundance and almost simultaneously on 18- to 24-inch-tall plants. The peppers begin to mature about 75 days after planting.

'Long Red Cayenne': These peppers bear extra-hot pods that are 5 inches long and less than 1 inch wide. When ripe, at least 75 days after planting, they turn bright crimson. Cayennes are dried and pulverized into spicy flakes for sprinkling on food. They are also good for adding to pickles, dropping whole into a dish, or canning.

'Espanole Improved': This chili is ready to harvest just 65 days after transplanting seedlings—a good choice for cool climates with a short, frost-free growing season. The fruits are hot and will ripen even in cool weather.

'Jalapeno': This bullet-shaped pepper—named after a Mexican town—has a bold, creeping burn that takes several seconds to catch up on the eater. It is especially good to pickle in vinegar and slice onto pizza, tacos, burritos, or almost any dish. Jalapenos may be stuffed with cream cheese, cheddar cheese, or sausage, and breaded and fried for appetizers called poppers. Jalapenos become chipotle peppers if dried and smoked. Folks who prefer milder peppers can try 'Tam Mild Jalapeno' which is half as hot as the original.

'Anaheim': These are classic chilis that grow into 8-inch-long, lanky fruit with moderately thick walls. They can be picked green and roasted for green chili or stuffed with cheese or meat for chili rellenos. Alternatively, they can be allowed to mature until red, then dried and hung in ristras (wreaths) or pulverized into chili powder. Harvest begins about 70 days after planting seedlings. People who prefer milder peppers might try 'Anaheim M'.

'Serrano': This is a plant with fiery hot peppers—slim, 2-inch-long, upright peppers that resemble candle flames. They mature to orange red on plants that grow up to 36 inches tall. The thin-walled fruit dries easily for use as decorations or can be pulverized into flakes to sprinkle on food. They are also good for pickling and salsas.

CILANTRO

The aromatic, sweet, and pungent foliage of coriander is harvested before the plants set seed and is called cilantro. It's used in salsas, tacos, chili, and other dishes. A cool-season annual, delicate, feathery leaves grow on stems more than 2 feet high. If allowed to go to seed, you may find self-sown volunteers springing up in the fall. The fruit can be harvested and broken open to release the edible coriander seeds inside.

MEXICAN MINT MARIGOLD

This is a marigold with a small flower and aromatic leaves that imitates tarragon. But unlike tarragon, which needs a cold winter rest, Mexican mint marigolds thrive in climates with little or no winter cold. They also can be grown as an annual during the frost-free summer season in cold climates. Used for centuries in South America, the leaves are good in herbal teas or any recipe calling for anise or tarragon. They also blend well with chicken, fish, sautéed vegetables, winter squash, salads, herbal vinegars, eggs, and beans.

ONIONS

As in many other types of cuisine, onions are important flavorings in Mexican food. You can use pungent storage onions or mild and sweet onions according to your taste preferences.

SQUASH

A variety of squash originated in Mexico where they are scrambled with eggs, sautéed with other vegetables, stuffed or buttered and baked, or put in soups and salads. Some Mexican favorites include cushaws, bearing long-storing, greenish fruit on speckled-leaved plants; hubbard squash with large, blue green–skinned fruit and sweet flesh; and big cheese types with flattened pumpkin shapes.

TOMATILLO

This relative of the tomato has a mild, tart flavor and a sturdy consistency that endears it to Mexican cuisine. Both green and purple varieties are available. Tomatillos take about 60 days from planting to harvest so are suitable even for cool-climate gardens.

TOMATOES

Anyone who has eaten a delicious taco or salsa knows tomatoes—particularly sweet, fresh, home-grown tomatoes—are an integral ingredient. Many of the other tomatoes included in this book can also do the job. Another option is to grow authentic, Mexican heirloom tomatoes including semi-wild 'Chiapas' and 'Ciudad' tomatoes with small but sweet fruit. (Seeds are available through Native Seeds/SEARCH source listed in Appendix B). You also can find hollow Mexican tomatoes such as 'Large Ribbed Zapotec', 'Yellow Ruffled', and 'Mexicali'—all of which are great for stuffing.

Mildly spicy 'Mulato Island' is great for making stuffed rellenos. (Photo courtesy of Thompson and Morgan)

SCALE OF PEPPER HEAT

MILD: cherry, bell, pimiento
MEDIUM: ancho, poblano, anaheim
HOT: jalapeno, chipotle (smoke-dried jalapeno)
VERY HOT: piquin, cayenne, tabasco, serrano
SUPER HOT: habanero, Thai

'Hot Claw' is one of the most attractive, and hottest, of chilis.

THE RECIPES

Produce from your Mexican Sun Garden will be perfect in the following recipes.

Soup

GAZPACHO (ICED VEGETABLE SOUP)

6 tomatoes

1 medium cucumber, peeled, seeded, and chopped

1 medium onion, finely chopped

1 small green pepper, finely chopped

1 small clove garlic, sliced

2 tablespoons corn oil

2 teaspoons red wine vinegar

1 teaspoon salt

1/2 teaspoon hot pepper sauce

2 tablespoons cilantro, chopped

Loosen tomato skins by dipping in boiling water for a few seconds or until skins begin to split. Set aside to cool, then peel off skins with sharp knife. Coarsely chop tomatoes.

Make tomato juice by pureeing two tomatoes with garlic, salt, hot pepper sauce, oil, and vinegar.

Combine tomatoes, tomato juice, cucumber, onion, green pepper, and cilantro in a large bowl. Chill at least 1 hour.

YIELD: Serves 6

Side Dishes

SPICED WINTER SQUASH

———

3 *pounds squash*

1/2 *cup brown sugar, packed*

4 *teaspoons margarine*

2 *teaspoons fresh Mexican mint marigold, chopped*

Preheat oven to 350°F. Cut squash in half and scoop out seeds. With a sharp knife, make 6 to 8 shallow slices into the flesh of each squash half, using care not to cut through the squash rind. Cream sugar with margarine and divide between the two squash halves, using the back of a spoon to spread the mixture over the furrowed squash. Place rind down in a large baking dish, cover, and bake for 40 minutes or until tender. Cut into slices and set on a serving dish. Stir mint marigold leaves into syrup left in baking dish. Pour over squash and serve.

YIELD: Serves 8

MEXICAN VEGETABLES

———

1 *tablespoon margarine*

1 *onion, peeled and chopped*

2 *cloves garlic, peeled and minced*

1 *green pepper, seeded and chopped*

1 *cup corn kernels (from 3 ears)*

1 *cup zucchini, sliced*

1 *cup yellow squash, sliced*

3 *tomatoes, diced*

2 *cups rice, cooked*

Melt margarine in large skillet and sauté onion, garlic, green pepper, corn, zucchini, and yellow squash, stirring to prevent sticking or browning. Add tomatoes, cover, and simmer on low for 15 minutes. Serve over cooked rice.

YIELD: Serves 8

Main Courses

SAUSAGE-STUFFED POBLANOS

—

1/2 pound sausage

1 clove garlic, minced

1/2 small onion, chopped

1-1/2 cups rice, cooked

1-1/2 cups Monterey jack cheese, grated

1 tablespoon cilantro, minced

15 to 18 poblano peppers

Preheat oven to 350°F. Cook sausage in a large skillet, crumbling it into small pieces. Drain fat and transfer sausage to a large mixing bowl. Add garlic and onion to skillet, sauté until soft. Mix garlic, onion, rice, cilantro, cheese, and sausage in large bowl.

Wash peppers and cut off the stems. Scoop out seeds without breaking pepper open, wearing gloves if desired to keep hot flavorings off your skin. Fill each pepper with stuffing. Set stuffed peppers in a large baking dish, leaning peppers on each other if necessary to keep upright. Bake covered for 30 minutes.

YIELD: Serves 4–6

VARIATION: This sausage stuffing can also be used for approximately 6 larger bell peppers.

BLACK BEAN TORTILLAS

—

2 cups dried black beans

1/2 pound ground beef

1/2 cup roasted green chilis, chopped

1 clove garlic, minced

2 onions, chopped

2 tomatoes, chopped

1/2 cup cheddar cheese, grated

12 tortillas

Presoak dried beans overnight, covered with water. Cook black beans by simmering in fresh water for 90 minutes. When tender, drain.

In a large skillet, brown the ground beef with garlic and one onion. Drain out fat. Stir in beans and chilis. Heat for 10 minutes, stirring occasionally. Serve in tortillas with grated cheese, chopped tomatoes, and onions.

YIELD: Serves 4

Seasoning

ROASTED GREEN CHILIS

---

12 green chilis

Wash chilis and lay on a cookie sheet. Set under broiler until surface tans, often accompanied by a popping sound. Turn peppers over to tan another side. Repeat several times until peppers are completely cooked. Remove peppers from broiler and put in a clean paper bag. Set aside for 10 minutes. Transfer to a cutting board. Remove stem and peel off skin. Use right away or freeze.

VARIATION: Any large pepper roasts well and is a welcome addition to salads, casseroles, pasta, rice, and other dishes.

Tomatillos come encased in a papery husk, which must be shed to reveal the green fruit.

*A*PPENDIX A: ENCYCLOPEDIA OF CROPS

After browsing through this book, you may have a good idea of the foods you want and the designs that will look best in your yard. Now you need the details on how to make these foods grow to be their best. This is where the Encyclopedia of Crops comes in.

Crops are listed alphabetically by their common names. They include the following quick reference information.

Appearance/Flavor: A handsome garden design uses plants in a variety of shapes and textures. Blending, for example, low, bushy, and vining plants provides pleasant diversity. Flavor references explain whether harvested crops are sweet, pungent, peppery, mild, or some other flavor.

Garden Color: This identifies the decorative color(s) of the plant, which can add to the beauty of your garden.

Life Cycle: Plants that are annuals produce their harvest within a single growing season and die at the end of the year. Perennials grow and produce for several to many years. There also are a few biennials, producing foliage the first year and flowers, seeds, and fruits the following year. A number of crops grown as annuals, including onions, leeks, chicories, and radicchios, are actually biennials but are seldom given the chance to grow a second year. Some plants that are biennial or perennial occasionally are grown for one season like annuals; in this case, both life cycles will be listed.

Interplanting crops such as Chinese cabbage and Swiss chard makes the most of limited space and provides interesting contrasts in form and color.

Hardiness: Perennial plants exhibit varying tolerances for cold and heat, which is called hardiness. The United States is divided into a range of hardiness zones, starting at subtropical Zone 10 at the tip of Florida to Zone 2 in the coldest reaches of Alaska. The range of zones within which a perennial is hardy and will grow is indicated under this heading.

Temperature Preference: Cool-season crops prefer weather averaging approximately 50° to 70°F and can tolerate some light frost. Warm-season crops need frost-free weather ideally from 60° to 85°F.

Sun and Shade: Crops in this book are suitable for either full sun—at least six hours of sun a day; or light shade—four to six hours of sun a day.

Spacing: To allow gourmet crops sufficient room to thrive, give each plant enough garden space to mature without becoming entangled in neighboring plants. Refer to spacing recommendations.

In addition to these quick reference items, each entry provides details on ideal growing conditions, care tips, and problem prevention.

ANGELICA (*Angelica archangelica*)

Appearance/Flavor: Upright/anise
Garden Color: White flowers
Life Cycle: Perennial or biennial
Hardiness: Zones 3 to 7
Temperature Preference: Cool
Sun and Shade: Sun or light shade
Spacing: 3 feet apart

GROWING GUIDELINES: This herb has angelic associations and anise undertones. It soars 6 feet high with wide clusters of small, white flowers the second year of growth. Plant angelica seedlings—available at specialty herb nurseries—in fertile and moist soil amended with extra compost before planting. Greenhouse grown seedlings should be planted after spring frost passes. Once angelica is established in your yard, it may produce its own seedlings that can be carefully dug—without damaging the young roots—and moved to a new location in spring.

CARE TIPS: Water new plantings with a water-soluble fertilizer. Mulch with several inches of compost in spring and water as needed to keep the soil moist. Cut back flower stalks when they arise during the second year of growth to prevent the plant from dying after bloom. Or allow the flowers to mature and set seeds, which may sprout if allowed to fall to the ground and germinate undisturbed.

PROBLEM PREVENTION: Aphids—small, pear-shaped sucking insects that cling to young stems or flowers—can be washed away with the garden hose or sprayed with insecticidal soap.

APPLE (*Malus* spp.)

Appearance/Flavor: Large upright/sweet
Garden Color: White flowers, red or yellow fruit
Life Cycle: Perennial
Hardiness: Zones 3 to 9
Temperature Preference: Variable
Sun and Shade: Sun
Spacing: 6 feet apart for dwarfs, 25 feet apart for full-sized trees

GROWING GUIDELINES: There are many kinds of apples—red, yellow, green, sweet, tart—and many types of apple trees—dwarf (naturally small), semidwarf (medium-sized), and standard (full-sized). In a mixed gourmet garden it's best to grow dwarfs, which leave plenty of room for other crops. Also useful are naturally compact, spur-type trees with short fruiting branches. Ask your local Cooperative Extension Service agent or a reliable local nurseryman what cultivars and dwarfing root stocks (used to make apple trees small) are best suited for your climate and soil. To produce apples, apple trees need cross-pollination, exchanging pollen with a different yet compatible cultivar. When choosing which two cultivars to grow, make sure they are compatible cross-pollinators.

Get certified disease-free trees, which will probably arrive in earliest spring in cool climates or possibly fall in warm climates. Plant them in a site with well-drained but moist soil of average fertility that is protected from strong winds. For spring planting, it's helpful to prepare the garden a season ahead of time so the trees can be planted without delay. Keep the tree moist until it's well established and growing strongly.

CARE TIPS: Fertilize apple trees in spring using a balanced, granular fertilizer. Increase the amount used to encourage more growth or decrease fertilizer to slow growth. Mulch to keep the soil moist and discourage weeds. Water during dry weather. Because dwarf trees often have brittle roots that can snap off in wind storms, anchor them to a flexible but sturdy orchard stake set close to the tree trunk. Use a soft, biodegradable tie so the trunk will not be damaged as it grows.

Dwarf trees will take several years to begin bearing fruit—which is still faster than larger trees. Spend these years wisely training the plant into a productive form—a shape that provides every limb with sunshine. The most popular training system is called central leader. It has one main trunk rising up the center of the plant and evenly spaced side branches emerging in different directions along it. Here is how a central leader plant is trained.

- Cut back a newly planted, year-old tree in early spring to about 2 feet high.

- As new branches sprout along the trunk, choose the strongest growing central one to become the new trunk, and three or four side branches (emerging in different directions and separated by about 4 inches of trunk) to become lateral branches. Remove all other growth.

- To encourage maximum productivity from new, lateral branches, weight them by hanging a can or clothespins on the end of the branch. This pulls the branch down slightly making it grow more horizontally, becoming stronger and more fruitful.

- The following spring, cut back the lateral branches by one-third to encourage them to produce side branches and remove any unwanted branches sprouting low on the trunk. When the trunk has risen several feet above the previous set of branches, choose another three or four lateral branches to keep and remove any others. Allow the main trunk to continue to grow undisturbed.

- In subsequent years, thin out thick growth and unwanted branches to keep the main framework open.

PROBLEM PREVENTION: Beginning with disease-resistant cultivars such as 'Liberty' and 'Prima' is the best way to prevent problems. To discourage apple maggots—fly larvae that tunnel into fruit—hang four red spheres coated with sticky tanglefoot in each tree from several weeks after bloom through the end of August. These catch egg-laying flies before they can attack the young fruit. Hang codling moth traps in spring to identify when adults become active and spray before moths can lay eggs, preventing the larvae from tunneling into young fruit. Pick up any fruit that falls to the ground prematurely—they are likely to harbor tunneling pests and their destruction will prevent further spread.

ARUGULA (*Eruca vesicaria*)

Appearance/Flavor: Low leafy/mustard-garlic
Garden Color: Medium to dark green
Life Cycle: Annual
Temperature Preference: Cool
Sun and Shade: Sun
Spacing: 6 inches apart

GROWING GUIDELINES: The lobed leaves of arugula emerge quickly after sowing, providing a most interesting culinary carpet. Arugula grows best in moist, fertile soil, abundantly enriched with compost, but will tolerate heavy or slightly light soils as well. Sow new seeds every two to three weeks during spring, late summer, and fall—and in warm climates, even winter—for a regular harvest of arugula.

CARE TIPS: For quick growth and optimum flavor, keep arugula watered in dry weather. Fertilize with a water-soluble fertilizer every three weeks.

PROBLEM PREVENTION: Flea beetles—tiny, black leaf munchers—may Swiss cheese the leaves with little holes. At the first sign of these pests, cover the planting with a floating row cover, a lightweight fabric that keeps flying pests off.

ASPARAGUS (*Asparagus officinalis*)

Appearance/Flavor: Upright ferny/mild
Garden Color: Medium green
Life Cycle: Perennial
Hardiness: Zones 2 to 9
Temperature Preference: Varied
Sun and Shade: Sun
Spacing: 18 to 24 inches apart

GROWING GUIDELINES: The slender shoots of asparagus arise in spring to provide gourmet spears for the kitchen. Those left growing quickly fill out into feathery fronds that form a handsome hedge or foliage plant in the garden. Start with year-old bare root plants from a reliable nursery. The cultivar should be disease resistant and well suited for your area.

Provide well-drained and well-manured soil for best growth. Work a thick layer of composted manure into the soil before planting. Plant a row of asparagus in a trench or an individual plant in a hole, both dug about 10 inches deep. Set the asparagus crown, where the roots and shoots meet, 6 to 8 inches deep in a small mound of soil. Cover with several inches of soil and fill in the remainder once the new spears are growing. Water to keep moist until established.

CARE TIPS: Mulch with 2 to 4 inches of composted livestock manure each spring. Allow asparagus plants to grow for several years before cutting the first harvest. This lets the plants become strong enough to last a lifetime. Once the plants are bushy and producing plump thumb-sized spears, begin harvesting for several weeks in spring and gradually extend that period up to a month.

PROBLEM PREVENTION: To prevent perennial weeds and lawn grass from working their way into an asparagus bed, separate growing areas from lawn with a submerged landscape timber or other garden edging. Mulch thickly and pull any weeds before they become entangled in the asparagus. Cut off the yellow asparagus fronds in fall to remove winter hiding places for asparagus beetles.

 BASIL (*Ocimum basilicum*)
Appearance/Flavor: Bushy/aromatic
Garden Color: Light to medium green or purple
Life Cycle: Annual
Temperature Preference: Warm
Sun and Shade: Sun or light shade
Spacing: 6 inches apart for small plants to 18 inches apart for large plants

GROWING GUIDELINES: Basil comes in many varieties from small-leaved bush forms that only get 6 inches high to large, lettuce-leaf types that can reach several feet tall. All have a lovely clovelike flavor, some with undertones of lemon, cinnamon, licorice, and other flavors. Basil grows easily from seed which can be sown directly outside in the garden after spring frosts pass or prestarted indoors several weeks earlier. Use care to avoid disturbing basil seedling roots when transplanting. Grow in moist but well-drained soil of average fertility. After planting, water with a water-soluble, transplant fertilizer.

CARE TIPS: Water as necessary to maintain even soil moisture. Harvest by pinching off sprigs as needed or by cutting plants back by one-third every three weeks or so through the summer. To encourage quick resprouting, water with water-soluble fertilizer after a major harvest. When temperatures become cool in late summer or fall, growth becomes sluggish and foliage can become off-flavored.

PROBLEM PREVENTION: Pinch off flowers as they bud to prevent seed set which reduces yields and hastens plant death. Swarming Japanese beetles can attack basil. Cover plants with floating row covers to keep beetles off.

BEANS, BROAD (*Vicia faba*)
Appearance/Flavor: Upright/mild
Garden Color: White flowers with black centers
Life Cycle: Annual
Temperature Preference: Cool
Sun and Shade: Sun
Spacing: 4 to 6 inches apart

GROWING GUIDELINES: Broad beans, which grow on sturdy upright stems—18 inches to 4 feet high depending on the cultivar—have plump pods and large, edible seeds inside. The seeds are enclosed in a milky skin that should be removed before eating. Provide cool, well-drained soil of average fertility. Raised beds work well if planting in early spring when soils tend to be wet. Where winters are mild, broad beans can also be planted in the fall. Setting seeds in double rows 12 to 18 inches apart allows stems to lean on each other for extra support when burdened with large pods.

CARE TIPS: Broad beans can produce their own nitrogen fertilizer but must be innoculated with a special strain of nitrogen fixing bacteria. Look for a strain labeled specifically for broad or fava beans and apply to the seeds or furrow before planting. During warm weather, be careful to keep plants mulched and irrigated to prevent premature fading. When the harvest is over, cut the stalks and put in a compost pile but leave the roots in the ground. They will decay and enrich the soil with extra nitrogen.

PROBLEM PREVENTION: Aphids—small, soft bodied sucking insects—can infect broad beans with a plant virus that limits productivity. Watch for aphids and spray immediately with insecticidal soap, repeating as needed to prevent reinfestation.

BEANS, SNAP and **LIMA** (*Phaseolus vulgaris, P. limensis, P. lunatus*)

Appearance/Flavor: Low bushy or vining/mild
Garden Color: Light to medium green
Life Cycle: Annual
Temperature Preference: Warm
Sun and Shade: Sun
Spacing: 4 inches apart for bush beans, 8 inches for pole beans

GROWING GUIDELINES: If there was an all-American vegetable, the bean would surely be it. Snap beans are grown for their tender, young bean pods and lima beans for their fat, buttery seeds, harvested when mature. Bush types grow about 12 inches high and are ideal for planting in double rows which form a canopy of greenery that shades out weeds. Pole beans—vines grown on trellises or poles—reach about 6 feet high and are exceptionally productive. Snap and lima beans grow best in warm, well-drained, moderately fertile soil, ideally 70° to 80°F, although some cultivars have cool soil tolerance, which allows for slightly earlier planting in cool climates. Plant the seeds directly in the ground when temperatures are right.

CARE TIPS: First-time bean growers should apply a nitrogen-fixing bacterial innoculant to the seeds or planting furrow before sowing the seeds. The bacteria live in round nodules on bean roots, capturing nitrogen from the air and changing it to a form that the beans can use as fertilizer.

PROBLEM PREVENTION: Bean beetles—which resemble brown ladybugs—and their soft, bristly, yellow larvae can damage bean foliage and pods. Pick beetles and larvae off bean plants and step on them or fight them with parasitic wasps available from mail-order catalogs. (Sources are listed in Appendix B.) Bean beetles can also be killed with a pyrethrin spray. When they are done producing, remove bean plants, cutting off plant tops (leave the roots to decay and add nitrogen to the soil) and put them in a sealed garbage bag for several weeks to kill any remaining bean beetles or their larvae. To discourage bean diseases, pull up any plants with distorted growth or severely mottled or curled leaves and put them in your garbage can—not the compost pile. Avoid working amid bean plants when they're wet so you won't spread disease spores.

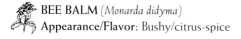

BEE BALM (*Monarda didyma*)
Appearance/Flavor: Bushy/citrus-spice

Garden Color: Red, purple, white, or pink flowers
Life Cycle: Perennial
Hardiness: Zones 4 to 8
Temperature Preference: Varied
Sun and Shade: Sun to light shade
Spacing: 2 to 3 feet apart

GROWING GUIDELINES: What a wonderful surprise it is to find bee balm or its relatives growing wild along a stream bank. It is Nature's gift to America—a delightful, native plant with many uses. Bee balm has spicy, citrus-scented leaves and shaggy, red, pink, purple, or white flowers; both flowers and foliage are edible. Give it moist and rich soil, adding extra compost before planting.

CARE TIPS: Irrigate as necessary and mulch to keep the soil damp in dry weather. Fertilize in spring with a balanced, granular fertilizer. Bee balm sends out new growth on runners to fill up a space 3 feet or more across. To prevent it from overrunning nearby plants or from aging and hollowing out in the center, dig up the plant and divide it into segments every couple years. Refresh the soil with compost and replant the healthiest division.

PROBLEM PREVENTION: Most cultivars of bee balm are susceptible to powdery mildew, which disfigures the plant, covering the foliage with powdery white spores that look like felt and render the plant inedible. Avoid it by planting disease-resistant cultivars such as 'Marshall's Delight'. Disease-stricken plants can be cut back to the ground and allowed to resprout with fresh, clean foliage.

BEETS (*Beta vulgaris*)
Appearance/Flavor: Low leafy/sweet
Garden Color: Dark green leaves and red stems
Life Cycle: Biennial/annual
Temperature Preference: Cool
Sun and Shade: Sun
Spacing: 3 to 4 inches apart for full-sized beets, 1 to 2 inches apart for baby beets

GROWING GUIDELINES: Beets, which have sweet, swollen red or golden roots and edible leaves, are grown as annuals. But because they usually don't flower until the second year, they are actually biennials. Beets grow easily in loose, deep, well-drained soil of average fertility. Plant the seeds directly in the garden in spring for summer harvests or in late summer for fall harvests. Beets may also grow during winter in warm climates.

CARE TIPS: Sometimes several plants will emerge from what appears to be a lumpy seed but actually is a fruit with several seeds inside. Thin out the extra plants and pull any weeds that appear so the beets won't become overcrowded. Protect shallow beet roots by hoeing with care and hand weeding around beet plants. Mulch and water to keep the soil moist.

PROBLEM PREVENTION: Prevent premature bolting by planting beets after spring temperatures become moderate.

BLACKBERRIES (*Rubus* spp.)

Appearance/Flavor: Tall bushy/sweet
Garden Color: White flowers, red or black berries
Life Cycle: Perennial
Hardiness: Zones 5 to 9
Temperature Preference: Varied
Sun and Shade: Sun
Spacing: 3 feet apart for thorny cultivars, 5 feet apart for thornless cultivars

GROWING GUIDELINES: Blackberries come in two types: traditional thorny types (once believed to be home to poisonous snakes) and newer thornless types with arching canes that benefit from trellising. The dozens of cultivars available vary in temperature preferences. Ask your local Cooperative Extension Service agent which cultivars grow best in your area. Provide fertile and well-drained soil in a location with free air circulation but without strong winds. Plant as far as possible from any wild blackberries—a potential source of diseases. In cool climates the best time to plant is spring; in warm climates fall may be better.

CARE TIPS: Blackberries need special pruning to keep them rejuvenated and prevent overcrowding. In spring, cut off all but the seven strongest canes on each plant—the result being better health and larger berries. Trim side branches on these canes back to about a foot long. At the same time, apply a balanced fertilizer and a compost mulch. After picking the berries, cut the fruiting canes back to the ground—they won't fruit again. But leave the new canes which will bear next year's crop. Irrigate during dry weather to keep the soil evenly moist.

PROBLEM PREVENTION: Always start with disease-free blackberry plants from a reliable nursery. Remove any canes or plants that grow distorted or are covered with leaves encrusted with orange rust disease. Bag these, as well as old leaves and canes, and throw them out in the garbage rather than composting them. Using lime-sulfur sprays in spring just as blackberry buds are breaking can help prevent several other diseases.

BLUEBERRIES (*Vaccinium corymbosum*)

Appearance/Flavor: Bushy/sweet
Garden Color: White flowers, red and blue berries
Life Cycle: Perennial
Hardiness: Zones 4 to 7
Temperature Preference: Varied
Sun and Shade: Sun to light shade
Spacing: 6 feet apart

GROWING GUIDELINES: Delicious blueberries dwell on handsome landscape plants with pretty white flowers in spring and red foliage in fall. One caution: Blueberries turn blue long before they become sweet. Wait until the plant is covered with blueberries and sample a few before picking a large harvest. Highbush blueberries are discussed here, but far-north gardeners may grow lowbush or half-high blueberries, and southern gardeners may grow heat-tolerant, rabbiteye blueberries. Ask your nurseryman for recommendations of cultivars suitable for your climate. Blueberries need special soil for success. It must be moist but sandy, well drained and very acidic, with a pH around 4.5. Naturally acidic soils can be made suitable by adding extra peat moss to make them light and moisture retentive. Sulfur can be added regularly to lower the pH of less acid soils.

CARE TIPS: Mulch after planting with pine needles mixed with bark mulch to keep shallow blueberry roots moist and reduce problems with weeds. Irrigate as necessary to keep soil moist during dry weather. Once plants mature, prune out several of the oldest branches in early spring each year so vigorous, new branches can take their place.

PROBLEM PREVENTION: Blueberry maggots may attack young berries, tunneling into and ruining them. Like apple maggots, blueberry maggots can be caught on sticky, red balls—one hung in each bush before the berries show a hint of blue. Remove any dead or dying branches, disinfecting the pruning shears with Lysol® before cutting into healthy tissue. Remove and destroy any berries that are shriveled or otherwise damaged or diseased.

BROCCOLI (*Brassica oleracea*)
Appearance/Flavor: Upright/mild
Garden Color: Blue-green leaves, yellow flowers
Life Cycle: Annual
Temperature Preference: Cool
Sun and Shade: Sun
Spacing: 18 inches apart
GROWING GUIDELINES: Broccoli, while not always high on America's political agenda, is easily cultivated for its large clusters of plump flower buds. Provide moist, rich soil. Plant in spring for summer harvest and summer for fall harvest. Broccoli can also be grown during winter in warm climates. Where there is a long growing season, broccoli can be planted from direct-sown seeds; elsewhere give it a six-week headstart indoors and transplant it outside as a seedling. Apply a water-soluble fertilizer when transplanting or as soon as direct-sown seedlings arise.

CARE TIPS: Keep broccoli plants growing steadily so heads will be sweet and mild. Irrigate as necessary to keep soil moist and apply a granular fertilizer three weeks after planting and every month thereafter. Harvest as soon as the broccoli heads swell. If allowed to sit, they will burst open into flowers, which although edible and pretty sprinkled on a salad, are not as satisfying as broccoli heads.

PROBLEM PREVENTION: Rotate planting sites so broccoli doesn't grow in the same place twice. It's also helpful to avoid using the previous planting sites of related plants such as cabbage, cauliflower, and kohlrabi. Green cabbage worms, which blend in with the head perfectly, can be kept at bay by covering plants with floating row covers, or they can be killed by spraying with Bt, a bacterial disease of caterpillars. Soak the harvested heads in salt water for 10 minutes before cooking to dislodge any remaining caterpillars.

 BROCCOLI RAAB (*Brassica rapa*)
Appearance/Flavor: Upright/mild-peppery
Garden Color: Medium green leaves
Life Cycle: Annual
Temperature Preference: Cool
Sun and Shade: Sun
Spacing: 5 inches apart
GROWING GUIDELINES: Broccoli raab, also called sprouting broccoli, is actually a form of turnip that pro-duces small, plump flower buds reminiscent of broccoli sprouts. You can grow fast-maturing broccoli raablike let-tuce, sowing a sprinkling of seeds every two weeks through-out the cool growing season. Plant in moist and fertile soil.

CARE TIPS: Irrigate as needed to keep soil moist so plants can grow steadily and remain mild flavored. Apply a balanced, granular fertilizer as soon as the seedlings come up. Harvest as soon as you see the plump buds and before they open into flowers.

PROBLEM PREVENTION: Keep flea beetles and other pests off broccoli raab by covering newly sown seeds with floating row covers.

 BRUSSELS SPROUTS (*Brassica oleracea*)
Appearance/Flavor: Upright/mild
Garden Color: Blue-green to medium green leaves
Life Cycle: Biennial/annual
Temperature Preference: Cool
Sun and Shade: Sun
Spacing: 18 to 24 inches apart
GROWING GUIDELINES: Brussels sprouts, which pro-duce small, tender miniheads at the axis of each leaf petiole, can survive winter temperatures down to about 20°F. This makes them ideal for planting in late spring and harvesting in fall. In warm climates, plant in summer or fall to harvest during winter or spring. Provide, as for broccoli and related plants, moist and fertile soil. Brussels sprouts take a long time to mature so prestart seedlings indoors, six weeks before planting time.

CARE TIPS: Fertilize after planting with a water-soluble, transplant solution and six weeks afterward with a balanced, granular fertilizer. Mulch with compost and water when the weather is dry. Pick the sprouts when they are plump and firm, before they open up to become loose and leafy.

PROBLEM PREVENTION: Aphids—small, pear-shaped, sucking insects—may attack brussels sprouts with a vengence, particularly plants that are weakened by less-than-ideal grow-ing conditions. Wash aphids off with a strong blast from a hose and/or spray with insecticidal soap to kill the aphids. Plant in a site where no brussels sprouts or related plants grew the year before to discourage pest and disease build-up.

 CABBAGE (*Brassica oleracea*)
Appearance/Flavor: Rounded/mild

Garden Color: Purple, red, or blue-green leaves
Life Cycle: Biennial/annual
Temperature Preference: Cool
Sun and Shade: Sun
Spacing: 18 inches apart for small cabbages, 24 inches apart for large cabbages

GROWING GUIDELINES: Cabbages—which whorl tender succulent leaves into a compact head—are among the easiest crops to grow. Choose from early cabbages which can be planted in spring (whenever the weather becomes mild) for summer harvest, or try late cabbages, planted in early summer for harvest in late fall and suitable for storing in a cold refrigerator or root cellar for several months. Cabbage can also be started in fall for a winter or early spring crop in warm climates. Plant in moist, fertile soil, prestarting seedlings indoors four to six weeks before the intended transplant time.

CARE TIPS: Fertilize every six to eight weeks with a complete, granular fertilizer, mulch with compost, and water to keep the soil moist. Harvest mature cabbage heads promptly in wet weather, otherwise they may swell and crack.

PROBLEM PREVENTION: Cabbage worms, as on broccoli, can be a pest. The green caterpillar blends in with the foliage but leaves telltale, dark droppings and hole-riddled foliage behind. They can be controlled by covering plants with floating row covers or spraying with Bt, a bacterial disease of caterpillars.

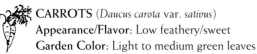

CARROTS (*Daucus carota* var. *sativus*)
Appearance/Flavor: Low feathery/sweet
Garden Color: Light to medium green leaves
Life Cycle: Biennial/annual
Temperature Preference: Cool
Sun and Shade: Sun
Spacing: 3 to 4 inches apart

GROWING GUIDELINES: Delicate, feathery leaves on carrots give little clue as to the plump, sweet roots hiding below the ground. When the shoulders swell, it's time to gently unearth one carrot and evaluate its size. A ripe and ready carrot is deep orange and filled out down to the tip. Long carrots need deep, loose soil—free of rocks and tight clay down to at least 12 inches deep. In less than ideal soils, grow shorter rooted, less temperamental cultivars. When temperatures become mild,

direct sow carrots outdoors in spring for summer harvest or in mid to late summer for fall harvest. In warm climates, carrots can be grown during winter as well. Even in cold climates, if heavily mulched, some carrot roots may last the winter providing a sweet harvest in earliest spring.

CARE TIPS: Carrot seeds are a trick to germinate. Seedlings cannot push up and out of soil that is at all heavy or crusted. Plant shallowly in rows or sweeps and cover with a light blend of sand mixed with compost. It also helps to top the planting area with a floating row cover which softens and breaks up raindrops that could compress the soil. The seeds are small and easy to plant too thickly. This is easily solved by mixing seeds with coarse sand before planting or buying pelleted seeds, coated with clay for easier handling.

PROBLEM PREVENTION: After carrot seeds germinate, leave the floating row covers on to prevent carrot flies from laying eggs near the carrots—the eggs hatch into maggots that can riddle the roots. Also some new cultivars are maggot resistant, eliminating the need for long-term row cover use. Rotate carrot planting sites to prevent pest buildup.

CAULIFLOWER/BROCCOFLOWER (*Brassica oleracea*)
Appearance/Flavor: Upright/mild
Garden Color: Blue-green leaves, white, green, or purple heads
Life Cycle: Biennial/annual
Temperature Preference: Cool
Sun and Shade: Sun
Spacing: 18 inches apart

GROWING GUIDELINES: Cauliflower and its green-headed brother, broccoflower, sprout tender heads of immature flower buds. Cauliflower also comes in purple-headed forms, which, like broccoflower, are easier to grow than the temperamental white heads. All forms prefer rich, fertile soil that is moist but well drained. Add extra compost before planting. Start cauliflower from seedlings, germinated indoors six weeks earlier. Cauliflower demands mild, cool temperatures, hovering around 55° to 60°F ideally. It is less tolerant of frost than broccoli, and it may be better to plant after the last spring frost rather than before it. If planted earlier, cover with a floating row cover for protection. After transplanting, water with a diluted complete fertilizer.

CARE TIPS: Side-dress with a balanced, granular fertilizer every six weeks after planting. Irrigate any time the weather becomes dry. Expanding heads of white-headed types need protection from the sun, accomplished with a process called blanching. If nearby leaves are long enough, you can tie them over the head when you see the first bud clusters. Otherwise you can cover the head with a paper grocery bag, tying the open end around the stem.

PROBLEM PREVENTION: Like other cabbage family members, cauliflower can be attacked by cabbage worms. Floating row covers and Bt help deter them.

CHERVIL (*Anthriscus cerefolium*)
Appearance/Flavor: Feathery/anise
Garden Color: White flowers, light green foliage
Life Cycle: Annual
Temperature Preference: Cool
Sun and Shade: Light shade
Spacing: 6 to 12 inches apart

GROWING GUIDELINES: Chervil, a favorite in French cuisine, has finely cut leaves with a delicate anise flavor. It is a quick-growing plant, ideal to sow directly in the garden in spring or late summer, or even fall or winter in warm climates. For fresh chervil most of the year, plant seeds every three weeks and grow chervil indoors in pots during the winter. Pluck off the foliage early on; it becomes scanty once the plant begins to flower. Provide moist, fertile, and well-drained soil. Fertilize with a water-soluble fertilizer when seedlings first emerge.

CARE TIPS: Irrigate during dry weather and mulch to help keep the soil moist and cool, especially if planting in full sun.

PROBLEM PREVENTION: Grow cultivars such as 'Brussels Winter' that are slower to bolt to flower.

CHICORY (*Cichorium intybus*)
Appearance/Flavor: Low leafy/mild-bitter
Garden Color: Medium to dark green or red
Life Cycle: Biennial/annual
Temperature Preference: Cool
Sun and Shade: Sun
Spacing: 2 inches apart for mesclun, 8 inches apart for rosettes

GROWING GUIDELINES: Chicory—a relative of the blue-flowered roadside chicory, endive, and escarole—is grown for its lettucelike leaves. The slightly bitter flavor blends well in mesclun mixes of assorted baby greens. Chicory is particularly easy to grow because it is a biennial and not likely to bolt to seed the first season of growth. The foliage is most succulent and mild in the cool weather of spring and fall, winter in warm climates. Direct sow chicory in spring, late summer, or even fall in warm climates. Provide moist, fertile soil.

CARE TIPS: Feed with a complete, water-soluble fertilizer every four weeks throughout the growing season.

PROBLEM PREVENTION: Avoid planting chicory too early in the spring. If plants are exposed to cold temperatures, they may bolt prematurely.

CHIVES (*Allium schoenoprasum*)
Appearance/Flavor: Upright/onion
Garden Color: Lavender flowers
Life Cycle: Perennial
Hardiness: Zones 4 to 8
Temperature Preference: Varied
Sun and Shade: Sun
Spacing: 18 inches apart

GROWING GUIDELINES: With round, upright leaves and globular tufts of purple flowers, chives can be an impressive sight. The onion flavor is great for cooking or in salads. A few, small leaves can grow into a thick clump if given moist, rich soil and a little compost for mulch. Plant seedlings, divisions from a friend's garden, or nursery plants in spring or fall.

CARE TIPS: To renew big old plants, dig them up and cut them into pieces with a sharp garden spade. Replant the healthiest section in fresh soil, well amended with compost.

PROBLEM PREVENTION: To prevent aggressive self sowing, remove lavender flowers (and drop them into salads or herbal vinegars) before they can set seed.

CILANTRO (*Coriandrum sativum*)
Appearance/Flavor: Feathery/pungent
Garden Color: White flowers
Life Cycle: Annual
Temperature Preference: Cool
Sun and Shade: Sun
Spacing: 4 inches apart

GROWING GUIDELINES: Cilantro is the foliage of the coriander plant, which is also grown for its orange spice–flavored seeds. Stems to 2 feet high are clad in finely cut leaves, which have a unique sweet, pungent flavor. The foliage begins to diminish when the plant starts to produce delicate sprays of flowers. Provide moist, fertile soil, enriched with extra compost before planting. Plant the seeds directly in the garden as soon as the weather becomes mild in spring.

CARE TIPS: Plant seeds every couple weeks throughout the summer, into fall in mild climates, for a continual supply of cilantro leaves.

PROBLEM PREVENTION: Because coriander goes to seed quickly, especially during the summer, grow slow-bolting cultivars.

CORN (*Zea mays*)
Appearance/Flavor: Tall upright/sweet
Garden Color: Medium green with yellow or purple highlights
Life Cycle: Annual
Temperature Preference: Warm
Sun and Shade: Sun
Spacing: 12 to 15 inches apart

GROWING GUIDELINES: Many kinds of corn await growing: yellow, white, or yellow and white bicolors; old-fashioned, starchy, cornmeal corn; quick-growing, mild, early corn; full-flavored late corn; classic sweet corn; extra-high-sugar, supersweet corn; and slow-to-become-starchy, extended-sugar corn. All of these types of corn need rich moist soil, amended with extra composted livestock manure before planting. Direct sow corn seeds when spring frosts pass and the soil becomes warm to the touch, about 70°F. One exception is supersweet corn, which needs very warm temperatures, in the 80s for good germination. Plant in blocks with at least 4 rows side by side to ensure good polination, the prerequisite for kernal development. Seeds can be planted as close as 7 inches apart, and thinned to a foot apart when still small. (Supersweet corn should be planted later than others to avoid contact with other corn pollen that will make the ears less sweet.)

CARE TIPS: Once corn seedlings are growing strongly, side-dress with a balanced, granular fertilizer and repeat every six to eight weeks. To make stalks sturdier and less likely to tip in windstorms, mound soil up around the base of the stalk. Roots will develop and grow into the mounds of earth.

PROBLEM PREVENTION: A number of different pests like corn ears just as much as you do. To prevent raccoon harvesting, surround the garden with an electrified wire fence—one zap from that and raccoons are unlikely to bother the corn. Treat young corn silks with powdered Btk (*Bacillus thuringiensis* var. *kurstaki*, a bacterial disease of caterpillars) to prevent caterpillars such as ear worms and corn borers from getting into the developing kernels. It also helps to put mineral oil on older silks. The corn ear worm is present in warm climates much of the year and moves to the north in midsummer.

CRESSES (*Lepidium sativum* or *Barbarea verna*)
Appearance/Flavor: Low leafy/peppery
Garden Color: Medium to dark green foliage
Life Cycle: Annual
Temperature Preference: Cool
Sun and Shade: Sun
Spacing: 2 inches

GROWING GUIDELINES: These are quick-growing, pepper-flavored plants that are ideal for blending into mesclun mixes of baby greens. Direct sow in fertile, moist soil, watering with a water-soluble, balanced fertilizer once seedlings emerge. Plant in spring for harvest several weeks later, replanting every two weeks for an extended harvest season. Cresses are also easy to grow in a flat or pot placed in a sunny window, patio, or under lights.

CARE TIPS: Water during dry weather so cresses can stay tender and mild.

PROBLEM PREVENTION: Prevent damage from foliage-eating pests such as flea beetles by covering cress with a floating row cover.

CUCUMBERS (*Cucumis sativus*)
Appearance/Flavor: Vining/mild
Garden Color: Yellow flowers, medium to dark green foliage
Life Cycle: Annual
Temperature Preference: Warm
Sun and Shade: Sun or light shade

Spacing: 10 inches apart on trellises; if untrellised, in hills spaced 2 to 3 feet apart for compact vines, 4 feet apart for standard vines

GROWING GUIDELINES: Cucumbers, with their thirst-quenching fruit sprouting from lanky or squat vines, grow best in rich soil with good fertility and high organic content. Add compost before planting. In cool climates, prewarming the soil with black or green plastic mulch allows for a faster start. Wait until the last spring frost passes and direct sow or transplant seedlings started indoors two to four weeks earlier. When transplanting, use care not to disrupt cucumber roots. Plant in rows beside a trellis or in hills—mounds of rich soil heaped up about 6 inches high and about 18 inches across. Plant five seeds per hill, thinning out all but the two or three strongest seedlings. Or transplant two seedlings per hill. For extended harvest, plant another wave of cucumber seeds or seedlings four weeks, or, in areas with long growing seasons, eight weeks later. Use a water-soluble fertilizer when transplanting.

CARE TIPS: Apply a sprinkling of balanced, granular fertilizer every six to eight weeks. Mulch around plants to keep the soil moist and discourage weeds. Once cucumbers begin fruiting, pick through the vines every day to find cucumbers when they are young, plump, and firm. If cucumbers are allowed to age on the vine, the plant will stop producing new fruit. Water if the weather becomes dry and after applying granular fertilizer to make sure the roots are not damaged by fertilizer salts.

PROBLEM PREVENTION: Cucumbers may be plagued by cucumber beetles. These black-and-gold striped beetles can consume entire seedlings. On older plants they tend to cluster on new growth and in flowers, consuming foliage and limiting fruit set. But what's worse is that they infect plants with bacterial wilt, which is deadly to cucumber vines. To prevent attacks on young plants, cover newly sown seeds or newly planted seedlings with floating row covers to keep away beetles. Unless the cultivar needs no fertilization, remove the row covers once the vines get to be a couple feet long and have several flowers each. At that time, eradicate cucumber beetles with pyrethrins or rotenone, if necessary. Because they are most active at night, this is a good time to spray.

 CURRANTS, BLACK (*Ribes nigrum*), **RED** or **WHITE** (*R. hybrid*)
Appearance/Flavor: Bushy/sweet
Garden Color: Yellow flowers, white or red fruit
Life Cycle: Perennial
Hardiness: Zones 3 to 7
Temperature Preference: Cool
Sun and Shade: Sun to light shade
Spacing: 5 to 7 feet apart for black, 4 to 6 feet apart for white or red

GROWING GUIDELINES: Currants, which grow into handsome bushes with three-lobed leaves and showy sprays of berries, can blend easily into the landscape. The flavor of the berries varies, and it's wise to sample some before choosing which bush to plant. Plant in moist, fertile, and well-drained soil, adding extra compost before planting.

CARE TIPS: Apply a high-potassium fertilizer in spring and keep the planting area mulched so it will be cool and moist. Water as needed to keep the soil moist during dry weather.

PROBLEM PREVENTION: In areas where white pine blister rust is a problem, cultivation of currants may be banned. Elsewhere, look for rust-resistant cultivars to avoid any complications.

 DILL (*Anethum graveolens*)
Appearance/Flavor: Upright/aromatic
Garden Color: Yellow flowers
Life Cycle: Annual
Temperature Preference: Warm
Sun and Shade: Sun
Spacing: 12 inches apart

GROWING GUIDELINES: Dill has it all. It harbors a wonderful flavor, one of the best to combine with summer squash, rice, and potatoes. With ferny leaves of dark green and open heads of yellow flowers on a slender, stately form, it adds distinction to a garden of lower growers and also merits use in flower arrangements. Sow dill directly from seeds, planting in well-drained soils of moderate fertility when the danger of frost has passed. For a continuing dill supply, plant new seeds every couple weeks until midsummer. Pick dill leaves while fresh and green; harvest dill seed when the heads start to turn brown. You can also use young flowers like dill weed.

CARE TIPS: If growth is slow, you can fertilize dill with a low nitrogen fertilizer.

PROBLEM PREVENTION: The caterpillars of black swallowtail butterflies may feast on dill. Consider it a donation made to encourage more butterflies around the yard.

 EGGPLANT (*Solanum melongena* var. *esculentum*)
Appearance/Flavor: Bushy/mild
Garden Color: Purple, pink, white, or orange fruit
Life Cycle: Perennial/annual
Temperature Preference: Warm
Sun and Shade: Sun
Spacing: 18 inches apart

GROWING GUIDELINES: Eggplants, a few varieties of which bear white globular fruits reminiscent of their namesake, come in purple, pink, lavender, and a variety of other colors. Plant eggplant seedlings, started indoors eight weeks before the last spring frost, once the soil and weather become warm. Eggplants—like their relatives tomatoes and peppers—do best in a moist but well-drained, fertile soil. Add extra compost before planting. When transplanting seedlings, water with a balanced, water-soluble fertilizer.

CARE TIPS: If growth is slow, sprinkle on a complete granular fertilizer three or four weeks after planting. Most cultivars set fruit poorly in temperatures under 70°F but can be kept warmer by covering them with a floating row cover to hold in the sun's heat. Harvest the eggplants when the fruit is firm and glossy-skinned, before the seeds mature and darken. Use a knife to cut the fruits free; the stems are tough and fibrous.

PROBLEM PREVENTION: Flea beetles are attracted to eggplants and can drill enough small holes in the foliage to consume the entire plant if not treated. When hardening off seedlings or situating container-grown plants, place them on a table over 3 feet high, where flea beetles have difficulty finding them. When putting eggplants in a garden, cover seedlings with floating row covers. Spray mature plants with sabadilla, pyrethrin, or rotenone. Avoid planting in sites where tomatoes, potatoes, or peppers were recently grown.

 ENDIVE/ESCAROLE (*Cichorium endivia*)
Appearance/Flavor: Low leafy/mild-bitter
Garden Color: Light to dark green

Life Cycle: Biennial/annual
Temperature Preference: Cool
Sun and Shade: Sun
Spacing: 4 inches apart for mesclun; 8 inches apart for small heads; up to 12 inches apart for large heads

GROWING GUIDELINES: These leafy vegetables resemble lettuce in all but their flavor, which is mild with undertones of chicory bitterness. Endive has succulent, narrow, curly leaves—very decorative. Escarole has thinner leaves nestled in broad heads. (Both are related to Belgian endive, a mild, tender baby head sprouted during winter from a thick chicory root grown the season before.) Sow seeds or transplant seedlings started indoors four to six weeks earlier beginning in spring. Seeds can be sown every three weeks throughout the spring, summer (if cool), and into fall or winter in warm climates. Provide rich, moist, and fertile soil.

CARE TIPS: To keep endive and escarole growing quickly, apply a water-soluble, balanced fertilizer upon transplanting and every three weeks afterwards. Some people prefer to blanch their endive and escarole to make it milder and creamier before harvesting. For a week or two before harvesting, tie long outer leaves over the head to wrap it in darkness, just like blanching cauliflower.

PROBLEM PREVENTION: The fastest growing endives, which can be ready to harvest in a month and a half, should be picked as soon as the heads are full and substantial—they can rot at the base if allowed to linger in the garden. If aphids attack, wash them off with a spray from the garden hose or kill them with insecticidal soap. Treat promptly to prevent them from multiplying. To prevent premature bolting, wait until spring weather becomes mild before planting.

 FENNEL, BRONZE (*Foeniculum vulgare*), **FLORENCE** (*F. vulgare* var. *azoricum*)
Appearance/Flavor: Ferny/anise
Garden Color: Yellow flowers, bronze or light to medium green foliage
Life Cycle: Perennial/annual
Hardiness: Zones 5 to 9
Temperature Preference: Varied
Sun and Shade: Sun
Spacing: 12 inches apart

GROWING GUIDELINES: Bronze fennel is a perennial with feathery, maroon leaves grown up to 2 or 3 feet high that look lovely in a flower or kitchen garden and have a pleasant anise flavor. Florence fennel, which is grown like an annual, has feathery green leaves about 2 feet high and a basal bulb of swollen stems which resembles celery but has a delicate anise flavor. Both may produce fragrant fennel seeds, useful in baking. Bronze fennel grows best in well-drained soil of average fertility but Florence fennel requires more substance—moist, fertile soil. Direct sow seeds in mid to late spring, when the weather becomes mild. Or transplant young bronze fennel plants from the nursery, taking care not to disturb the roots when planting.

CARE TIPS: Florence fennel will need irrigating whenever the weather becomes dry. If allowed to set seed, both kinds of fennel may self sow. If your garden has no place for self-sown seedlings, remove flower heads before seed become ripe. Swallowtail butterfly caterpillars will feed on fennel; allow them to stay undisturbed, and you will soon find beautiful butterflies frequenting your garden.

PROBLEM PREVENTION: Avoid planting Florence fennel in cold, early-spring weather and use care to not disturb the roots, which can cause premature flowering and reduced bulb size. Bolt-resistant cultivars of Florence fennel have fewer problems with premature flowering.

GARLIC (*Allium sativum*)
Appearance/Flavor: Upright/garlic
Garden Color: Medium green
Life Cycle: Perennial/annual
Hardiness: Zones 3 to 8
Temperature Preference: Cool
Sun and Shade: Sun
Spacing: 4 inches apart

GROWING GUIDELINES: Hailed as the herb for gourmet cooking and good health, garlic can hardly be ignored in any garden. This is particularly true because of the many types of hard-to-find garlic that can be grown at home. Long-storing and pungent, grocery-store silverskin or soft-neck garlic grows well in California, where many large garlic farms are located. Home gardeners can cultivate hard-neck garlics, such as rocambole, purple stripe, or porcelain, which have varying flavors and athletic flower stalks that twist as they rise. The flower stalks can be removed to encourge better bulb development or allowed to grow and harvested for flower arrangements.

Garlic, with its shallow, greedy roots, grows best in moist but well-drained, fertile soil. Add extra compost to the soil then plant cloves in late summer or early fall.

CARE TIPS: Newly planted garlic cloves begin rooting underground, where the activity remains unseen, and send up foliage promptly in spring. Keep the soil moist by irrigating and mulching between bulbs. Pull out any weeds that arise. Garlic foliage begins to yellow and fall over in summer—a dormant period perfect for harvesting bulbs. Store bulbs in mesh bags in a cool, airy location and save a few of the best bulbs to replant at the end of summer. Soft-neck garlic can be braided as the leaves begin to dry, making handsome strings of garlic heads which can be artistically intertwined with dried chili peppers or flowers.

PROBLEM PREVENTION: Garlic is unattractive to plant-eating pests, but it will rot if planted in soggy soil. If water doesn't drain freely, raise the garden and add extra sand and compost before trying garlic. Rotate the planting site with crops other than onions, which are related.

GERANIUMS, SCENTED (*Pelargonium* spp.)
Appearance/Flavor: Bushy/fruity, floral, or spice
Garden Color: Pink, purple, or white flowers; silver to medium or dark green leaves, some variegated
Life Cycle: Perennial/annual
Hardiness: Zones 9 to 10
Temperature Preference: Warm
Sun and Shade: Sun
Spacing: 18 inches apart

GROWING GUIDELINES: Scented geraniums, a pleasure to grow and handle, have rounded or deeply cut leaves exuding a variety of aromas. Some such as lemon and rose geraniums are suitable for teas, cakes, or layering in sugar to infuse a pleasant aroma. The flowers are petite and come in pink, purple, or white. Scented geraniums can reach 18 to 36 inches high, depending on the variety. Plant young scented geraniums (usually grown from stem cuttings instead of seed) in spring after the last frost passes. Provide well-drained soil of average fertility.

CARE TIPS: Pinch off the stem tips to harvest sprigs for indoor use and the plant will grow more bushy. In cool climates, potted plants can be brought indoors and kept in a sunny window or under lights until moving outdoors in the spring.

PROBLEM PREVENTION: When wintering indoors, scented geraniums can be susceptible to whiteflies—sucking insects that look like light-colored gnats. Control them by spraying with insecticidal soap.

GOOSEBERRIES (*Ribes uva-crispa* or *hirtellum*)
Appearance/Flavor: Tall bushy/sweet
Garden Color: Green or pink berries
Life Cycle: Perennial
Hardiness: Zones 3 to 7
Temperature Preference: Cool
Sun and Shade: Sun or light shade
Spacing: 5 feet apart

GROWING GUIDELINES: Gooseberries, with handsome lobed leaves, prickly thorns, and unusual, translucent berries, look like a decorative shrub but produce a bountiful harvest. Gooseberries get to be about 5 feet high and equally wide and have green or pink berries. Start with a healthy nursery plant, set out in early spring or fall in warm climates. Provide moist, fertile soil, with extra compost added before planting.

CARE TIPS: Fertilize each spring with a balanced, granular fertilizer topped with compost mulch. In late winter, before leaves emerge, remove a few of the oldest branches so new ones can take their place. Water as necessary to keep the soil moist during dry weather.

PROBLEM PREVENTION: Mildew disease can plague susceptible gooseberries but may be avoided by planting mildew resistant cultivars such as 'Pixwell' and 'Poorman'. Borers may tunnel into stems, leaving little piles of sawdust behind. Cut them out to prevent spreading.

HORSERADISH (*Armoracia rusticana*)
Appearance/Flavor: Upright/spicy
Garden Color: Medium green
Life Cycle: Perennial
Hardiness: Zones 3 to 8
Temperature Preference: Varied
Sun and Shade: Sun
Spacing: 6 to 18 inches apart

GROWING GUIDELINES: Horseradish—most pungent if eaten fresh—has lanky, zippy-flavored roots and long, coarse, flat-bladed leaves growing up to 3 feet tall. Start horseradish from root cuttings or divisions in early spring or fall, planting them in rich, moist, but well-drained soil. The roots grow best if the soil is loosened to at least 2 feet deep. Under these ideal conditions, the plant will grow and spread, even to the point of becoming weedy. It can survive, even prosper, in less than ideal soils—slightly dry or of modest fertility.

CARE TIPS: Water when necessary to keep the soil moist, especially for several months after planting. Fertilize if necessary to encourage new growth. Harvest in fall when the foliage dies back to the ground.

PROBLEM PREVENTION: Once established, horseradish can be an aggressive grower. To prevent excessive spreading, dig up the entire plant every year or two, using most of the roots and replanting just a few.

JERUSALEM ARTICHOKE (*Helianthus tuberosus*)
Appearance/Flavor: Tall upright/mild
Garden Color: Yellow flowers
Life Cycle: Perennial
Hardiness: Zones 2 to 9
Temperature Preference: Varied
Sun and Shade: Sun
Spacing: 18 inches apart

GROWING GUIDELINES: This uniquely named plant is American—not from Jerusalem—and is grown for its mild and crunchy, tuberous roots, not for its artichokelike buds. The Jerusalem artichoke is a perennial sunflower and, like horseradish, a notorious spreader likely to carve a large niche for itself in the garden. The plants can reach 8 to 12 feet tall, sometimes flowering and sometimes not. Below the ground their roots spread, producing 3- to 4-inch-wide bumpy tubers, which taste like water chestnuts. Plant the tubers in spring or fall in well-drained soil of average fertility, although the plants will grow in almost any soil. In fall after the stems die back, dig up all the tubers and replant a few for next year, although the plants usually come back anyway sprouting from tiny pieces of tuber left behind.

CARE TIPS: For the sake of orderliness, it's wise to pull weeds out of a Jerusalem artichoke bed, although the Jerusalem artichokes could crowd out many weeds. Mulch around the plants with compost to fertilize and maintain soil moisture.

PROBLEM PREVENTION: Jerusalem artichokes are best grown in a separate bed to avoid overpowering other plants.

KOHLRABI (*Brassica oleracea*)
Appearance/Flavor: Low/mild
Garden Color: Blue-green leaves, white or purple bulbs
Life Cycle: Biennial/annual
Temperature Preference: Cool
Sun and Shade: Sun
Spacing: 4 inches apart

GROWING GUIDELINES: Kohlrabi, with crispy, white-fleshed, swollen stems, can be ready to harvest about a month and a half after planting. An intriguing looking plant, their smooth, lobed leaves arise above swollen stems resembling little space-ships. Kohlrabi are available in greenish white or purple. Provide rich, moist, and well-drained soil, adding compost before planting. Plant seeds, or transplant seedlings started indoors four weeks earlier, in spring when temperatures become mild. Replant in summer for fall harvest. In mild climates plant in fall or winter.

CARE TIPS: Apply a balanced, water-soluble fertilizer when transplanting or once seedlings emerge. A balanced, granular fertilizer can be added three weeks later, if needed. Pick kohlrabi when the bulbs are small, tender, and crisp, about 2 to 3 inches in diameter.

PROBLEM PREVENTION: To prevent problems with root maggots, cover the plants with a floating row cover. Avoid planting where related plants—cabbage, broccoli, cauliflower, turnips, or rutabagas—have recently grown.

LAVENDER, ENGLISH (*Lavandula angustifolia*)
Appearance/Flavor: Bushy/perfumed
Garden Color: Lavender-blue flowers, silver leaves
Life Cycle: Perennial
Hardiness: Zones 5 to 9
Temperature Preference: Varied
Sun and Shade: Sun
Spacing: 12 inches apart

GROWING GUIDELINES: English lavender, which has silvery needlelike leaves and upright spikes of lavender-blue flowers, releases a wonderful aroma. Although usually used for perfumes or other fragrant products, a little bit of lavender can add a gourmet touch to baked goods. Lavender plants can grow 12 to 24 inches high, depending on the cultivar and also on the climate. In colder climates, it is likely to die back some during winter and require substantial pruning in spring. Like other silver-leaved herbs, lavender needs sharply drained soil, ideally sandy and loose. In other soils it can be planted in a raised bed, amended with plenty of coarse sand. Start with nursery-grown plants—propagated from cuttings or seed—and plant when the weather is mild, in spring or early fall.

CARE TIPS: Mulch lavender plants with an inch layer of coarse sand which helps to keep the bottom of the plant dry. Water if the weather becomes dry while the plant is getting established but once it is growing strongly, lavender can tolerate mild droughts without irrigation. In spring, once the new leaves begin to emerge (which can be later than most other plants), trim off dead branches. Harvest flowers while in bud; cut off any flower stems you missed after bloom is completed.

PROBLEM PREVENTION: To prevent excessive winter damage in cold climates, cover dormant plants with pine boughs once the soil is frozen. Remove the boughs as soon as the soil begins to thaw in spring.

LEEKS (*Allium ampeloprasum*)
Appearance/Flavor: Upright/mild onion
Garden Color: Blue-green leaves
Life Cycle: Biennial/annual
Temperature Preference: Cool
Sun and Shade: Sun
Spacing: 6 inches apart

GROWING GUIDELINES: The cool blue foliage of leeks begins at a plump layered base and stretches up 12 to 18 inches high. Because leeks are actually biennials, they can be grown like an annual during a single growing season with little concern about bolting to seed. Or they can be allowed to overwinter and harvested the following spring. They yield thick, white stems of succulent and mild onionlike flavor. Like other onions, plant leeks in rich, moist, but well-drained soil. Add extra compost before planting. Transplant leek seedlings, started indoors 10 to 12 weeks earlier, once spring weather turns mild. Set the seedlings in a trench about 4 inches deep.

CARE TIPS: Fertilize when transplanting seedlings with a water-soluble transplant fertilizer and follow up with a balanced, granular fertilizer six weeks later. Pull up any weeds that appear and water as needed to keep the soil moist. As the plants grow, hill up soil around the base; the absence of light helps the basal bulb become creamy-colored, succulent, and mild. When harvesting, plan to dig leeks because they may snap off if pulled up. Bring in early leeks, which are not highly cold tolerant, before winter arrives. Late leeks may be able to last outdoors if covered with a thick mulch of hay.

PROBLEM PREVENTION: Rotate the planting site, growing leeks where no other onions have grown recently.

LEMON BALM (*Melissa officinalis*)
Appearance/Flavor: Bushy/lemon
Garden Color: White flowers, medium green leaves
Life Cycle: Perennial
Hardiness: Zones 4 to 9
Temperature Preference: Varied
Sun and Shade: Sun or light shade
Spacing: 18 inches apart

GROWING GUIDELINES: Lemon balm, with cute, scalloped leaves on a plant that can grow 30 inches high, has an intense lemon flavor that makes it a pleasure to be around. Start with nursery plants, divisions, seeds, or seedlings, planting them in spring or fall in well-drained soil of average fertility.

CARE TIPS: Provide water-soluble fertilizer when transplanting seedlings. Mulch with compost each spring; lemon balm needs little extra fertilizer. After several years, plants can grow as large as a bush. Dig up and divide the plant or replace it altogether with a new seedling.

PROBLEM PREVENTION: Lemon balm can self seed prolifically, taking over an entire garden if allowed. Cut the plants back by 6 inches when they begin to flower to prevent seed formation; use the removed sprigs in iced tea or fruit salads. Foliage tarnished by powdery mildew can be cut off, allowing the plant to resprout fresh foliage.

LETTUCE (*Lactuca sativa*)
Appearance/Flavor: Low leafy/mild
Garden Color: Red, bronze, light, medium, or dark green foliage
Life Cycle: Annual
Temperature Preference: Cool
Sun and Shade: Sun or light shade
Spacing: 2 inches apart for mesclun, 8 inches apart for leaf lettuce, 12 inches apart for head lettuce

GROWING GUIDELINES: Lettuce comes in a surprising variety of forms and colors—from finely cut to broad leaved, frilly rosettes to plump heads. Leaves range between lemon green, emerald green, pink, and ruby. They often reach about 12 inches tall but stretch up higher when bolting into flower. The plants grow best in moist, fertile soil with good drainage. Plant seeds or seedlings, started indoors four weeks earlier, when the weather becomes mild in spring. Continue to plant new crops of lettuce every two to three weeks throughout the growing season, even into winter in mild climates. In summer, heat-tolerant lettuce plants can be grown in light shade, under a bean teepee or beside trellised cucumbers. Fertilize newly planted or newly emerging seedlings with a water-soluble fertilizer.

CARE TIPS: Apply a balanced, granular fertilizer three weeks after planting. Water lettuce as needed to keep the soil moist. Mulch around the plants, especially in summer, to help keep the soil cool and reduce weeds. In frosty weather, cover lettuce with a floating row cover to hold in the sun's heat. Harvest outer leaves as needed or cut the entire plant before it begins to send up a flowering stalk. (The plant develops an unpleasant, bitter milky sap just before it flowers.) Once plants elongate, remove and compost them, replanting new seeds or seedlings.

PROBLEM PREVENTION: To discourage slugs, keep mulch away from the base of the plants. Riddle the planting area with beer traps—beer-filled margarine tubs sunken with the rim at the soil surface. Slugs will crawl in the traps and they won't be able to get out.

LOVAGE (*Levisticum officinale*)
Appearance/Flavor: Upright/celery
Garden Color: Yellow flowers, light green foliage
Life Cycle: Perennial
Hardiness: Zones 4 to 8
Temperature Preference: Varied
Sun and Shade: Sun or light shade
Spacing: 18 to 24 inches apart

GROWING GUIDELINES: Lovage has compound, toothed leaves that resemble celery with an amplified flavor. Lovage can stretch up 6 feet high when displaying sprays of golden flowers. Start with nursery plants or seedlings, started indoors six weeks earlier. Set them out in spring, after the last frost, or in warm climates they can be set out in late summer or fall, when the weather begins to cool off. Provide well-drained soil that is moist and fertile. Plan the original planting site carefully. Once established, lovage may not transplant easily.

CARE TIPS: Water new transplants with a water-soluble fertilizer. Six weeks later and each following spring, side-dress with a balanced, granular fertilizer. Mulch with compost and water when the weather becomes dry. Unless you want to harvest lovage seed, which can be used like celery seed, remove entire flower stalks promptly after flowering to prevent them from becoming unsightly.

PROBLEM PREVENTION: If leaf miners carve tunnels in the foliage, cut off and destroy the infested leaves.

MEXICAN MINT MARIGOLD (*Tagetes lucida*)
Appearance/Flavor: Bushy/anise
Garden Color: Yellow flowers, dark green leaves
Life Cycle: Perennial/annual
Hardiness: Zones 9 and 10
Temperature Preference: Warm
Sun and Shade: Sun
Spacing: 12 inches apart

GROWING GUIDELINES: This marigold is a blessing in warm climates, where it will grow for years. It can also be cultivated as an annual during frost-free seasons in northern climates. Unlike most bedding marigolds, Mexican mint marigolds have narrow leaves, small, yellow flowers to about 18 inches high, and a delightful anise aroma. Plant seedlings, started indoors about six weeks earlier, when the weather is mild and frost free in well-drained soil of average fertility.

CARE TIPS: Water with a water-soluble, transplant fertilizer and add a granular fertilizer six weeks later if needed to encourage growth. Pinch off stem tips and use them for cooking; this also makes the plant grow bushier. Mexican mint marigold, when grown as a perennial, can be cut back more severely if needed for rejuvenation. Bring potted plants indoors to a sunny window or light garden to winter them over in cold climates. Or root a healthy stem sprig in water to transplant into a pot for winter.

PROBLEM PREVENTION: Finding a source of this plant can be challenging in northern climates, but it is available through mail-order herb suppliers.

MELON, MUSK and HONEYDEW (*Cucumis melo*)
WATERMELON (*Citrullus lanatus*)
Appearance/Flavor: Vining/sweet
Garden Color: Yellow flowers; light to medium green foliage (musk melons); blue-green foliage (watermelon)
Life Cycle: Annual
Temperature Preference: Warm
Sun and Shade: Sun
Spacing: Hills spaced 2 to 3 feet apart

GROWING GUIDELINES: Melon plants form graceful vines with tropical-looking leaves and subtle tan or green melons hiding below. The most decorative is 'Moon and Stars' watermelon with golden splashed foliage and golden moons and stars on the melon rind. Melons can be planted from seeds or seedlings, started indoors three to four weeks earlier. Seedless watermelons can be a little tricky to get to sprout. Keep them warm—about 80°F—and plant with the narrow, pointed end up so the seedling can easily slip out. The soil should be rich, moist, and fertile. Mound it up into 6-inch-high and 18-inch-wide hills, well amended with compost. Set melon seeds or seedlings out when the danger of spring frost has passed and the soil is thoroughly warm, ideally 75°F. Plant five seeds per hill, thinning out all but the two or three strongest plants or transplant two prestarted seedlings per hill. Covering the planting hill with black or green plastic mulch helps warm the soil and keep out weeds.

CARE TIPS: Apply a balanced, water-soluble fertilizer when transplanting seedlings or when new seedlings arise. Follow four weeks later with a balanced, granular fertilizer. If planting beside a trellis, work vines onto the trellis initially to be sure they will climb. Water as needed to keep the soil moist but cut back when the melons are ripening. This concentrates flavor. If grown on a trellis, support melons with a sling made out of an old nylon stocking.

PROBLEM PREVENTION: Cover newly planted melon seedlings with floating row covers to keep off cucumber beetles, which carry a wilt disease that causes melon vines to wilt and die. Watermelons, fortunately, are less prone to damage. Leave the floating row cover in place until several sets of flowers have formed and bees are required for pollination and fruit set. When you remove the row cover, watch the plant closely for cucumber beetles. If you see any, spray with pyrethrum or rotenone.

Powdery mildew—a disease that weakens plants—often attacks later in the summer when nights become cool. Starting melons early in the growing season gives them a better chance of avoiding it.

 MUSTARD (*Brassica* spp.)
Appearance/Flavor: Low leafy/spicy
Garden Color: Yellow flowers; bronze, dark to medium green foliage
Life Cycle: Annual
Temperature Preference: Cool
Sun and Shade: Sun
Spacing: 2 inches apart for mesclun, 10 inches apart for full-sized rosettes

GROWING GUIDELINES: Mustard plants, producing spicy seeds used to make mustard, has spicy foliage good for clipping young and adding to salads. Some mustards have beautiful burgundy or purple leaves, lovely both in the garden and in the salad bowl. Sow mustard seeds directly in a moist, rich soil as soon as the weather becomes mild in spring. Plant new mustard seeds every two or three weeks during cool, mild weather for fresh harvests.

CARE TIPS: Fertilize when the plants emerge and every three weeks thereafter with a water-soluble fertilizer. Water as needed to keep the soil moist, which encourages milder flavored plants. Harvest when plants are bite-sized, well before they bolt to seed and the leaves become excessively hot.

PROBLEM PREVENTION: Cover young mustard plants with floating row covers to prevent them from becoming riddled with flea beetle holes. Uproot flowering plants to prevent them from setting seed, which can sprout up everywhere like a weed.

 NASTURTIUM (*Tropaeolum majus, T. minus*)
Appearance/Flavor: Bushy or vining/peppery
Garden Color: Red, yellow, pink, orange flowers; medium green to white variegated foliage
Life Cycle: Annual
Temperature Preference: Warm
Sun and Shade: Sun
Spacing: 8 inches apart for bush forms, 18 inches apart for vining forms

GROWING GUIDELINES: Nasturtiums are versatile flowers—as delightful in a salad bowl as in a garden. The brightly colored flowers and round, shield-shaped leaves have a peppery flavor similar to watercress. The seeds, when pickled, resemble capers. Nasturtiums grow in bush forms 12 to 18 inches high or in vining forms that can creep or climb. Nasturtium seeds start quickly if direct sown outdoors once the danger of spring frost passes and the soil becomes warm. Plant in well-drained soil of average fertility.

CARE TIPS: Fertilize when seedlings arise with a water-soluble fertilizer. After the first flush of blooms fade, cut the old flowers off and fertilize again for a second round of flowering. Repeat as needed throughout the growing season.

PROBLEM PREVENTION: Aphids—pear-shaped sucking insects—love nasturtiums. Watch for them and knock them off with a spray from the garden hose or kill them with insecticidal soap. It's important to catch aphids before they swarm the entire plant, so be on the alert.

 ONION (*Allium cepa*)
Appearance/Flavor: Upright/onion
Garden Color: Medium green
Life Cycle: Biennial/annual
Temperature Preference: Varied
Sun and Shade: Sun
Spacing: 4 inches apart

GROWING GUIDELINES: Cylindrical onion leaves shaped like narrow tubes stand like soldiers in a row or wide bed, flopping over in summer to reveal the plump bulb shoulders emerging from the soil. Bulbs can be white, yellow, or red with round or flattened shapes. Onions are of two varieties. Long-day onions for northern areas are grown in spring and summer and produce bulbs once summer days exceed 15 to 16 hours long. Short-day onions grow during mild fall or early spring weather when the days are shorter. They need 11- to 12-hour-long days to form bulbs.

In spring as soon as the weather becomes mild, plant long-day onions from sets (small bulbs) or seedlings started indoors 10 to 12 weeks earlier. An early start, even under floating row covers to increase warmth, will be rewarded with larger bulb size. Plant southern onions when temperatures become cool and mild. Provide well-drained but moist, fertile soil, adding extra compost before planting.

CARE TIPS: Onions have shallow roots that are greedy for moisture and nutrients. Sprinkle a balanced granular fertilizer around young plants every four weeks while growth is active. Irrigate as needed to keep soil moist. Mulch and hand weed to prevent weeds from reducing bulb size. If bulbs are growing too closely, pull up the smaller onions and use them as baby onions or scallions.

PROBLEM PREVENTION: Rotate the planting site, planting where no onions, garlic, or leeks grew recently. Avoid wet soils which are certain to cause the bulbs to rot. Onion maggots, a kind of fly larvae, can tunnel into bulbs—not a pleasant sight. If these are a problem in your area, cover newly planted onions with a floating row cover to keep egg-laying female flies away.

OREGANO, GREEK (*Origanum vulgare* subsp. *hirtum*)
Appearance/Flavor: Bushy/aromatic
Garden Color: White flowers, medium green foliage
Life Cycle: Perennial
Hardiness: Zones 4 to 9
Temperature Preference: Varied
Sun and Shade: Sun
Spacing: 12 to 24 inches apart

GROWING GUIDELINES: Oregano, with its oval leaves on carefree stems that grow up, down, and sideways, comes in many varieties. Greek oregano is one of the best for flavor and is an intriguing looking plant sporting furry leaves on stems that reach up to 18 inches high. It grows best in well-drained soil of modest fertility. Plant a nursery-grown plant or a division in spring or late summer in cool climates, or fall in warm climates.

CARE TIPS: Apply a balanced, water-soluble fertilizer when planting seedlings or divisions. Keep the planting area moist until the transplant is growing strongly. Once well established, oregano can tolerate some drought. Adding a thin compost mulch to established plants may eliminate the need for additional fertilizing. Stop harvesting six weeks before the first fall frost to allow the plant to prepare for winter.

PROBLEM PREVENTION: Well-drained soil, parti-culary during winter, will prevent most problems with rot. Not every kind of oregano has great flavor—some are primarily decorative. Break a leaf and sample the aroma before buying a new plant. If there is no scent, keep looking.

PANSY (*Viola* x *wittrockiana*)
Appearance/Flavor: Low bushy/mild
Garden Color: Blue, red, yellow, purple, white, or orange flowers; dark green foliage
Life Cycle: Biennial/annual
Temperature Preference: Cool
Sun and Shade: Sun
Spacing: 8 inches apart

GROWING GUIDELINES: Pansies, with flat-faced, often bicolored flowers, are a handsome addition to a gourmet garden. They're great for garden-cheering edgings and interior patterns. What's even better is that the edible blooms can be used as a garnish or candied for pastries. Plant pansy seedlings in spring when the weather becomes mild or in the fall for early spring bloom. Seedlings can be started indoors six to eight weeks before planting time. Provide moist but well-drained soil of good fertility.

CARE TIPS: Water with a balanced, water-soluble fertilizer upon planting outdoors. When the first flush of bloom is over, cut off old flowers, apply a water-soluble fertilizer, and irrigate to keep the soil moist and encourage additional flowering.

PROBLEM PREVENTION: Well-drained soil will discourage rots. Plants that fizzle in midsummer may be stricken with spider mites, which can be treated with insecticidal soap; or the plants can be pulled up, sealed in garbage bags, thrown out, and replaced with something else. Heat-tolerant cultivars are less likely to struggle in summer.

PARSLEY (*Petroselinium crispum*)
Appearance/Flavor: Frilly/mild
Garden Color: Dark green
Life Cycle: Biennial/annual
Temperature Preference: Varied
Sun and Shade: Sun or light shade
Spacing: 10 inches apart

GROWING GUIDELINES: Parsley is available in frilly, curly leaf forms or broad, flat leaf, Italian forms—the latter cherished for its full flavor. Hamburg parsley forms a stout, aromatic root. Curly parsley gets to be about 12 inches high while Italian parsley grows to about 18 inches high. Parsley will flower, if allowed to grow a second year, sending up an umbrella-shaped flower cluster 2 feet high or taller. It dies after scattering its seed, which may then germinate into new plants. Parsley is best started from seedlings, sprouted indoors six weeks before the last spring frost. Plant them in rich, fertile, and moist, but well-drained soil.

CARE TIPS: Upon transplanting, water with a balanced, water-soluble fertilizer. Apply a balanced, granular fertilizer four weeks later. Mulch with compost to keep soil moist, but keep the compost a couple inches away from the base of the plant to discourage rot. If growth is sluggish after harvesting, apply additional water-soluble fertilizer. Foliage can be kept in good shape deep into winter by mulching around it with a thick bed of straw. New seedlings can be started in summer to move indoors into winter window gardens.

PROBLEM PREVENTION: If aphids attack indoors, wash them off in the sink or spray with insecticidal soap.

PARSNIP (*Pastinaca sativa*)
Appearance/Flavor: Upright/sweet
Garden Color: Medium green
Life Cycle: Biennial/annual
Temperature Preference: Cool
Sun and Shade: Sun
Spacing: 6 inches apart

GROWING GUIDELINES: Long, plump, white parsnip roots are a subterranean mirror image of their coarse, lanky leaves that can rise 2 feet high. Parsnips, like carrots, need a loose, sandy soil that is 12 to 18 inches deep. Direct sow the seeds in spring, when temperatures become mild. In warm climates, plant in the fall. The soil must stay moist the entire time the seeds are germinating—up to three weeks after planting—or they won't come up at all. It helps to run a soaker hose through the area and turn it on every day there is no rainfall.

CARE TIPS: Once seedlings are up, mulch around them to reduce weed problems. Fertilize with a granular fertilizer that is higher in potassium and phosphorus than in nitrogen. If heavily mulched with straw, parsnips may be able to survive winter outdoors in cold climates and be ready to harvest early in spring. Plan to dig deeply, rather than pull, to get the roots out whole.

PROBLEM PREVENTION: Canker-resistant cultivars escape unpleasant cankers that damage and discolor roots.

PEACHES, GENETIC DWARF (*Prunus persica*)
Appearance/Flavor: Tall upright/sweet
Garden Color: Pink flowers, yellow to orange or red fruit
Life Cycle: Perennial
Hardiness: Zones 5 to 9
Temperature Preference: Varied
Sun and Shade: Sun
Spacing: 30 inches apart for genetic dwarfs in containers or planters

GROWING GUIDELINES: Peach trees, with their long, glossy leaves and ruby-blushed fruit, now come in super dwarf sizes that can be grown in large pots. Potted peach trees will reach about 4 to 8 feet tall, bearing a small harvest of sweet, juicy peaches. Trees, shipped from the nursery in early spring, should be planted in a large container, at least 24 inches wide and 18 inches deep. Fill the container with a blend of 2 parts good garden soil, 1 part coarse sand, and 1 part peat moss.

CARE TIPS: Water as necessary to keep the soil moist—daily during hot, dry weather. Fertilize in spring with a half-strength, balanced, water-soluble fertilizer. Continue fertilizing every two to three weeks to midsummer, increasing the fertilizer concentration if necessary to encourage additional growth or prevent leaves from yellowing. If white salts begin to crust on the soil surface or pot, rinse the soil out by trickling a hose into it for 15 minutes and letting the water run freely out the bottom drainage holes. Thin out crowded growth as necessary to allow sunlight to reach every branch. In cold climates, bring the pot into an unheated garage in winter to protect it from severe winter cold. Every three years, uproot the tree, trim about 1 inch off the edge of the roots, and replant in fresh soil.

PROBLEM PREVENTION: Peaches need a regular spray program, beginning when the buds swell in spring. Ask your local Cooperative Extension Service for a spraying schedule useful for the pests and diseases prevalent in your area.

PEAS (*Pisum sativum*)
Appearance/Flavor: Vining/sweet
Garden Color: White flowers, blue green to green foliage
Life Cycle: Annual
Temperature Preference: Cool
Sun and Shade: Sun
Spacing: 2 inches apart on trellises

GROWING GUIDELINES: Pea plants, with pretty, waxy textured vines, white blossoms, and dangling pods, produce classic sweet peas (which require shelling) or edible pod peas (eaten pod and all). The shortest pea vines can be supported by branched twigs set beside the planting row. Full-sized vines need a 4- to 6-foot-high support—a trellis or fence—on which to climb. Sow pea seeds directly in the soil when the weather becomes mild in spring. The soil should be well-drained with average fertility. Treat pea seeds or the planting row with legume innoculant, a nitrogen-fixing bacteria which will allow the peas to produce their own fertilizer. A second or even third wave of pea crops can be planted in summer for late summer and fall harvest.

CARE TIPS: Water peas as needed to keep the soil moist. Harvest new pods promptly to encourage vines to continue producing. When vines are spent, cut them off and compost them. Allow nitrogen-rich roots to decay in the soil to nourish the next crop.

PROBLEM PREVENTION: Avoid touching pea vines when they are wet so you don't spread diseases. Use powdery mildew-resistant cultivars for a long, healthy harvest season. Spray away aphids with a garden hose or insecticidal soap. Pea enation, a virus common in the northwestern states, is avoided by planting resistant cultivars.

PEPPERS (*Capsicum annuum* var. *annuum*)
Appearance/Flavor: Upright bushy/mild or spicy
Garden Color: White flowers; red, yellow, purple, or orange fruit
Life Cycle: Perennial/annual
Hardiness: Zone 10
Temperature Preference: Warm
Sun and Shade: Sun
Spacing: 18 inches apart

GROWING GUIDELINES: Pepper plants, which can grow into little trees if potted and brought indoors for winter, have petite white flowers and produce a variety of peppers—large or small, hot or sweet, in green, red, yellow, or orange. Most grow to be 3 feet tall in a single season and even taller if kept alive for several years. Start pepper seedlings indoors eight to ten weeks before the last spring frost. For good germination, provide warm temperatures—80°F is ideal and can be provided in a cooler home by setting propagation pots on a soil-heating cable, available at

some full-service garden centers. Plant pepper seedlings outdoors after the last spring frosts pass and the garden soil becomes warm. Provide moist but well-drained and fertile soil.

CARE TIPS: Water newly planted seedlings with a balanced, water-soluble fertilizer. Apply a balanced, granular fertilizer six weeks later. Mulch around the plants to help keep the soil moist and reduce weeds. Water when the weather becomes dry. Pepper plants that threaten to tip over can be tied gently with strips of nylon hose to a bamboo stake set close to the main stem. To extend the harvest season, cover pepper plants with burlap at night to protect them from early frosts and allow them to ripen during the last warmth of autumn.

PROBLEM PREVENTION: Pepper performance can vary with the weather. Sweet peppers grow their best at about 75°F but often fail to fruit in temperatures much over 85°F. Hot peppers thrive up to about 85°F but may not fruit once the mercury tops 90°F. Smaller-fruited peppers are more adaptable to hot weather.

In the South, peppers can be troubled by leaf miners that etch off-colored tunnels through the leaves. This can be avoided by covering the young plants with floating row covers.

POTATOES (*Solanum tuberosum*)
Appearance/Flavor: Short vines/mild
Garden Color: White, pink, or lavender flowers; medium green foliage
Life Cycle: Annual
Temperature Preference: Warm
Sun and Shade: Sun
Spacing: 8 to 12 inches apart

GROWING GUIDELINES: Potatoes are the newest gourmet crop. Beneath compact vines develop tubers clad in red, blue, and tan skins with waxy golden or white flesh. Some are big bakers; others are tiny fingerlings the size of a man's thumb. Potatoes are not started from seed, like many other gourmet crops, but from seed potatoes. These are certified disease-free potatoes that can be planted whole or cut into pieces, with at least one eye or bud each. Another alternative is the new, tissue-culture-produced potato buds or minitubers. These are only about the size of a quarter but may grow more vigorously and have fewer disease problems than regular seed potatoes. Potatoes need well-drained, moist, and fertile soil, similar to tomatoes and peppers. But don't add any manure to the planting area—it could encourage diseases and excessive vine growth. Plant potato tubers from four weeks before to just after the last spring frost or plant them during summer for a fall harvest. Set tubers in double rows, placing the tuber in a trench about 8 inches deep. Cover each tuber with about 2 inches of soil.

CARE TIPS: As potato vines begin to grow, mound up the extra soil around the stems and cover with 6 inches of straw mulch. The new potato tubers grow from roots that develop above the seed potato within the hill of soil and mulch. Fertilize when the sprouts are several inches high with a low-nitrogen, granular fertilizer and keep the planting area moist, but not wet. Harvest tender, young, new potatoes when the vines begin to flower or wait until the vines die back to harvest mature potatoes. To store the potatoes in your basement for a few months, first let the skin cure for a week in warm temperatures, 85°F if possible. Always store tubers in darkness—in brown paper bags, dark corners of the cellar, or covered cardboard boxes—so they won't develop toxic green spots.

PROBLEM PREVENTION: Plant early and grow early-maturing cultivars to avoid Colorado potato beetles which can eat all the greenery off the leaves. Floating row covers also work well to keep out both potato beetles and flea beetles. You can also spray formulations of Bt blended for Colorado potato beetles on the young larvae of the beetle. Be sure the soil is well drained to avoid rots. Rotate the planting site every year to discourage other diseases. To prevent scab—ugly corky spots on potato tubers—grow scab-resistant cultivars or add enough sulfur to acidify the soil to below pH 6.

PUMPKINS (*Cucurbita pepo*)
Appearance/Flavor: Vining/sweet
Garden Color: Yellow flowers, yellow and orange fruit
Life Cycle: Annual
Temperature Preference: Warm
Sun and Shade: Sun
Spacing: Hills spaced 3 feet apart for compact cultivars, 6 feet apart for full-sized cultivars

GROWING GUIDELINES: Pumpkins, like Cinderella's carriage, magically swell an inch or two a day until they reach full size. Compact pumpkin plants for small gardens may only grow to 5 feet long and tend to produce small or medium-sized pumpkins. Full-sized plants may produce vines twice as long and could bear many small pumpkins or a few whoppers.

Provide pumpkins, like other squash, with fertile, highly organic soil, enriched with extra compost before planting. Rake soil up into hills—raised planting mounds about 6 inches high and 2 feet wide. Sow seeds directly in the hills or transplant seedlings started indoors three or four weeks earlier when the soil becomes warm and the danger of frost is past. Plant about five seeds per hill, removing all but the best one or two seedlings of full-sized cultivars and best two or three seedlings of compact cultivars. If there is not enough room for the vines to spread in all directions, plant fewer seeds or seedlings. To help warm the soil and eliminate weeds, planting areas can be covered with black or green plastic mulch.

CARE TIPS: Water seedlings with a balanced, water-soluble fertilizer to encourage a strong start. Fertilize every three weeks thereafter with a balanced, water-soluble fertilizer. Top the newly planted seedlings with floating row covers that will help prevent chills and keep pests off the susceptible young vines. Remove the row covers once several sets of flowers form. For the largest possible pumpkins, pinch off all but one or two pumpkins from each vine. To store pumpkins, pick them when the skin is so hard it can't be punctured with a fingernail and bring them indoors before temperatures drop below 40°F.

PROBLEM PREVENTION: Pumpkins, like cucumbers, are troubled by cucumber beetles, which can be kept off with floating row covers or killed with pyrethrin or rotenone. Pumpkin vines suddenly wilt if damaged by squash vine borers, which tunnel into the stem. Squeeze Btk (a bacterial disease of caterpillars) into the hole where the borer entered the vine or use a sharp knife to slice into the stem and skewer the borer.

RADICCHIO (*Cichorium intybus*)
Appearance/Flavor: Leafy/mild-bitter
Garden Color: Red to green leaves
Life Cycle: Biennial/annual
Temperature Preference: Cool
Sun and Shade: Sun
Spacing: 12 inches apart

GROWING GUIDELINES: Radicchio—a gourmet vegetable relatively new to America—has charming, petite heads that look a little like cabbage. They come in red or green with white veins and have an interesting mild-bitter flavor typical of chicory. The heads grow snuggled down in the center of a coarse, leafy plant. They emerge easily in newer varieties but in the older heirlooms may only sprout after the foliage is cut off. Plant seeds or seedlings, started indoors three or four weeks earlier, when the weather becomes mild in spring or in summer for a fall harvest. In southern climates, radicchio can also grow during winter. Provide well-drained but moist, fertile soil.

CARE TIPS: Apply a water-soluble, transplant fertilizer when planting seedlings or when new seedlings sprout. Add a balanced, granular fertilizer four weeks later. Once the crop has been growing for several months and is full and bushy, look down amid the leaves into the heart of the plant for the head. Once the head is full and measures about 3 inches across, cut it free. If the head is not there, wait another month and check again. If it still is not present, cut back the foliage and wait for the head to resprout.

PROBLEM PREVENTION: Look for early-maturing or heat-resistant cultivars in climates with a short, cool growing season. Some of the red-headed radicchios do not color until mature; be patient.

RADISHES (*Raphanus sativus*)
Appearance/Flavor: Low leafy/peppery
Garden Color: Medium green foliage
Life Cycle: Annual
Temperature Preference: Cool
Sun and Shade: Sun or light shade
Spacing: 2 inches apart

GROWING GUIDELINES: A mop of toothed radish leaves, growing about 4 inches high, gives little hint to the plump and colorful roots swelling below ground. But watch them closely so as to capture the roots when young, mild, crisp, and tender. The most popular radishes are shaped like little globes, but it's fun to try cylindrical French radishes. Large Oriental daikon radishes (said to resemble a woman's calf) can be grown like a rutabaga. Plant radish seeds directly in the soil beginning in early spring. For an extended supply of radishes, plant new crops every two weeks throughout the cool portions of spring, summer, and into fall—or even winter in mild climates. Provide well-drained soil of average fertility.

CARE TIPS: Fertilize only if growth is sluggish. If radishes bolt to flower, which often happens in summer, harvest the young seed pods. They're crunchy and a little spicy.

PROBLEM PREVENTION: To prevent cabbage maggots from riddling the roots, cover the planting area with a floating row cover to deter egg-laying females. Another alternative is to treat the soil with parasitic nematodes, subterranean hunters who prey on plant-eating pests and can be purchased through mail-order garden suppliers.

RASPBERRIES (*Rubus* spp.)
Appearance/Flavor: Bushy upright/sweet
Garden Color: White flowers; red, yellow, black, or purple fruit
Life Cycle: Perennial
Hardiness: Zones 3 to 8
Temperature Preference: Varied
Sun and Shade: Sun
Spacing: 2 feet apart for red and yellow raspberries, 3 feet apart for black and purple raspberries

GROWING GUIDELINES: Arching raspberry canes, grown in profusion beside a restraining trellis, look handsome in spring when full of white flowers and in summer or fall when burdened with plump, soft berries. Raspberry plants bear red, yellow, purple, or black fruit—each variety of plant has its own personality. Yellow and red are the hardiest, best in cool climates, while black is least hardy. Another choice to make is whether to grow summer-bearing raspberries that fruit in summer on second-year canes or everbearing raspberries, which fruit on second year canes in summer and again on new canes in the fall. Although everbearing may seem to be the better choice, they only work well if grown in an area with a long, warm fall that allows the final crop to ripen before frosts begin. Elsewhere, they can be pruned to harvest once, earlier in the growing season.

All of these raspberries need moist but well-drained, fertile soil situated in an area free of strong winds. Add extra compost before planting. Start with certified disease-free nursery plants, available unpotted as bare roots in early spring or in nursery pots later in the season. If planning to grow bare root plants, prepare the soil in fall so the plants can be put in the ground as soon as they arrive.

CARE TIPS: Apply a water-soluble, transplant fertilizer after planting. Established raspberries can be given a balanced, granular fertilizer in spring, as soon as growth begins. Water enough to keep the soil moist, but not wet, and mulch to slow evaporation and weed invasion. Raspberries grow best on a trellis which supports and separates the canes so they can all receive sun and fresh air. A simple wire fence, 5 feet high with three tiers of wires across it, will do. Use twist ties or strips of nylon stockings to secure the canes to the wires. Raspberries require some pruning to stay healthy and productive. Each spring, sort through the new canes and trim out small or weak ones, leaving three to six of the strongest canes per foot of row.

For a reliable and large crop from everbearing raspberries, cut off all the canes after they fruit. New canes that take their place will bear a bigger harvest earlier the following season.

On summer-bearing raspberries, remove all fruiting canes after they've been picked clean—they won't bear again. Leave the new canes to fruit next year.

Black and purple raspberries branch out, producing fruit on side branches of second-year canes. In summer, cut back new canes by about a foot to encourage more branching and more fruit for next year.

PROBLEM PREVENTION: Begin with certified, disease-free nursery plants, which will not introduce new diseases into the garden. Eliminate any wild blackberries or raspberries nearby, which could spread diseases. Prune as directed to encourage fresh air circulation and reduce problems with fungus diseases. Dig up, bag, and landfill any seriously sick plants to avoid disease spread. If these measures are not enough, a preventative spray program will be necessary. Ask your local Cooperative Extension Service agent for a program that will work against diseases common to your area.

ROSEMARY (*Rosmarinus officinalis*)
Appearance/Flavor: Bushy/aromatic
Garden Color: Blue flowers, dark green foliage
Life Cycle: Perennial/annual
Hardiness: Zones 8 to 10
Temperature Preference: Warm
Sun and Shade: Sun
Spacing: 2 to 3 feet apart

GROWING GUIDELINES: Rosemary—with needle-shaped leaves, bold flavor, and flashy blue flowers—serves as a wonderful evergreen shrub in warm climates and a good potted plant in cool climates. Rosemary comes in upright or creeping shapes, the latter suitable for a nice hanging basket or edging plant to cascade over a retaining wall. Rosemary needs a well-drained, sandy soil of moderate fertility. Where soils are less than light, raise the garden bed and add plenty of coarse sand to prepare a proper planting site. The alternative is to grow rosemary in a pot with 2 parts peat-based planting mix, 1 part coarse sand, and 1 part compost. Rosemary, which is usually started from cuttings, is available at many nurseries in spring.

CARE TIPS: Water newly planted rosemary to keep the soil moist until the plant begins growing actively. Once well established, it is drought tolerant and will only need watering during extended dry spells. Pinch off stem tips to harvest; or shear the entire plant to shape it—for example, for a knot garden—and bring in the clippings for cooking. If wintering a potted rosemary indoors, keep the plant in a bright window, let the soil dry out before watering again, and never let the soil become soggy. During cloudy weather, it may not be necessary to water at all.

PROBLEM PREVENTION: Good drainage (and avoiding overwatering potted plants) is essential to deter root rots.

ROSES (*Rosa* spp.)
Appearance/Flavor: Bushy/aromatic
Garden Color: White, pink, yellow, or purple flowers; red fruit
Life Cycle: Perennial
Hardiness: Zones 2 to 9
Temperature Preference: Varied
Sun and Shade: Sun
Spacing: 2 to 6 feet apart

GROWING GUIDELINES: Roses—low to large shrubs with glossy compound leaves—have showy white, red, pink, purple, and yellow flowers which are edible (if untreated with poisonous garden chemicals). Aromatic rose flowers and buds contain fragrant essential oils which can be added to herbal butters or light pastries with delectable results. Some roses also bear large, tart-flavored rose hips that are rich in vitamin C and ideal for teas. There are many kinds of roses. Among the most useful and aromatic are the old-fashioned shrub roses such as the French rose (*Rosa gallica*) and the damask rose (*R. damascena*), which bloom in early summer. Newer hybrid shrub roses tend to be easy care and fragrant with a longer blooming season. Roses vary in height from foot-high ground cover roses to 6- or 8-foot-tall shrub roses. Many pleasant intermediates are also available.

Plant roses, starting with top quality nursery stock, in rich and moist but well-drained soil. Add plenty of compost before planting and dig to loosen the soil deeply—24 inches deep if possible.

CARE TIPS: Apply a water-soluble, transplant solution after planting. Keep newly planted roses moist for the entire growing season, allowing them to get off to a strong start. Once well established, roses can tolerate occasional dry spells. Fertilize in spring and early summer with a balanced, granular fertilizer. Mulch with compost to improve the soil and discourage weeds. Pruning requirements vary according to rose type.

Cut back hybrid tea roses to about 6 inches high in early spring before growth resumes. Remove any dead, diseased, or spindly branches leaving as few as three of the sturdiest canes that are emerging and growing in different directions.

Shrub roses only need pruning to remove dead, damaged, or diseased branches.

PROBLEM PREVENTION: Avoid rot by planting in well-drained soil. Manage most insect pests with insecticidal soap. Grow disease-resistant cultivars to prevent black spot and other diseases.

 RUTABAGA (*Brassica napus*)
Appearance/Flavor: Leafy/sweet-mild
Garden Color: Medium green foliage, purple-topped root
Life Cycle: Biennial/annual
Temperature Preference: Cool
Sun and Shade: Sun
Spacing: 6 inches apart

GROWING GUIDELINES: Although the poor rutabaga bears the brunt of many jokes, it is a flavorful root with more potential than many realize. It is richer and sweeter than the turnip, growing to be plump and substantial. Rutabaga leaves, also larger than turnips, can reach 2 feet tall or taller. Direct sow rutabaga seeds in summer for fall harvest and winter cold storage (the roots will last for months). Provide moist but well-drained soil of average fertility.

CARE TIPS: Mulch newly sprouted seedlings with compost and add balanced, granular fertilizer if necessary to encourage new growth. Keep the planting site moist, especially during hot weather. Let roots sweeten by exposing them to several frosts before harvesting.

PROBLEM PREVENTION: Plant where no other cabbage family member—including cabbage, broccoli, cauliflower, kohlrabi, and turnip—has recently grown to avoid reoccurring prob-

lems. Keep off leaf-eating flea beetles and root-eating maggots by covering plants with a floating row cover.

 SAFFRON (*Crocus sativus*)
Appearance/Flavor: Low/aromatic
Garden Color: Lavender flowers
Life Cycle: Perennial
Hardiness: Zones 5 to 8
Temperature Preference: Varied
Sun and Shade: Sun
Spacing: 3 inches apart

GROWING CONDITIONS: Petite saffron crocuses, which resemble spring crocuses but emerge in the fall, have an aromatic tip in the center of the flower which is harvested for the saffron spice. The narrow leaves can grow to 12 inches long. Plant saffron crocuses in early fall in well-drained and fertile soil. They can be planted in and among low-growing, creeping herbs such as woolly thyme.

CARE TIPS: It is helpful to mark the location of saffron crocuses to avoid damaging them as they lie dormant in the soil.

PROBLEM PREVENTION: If chipmunks or rodents dig up crocus bulbs, enclose the bulbs in a fine wire mesh cage that they can't gnaw or scratch through. Don't confuse saffron crocus with autumn crocus (*Colchicum* spp.), which is unrelated and poisonous.

 SAGE (*Salvia officinale*)
Appearance/Flavor: Bushy/aromatic
Garden Color: Blue-purple flowers; silver, purple, yellow-green, or pink-marked foliage
Life Cycle: Perennial
Hardiness: Zones 3 to 8
Temperature Preference: Varied
Sun and Shade: Sun
Spacing: 18 inches apart

GROWING GUIDELINES: Garden sage, with silver, leathery leaves, is one of the classic herbs lauded by Simon and Garfunkle. It is lovely in the garden, with bright leaves growing on bushy plants to about 2 feet high. There are also purple, variegated gold and green, or tricolor pink, white, and green leaf forms. Garden sage needs well-drained soil of moderate fertility. In heavy soils, work in plenty of coarse sand and raise the bed before planting. Garden sage can be planted from seedlings, started indoors eight weeks earlier. Colored leaf forms can be purchased at garden centers or nurseries.

CARE TIPS: Keep newly planted sage moist until it begins growing actively. Once well established, it can withstand drought with only minimal watering. Pinch off tip sprigs for use in the kitchen. Cut back old, woody stems so fresh new stems can take their place. Stop harvesting heavily in late summer to let the plant prepare for winter.

PROBLEM PREVENTION: Providing good drainage is the key to preventing root rot.

 SAVORY, SUMMER and **WINTER** (*Satureja horensis* and *S. montana*)
Appearance/Flavor: Bushy/aromatic
Garden Color: Green
Life Cycle: Annual (summer savory)/perennial (winter savory)
Hardiness: Zones 5 to 9 (winter)
Temperature Preference: Warm (summer)/varied (winter)
Sun and Shade: Sun
Spacing: 12 to 18 inches apart

GROWING GUIDELINES: These savory sisters deserve wider use. They offer a unique flavor and almost needlelike foliage, with small pastel flowers in summer. Provide both with well-drained soil of moderate fertility. Start summer savory from seed 6 weeks before the last spring frost or look for seedlings in a well-stocked garden center. Winter savory, available in many herb nurseries, can also be started from divisions or cuttings. Fertilize with a mild fertilizer solution when transplanting outdoors. Additional fetilizer will only be needed if plants are reluctant to grow.

CARE TIPS: Harvest summer savory frequently, pinching off plant tips to prevent flowering and encourage bushiness. Shear winter savory in spring, trimming out old, brown branches, and divide every three years to rejuvenate.

PROBLEM PREVENTION: Where soils are too soggy, plants may suffer from rots.

 SHALLOTS (*Allium cepa*)
Appearance/Flavor: Upright/onion
Garden Color: Dark green
Life Cycle: Biennial/annual
Temperature Preference: Cool

Sun and Shade: Sun
Spacing: 6 inches apart

GROWING GUIDELINES: Shallots—an elegant French favorite of the onion family—have a delicious, mild flavor and a bulb divided into cloves, like garlic. The round, upright stems resemble onions. Separate and plant individual shallot cloves in fall where winters are mild or in spring in cold climates. Plant them in fertile, moist, and well-drained soil.

CARE TIPS: Shallots have shallow roots—greedy for moisture and nutrients. Sprinkle balanced, granular fertilizer around young plants every four to six weeks while growth is active. Irrigate as needed to keep soil moist. Mulch and hand weed to eliminate weed competition. When foliage yellows, dig up the shallots and replant the largest cloves for the next growing season. Store remaining shallots in mesh bags in a cool, dry, and airy location.

PROBLEM PREVENTION: Plant shallots where no onions or garlic recently grew. Cover with floating row covers to prevent problems with root maggots.

 SORREL, FRENCH (*Rumex scutatus*)
Appearance/Flavor: Leafy/lemony
Garden Color: Red-tinged seed pods, medium green foliage
Life Cycle: Perennial
Hardiness: Zones 4 to 9
Temperature Preference: Varied
Sun and Shade: Sun to light shade
Spacing: 12 inches apart

GROWING GUIDELINES: Sorrel has arrowhead shaped leaves, which are among the first greens to emerge in spring—a welcome sight. They are tender and juicy when young but get tougher as they mature. The leafy portion of the plant can reach 18 inches high. In summer, flowering stalks with clusters of distinctive, winged seeds stretch up to 4 feet high. Sorrel can be started from direct-sown seed, planted when temperatures become mild in spring, or from seedlings started indoors four weeks earlier and transplanted after the last spring frost. Provide moist but well-drained soil of average to rich fertility.

CARE TIPS: Sorrel grows vigorously in fertile soil and more slowly in average soil. For most households, a slow-growing plant, mulched with compost instead of fertilizer, will produce plenty of leaves. A commercial gardener, on the other hand, may want a quickly growing plant, and may apply extra fertilizer to stimulate additional growth.

PROBLEM PREVENTION: Sorrel, if allowed to go to seed, will spring up all over the garden. Remove flowering stalks to prevent this problem. Sorrel can also spread by root runners. If they spread too far in the garden, pull up any new sprouts and the underground runners they came from. This is easy to do in loose moist soil. One way to prevent aggressive spread is to grow sorrel as an annual, turning it under with a rototiller in the fall and replanting again in spring.

SPINACH (*Spinacia oleracea*)
Appearance/Flavor: Low leafy/mild
Garden Color: Dark green
Life Cycle: Annual
Temperature Preference: Cool
Sun and Shade: Sun or light shade
Spacing: 4 to 6 inches apart

GROWING GUIDELINES: Dark green, glossy leaved spinach—Popeye the Sailor's vitamin-rich, pick-me-up—comes with either intriguing crinkled leaves or straightforward, flat leaves, which are easier to wash before cooking. Spinach foliage is low growing, staying under about 1 foot high. It is easy to grow in moist, well-drained, and fertile soil during cool weather. In spring, when temperatures become mild, sow seeds directly in the garden. For an extended harvest, plant additional seeds every two weeks throughout the spring and also in late summer or fall, even winter in warm climates.

CARE TIPS: Fertilize newly emerged spinach seedlings with a water-soluble fertilizer. Follow two weeks later with another application if growth is slow. Protect plants from hard frost by covering them with a floating row cover. Irrigate as needed to keep the soil moist. Harvest promptly before the plant bolts to seed and the foliage diminishes.

PROBLEM PREVENTION: Plant disease-resistant cultivars and thin overcrowded plantings to avoid common foliage fungus diseases.

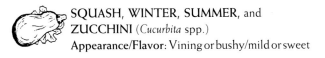

SQUASH, WINTER, SUMMER, and ZUCCHINI (*Cucurbita* spp.)
Appearance/Flavor: Vining or bushy/mild or sweet

Garden Color: Yellow flowers, medium to dark green foliage
Life Cycle: Annual
Temperature Preference: Warm
Sun and Shade: Sun
Spacing: Hills 2 feet apart for bush forms to 8 feet apart for full-sized vines

GROWING GUIDELINES: A variety of delicious crops are in the squash family, including pumpkins which are listed separately. They include mild-flavored summer squash and zucchini—quick growers and abundant producers. These squash often grow on bushy plants with huge, upright, tropical leaves. Winter squash—sweet and hard-skinned—grow on vines. They are covered in a carpet of foliage in summer, the leaves fading away in fall to reveal the plump squash below. Small-fruited vining squash can be grown on space-saving trellises. Squash planting time arrives after the last spring frost passes and the soil is warm. Form planting hills—mounds of soil 6 inches high and 18 to 24 inches wide—amended with a bucketful of compost. Direct sow seeds planting five seeds per hill and thinning to the best one or two seedlings for large-fruited squash, or two or three seedlings for medium-sized or small squash. Or transplant seedlings, started indoors three weeks earlier. If transplanting seedlings, use care not to damage or disturb the roots. Another crop of summer squash can be planted several weeks later for harvests in late summer and fall.

CARE TIPS: Water newly planted or newly emerging seedlings with a water-soluble fertilizer. Three weeks later, add a balanced, granular fertilizer to bush summer squash, and another dose of water-soluble fertilizer to vining types as the plants begin to stretch across the garden. Mulch with 4 to 6 inches of straw and water as needed to keep the soil moist. Or try mulching before planting with black or green plastic mulch, which thoroughly suppresses weeds. Pick summer squash when they are small, tender, and firm, checking the plants daily during the summer. Prompt harvesting encourages more fruit set and a longer harvest season. Let winter squash mature fully, until the shell can't be punctured by a fingernail. Bring them indoors to store in a cool place before temperatures drop below 40°F.

PROBLEM PREVENTION: Cover newly planted seeds or seedlings with floating row covers to prevent damage from cucumber beetles. Once several sets of flowers open, remove the cover and spray cucumber beetles with pyrethrin or rotenone. Cucumber beetles carry a bacterial wilt disease damaging to squash. Fortunately, spaghetti squash is less likely to be troubled by bacterial wilt than some other winter squash. To discourage vine borers—larvae that tunnel into squash stems and cause them to wilt—wrap panty hose around the bottom of the stem, close to the soil. Look for mildew-resistant squash cultivars that stay healthy late into the summer and fall.

STRAWBERRIES (*Fragaria* spp.)
Appearance/Flavor: Low leafy/sweet
Garden Color: White flowers, red fruit
Life Cycle: Perennial
Hardiness: Zones 3 to 10
Temperature Preference: Varied
Sun and Shade: Sun
Spacing: 12 inches apart

GROWING GUIDELINES: Petite strawberries have pretty three-parted leaves that turn crimson in fall and sparkling, white flowers in spring and summer. There are several types: alpine strawberries form small mounds and have little but highly flavored berries, while traditional strawberries are bigger and juicier. Of the traditional strawberries, classic June-bearing strawberries flower in mid-spring and produce a bumper crop of berries in June. Everbearers also fruit in June and produce another crop in fall. New day-neutral types flower and fruit off and on throughout the growing season.

Plant traditional strawberry plants as early as possible in spring, providing fertile, well-drained soil. Start with certified disease-free plants from a reliable nursery. Because these are often in bare root form and need to be planted immediately, it helps to prepare the strawberry bed as much as a season in advance. Alpine strawberry seedlings, started indoors eight weeks earlier, can be set out after the last spring frost.

CARE TIPS: Fertilize with a balanced, granular fertilizer in spring when the weather becomes mild. For four to six weeks after planting, pinch off any flowers that bloom. This eliminates the annual yield of June bearers, but will guarantee stronger plants in years to come. Everbearing strawberries can be allowed to fruit in fall. Day-neutral types will begin bearing fruit in midsummer. After several years, a strawberry patch may

decline in productivity; day-neutral plants may fade even earlier. This is a good time to rotate, eliminating those plants and replanting new plants in another site.

PROBLEM PREVENTION: To prevent damage to the early strawberry flowers, cover with floating row covers any time frost threatens in spring. In fall, mow off old leaves and rake them up to reduce the incidence of foliage diseases. Start with certified disease-free nursery plants and use disease-resistant cultivars to prevent an assortment of diseases. Remove and destroy any rotten berries to prevent disease spread.

SUNFLOWERS (*Helianthus annuus*)
Appearance/Flavor: Upright/nutty
Garden Color: Yellow, orange, bronze, or red flowers
Life Cycle: Annual
Temperature Preference: Warm
Sun and Shade: Sun
Spacing: 1 to 2 feet apart

GROWING GUIDELINES: Lofty sunflowers, bearing huge, black-centered, golden heads of crunchy seeds, can form a sizable perimeter boundary for the garden. The plants have broad, heart-shaped leaves and can grow to be 6 feet tall. (Cutting sunflowers—*Helianthus* x *multiflorus*—have many smaller flowers on branched plants and may not produce nutritious seeds.) Plant the seeds directly out in the garden when the last spring frost passes and the soil is warm. This is also the time to transplant seedlings started indoors two or three weeks earlier, using care not to disturb the roots. More seeds can be started every two to three weeks until early summer for an extended bloom season. Provide well-drained soil of average fertility.

CARE TIPS: Water young plants until well established. Fertilize with a balanced, granular fertilizer if growth is sluggish. If stems begin to tip, tie them to a sturdy stake set close to the main stem so it is not readily visible.

PROBLEM PREVENTION: Birds are likely to eat all the sunflower seeds if given half a chance. Bag developing heads with a paper grocery bag to keep birds off.

SWEET MARJORAM (*Origanum marjorana*)
Appearance/Flavor: Low bushy/aromatic
Garden Color: White flowers, silver-green foliage

Life Cycle: Perennial/annual
Hardiness: Zones 9 to 10
Temperature Preference: Warm
Sun and Shade: Sun
Spacing: 8 inches apart

GROWING GUIDELINES: Sweet marjoram, with small, rounded gray-green leaves and silver flower bud-balls, is an interesting looking plant made even more delightful by its wonderful, sweet-spice aroma and flavor. The plant, which is perennial in warm climates, can be potted up and brought indoors for winter in cold climates. Sweet marjoram reaches about 12 inches high and can be planted in spring after frosts pass. Plant nursery plants or seedlings started indoors six weeks earlier in well-drained soil of moderate fertility.

CARE TIPS: Water newly planted seedlings with a dilute solution of water-soluble fertilizer. Once the plant is growing vigorously (especially when topped with clusters of flower buds), clip off new growth to use in the kitchen. More water-soluble fertilizer can be applied after harvest to encourage the plant to resprout and be harvested again. Established plants will only need extra irrigation during drought.

PROBLEM PREVENTION: To escape problems with rot, plant only in well-drained soil.

SWISS CHARD (*Beta vulgaris*)
Appearance/Flavor: Upright/sweet
Garden Color: Red or dark to medium green leaves
Life Cycle: Biennial/annual
Temperature Preference: Varied
Sun and Shade: Sun
Spacing: 10 inches apart

GROWING GUIDELINES: Swiss chard—with its lovely, broad and tropical-looking leaves—comes in white-or red-stemmed forms, both of which provide sweet mild greens. The leaves can get to be 18 to 24 inches high. Because it is biennial, Swiss chard will grow all summer without bolting, although the most tender leaves are harvested young in the spring or fall. Direct sow the seeds in spring, when temperatures become mild. In warm climates, sow Swiss chard seeds in fall for late winter harvesting. Provide rich, moist but well-drained, and fertile soil.

CARE TIPS: When seedlings first emerge, water with a water-soluble, balanced fertilizer. Repeat every four to six weeks, or as needed to encourage rapid regrowth after harvesting.

PROBLEM PREVENTION: Cover plants during hard frosts to prevent damage.

TARRAGON, FRENCH (*Artemisia dracunculus* var. *sativa*)
Appearance/Flavor: Bushy/anise
Garden Color: Medium green
Life Cycle: Perennial
Hardiness: Zones 5 to 8
Temperature Preference: Varied
Sun and Shade: Sun
Spacing: 18 inches apart

GROWING GUIDELINES: Tarragon, a bushy plant with narrow leaves, has a strange habit of not setting seed—even if it does flower. Avoid its less talented brother, Russian tarragon, which is weak flavored and does produce seed. French tarragon is usually grown from divisions—which need periodic division to keep the twisting roots untangled. Plant French tarragon, which can get to be 3 feet high, in well-drained soil of average fertility. In heavy soil, add plenty of coarse sand before planting.

CARE TIPS: Keep new plantings moist until they begin growing strongly. Once well established, tarragon only needs watering during dry weather. Mulch with compost in spring to fertilize. Every three or four years, in the spring, renew the plant by digging up and dividing rooted sections, replanting the youngest and most vigorous sections.

PROBLEM PREVENTION: None common.

THYME (*Thymus* spp.)
Appearance/Flavor: Low creeping/aromatic
Garden Color: Pink, lavender, or white flowers; medium to dark green, silver or gold variegated, or silver leaves
Life Cycle: Perennial
Hardiness: Zones 4 to 9
Temperature Preference: Varied
Sun and Shade: Sun
Spacing: 12 to 18 inches apart

GROWING GUIDELINES: Dozens of varieties of thyme are available including narrow-leaf French, broad-leaf English, woolly, and lemon. All are low growing, sprouting small, aromatic leaves from wiry woody stems. Some are enhanced with silver or golden markings, even white, woolly foliage of uncommon interest. While a few types can be grown from seed, most cultivars come from divisions or stem cuttings. Plant any type of thyme in well-drained soil of moderate fertility. In heavy soils, add abundant coarse sand before planting. Plant nursery plants in the spring in cold climates and in the fall in warm climates.

CARE TIPS: Water new plants to keep the soil moist until growth accelerates. Mulch around the plants with coarse sand to keep the base of the plant dry and disease free. In spring, a little compost can be mixed in to fertilize the plant. This is also the time to cut back woody stems by one-third of their total length to encourage new growth. In three or four years, if the plant becomes too woody and barren, dig it up and divide off rooted sections. Rework the soil and plant the healthiest divisions.

PROBLEM PREVENTION: Good soil drainage is essential for eliminating rots. Reduce the potential for foliage diseases by thinning out thick clumps of stems, removing every third stem at the base so air can circulate freely.

 TOMATILLOS (*Physalis ixocarpa*)
Appearance/Flavor: Bushy/mild
Garden Color: Yellow flowers; purple-green leaves; yellow to brown fruit
Life Cycle: Annual
Temperature Preference: Warm
Sun and Shade: Sun
Spacing: 24 inches apart

GROWING GUIDELINES: The tomatillo—a relative of the tomato—bears green-gold fruit (like little apples) clad in papery Chinese lanternlike–husks. They grow on bushy plants that can get to be 2 or 3 feet high. Plant seedlings, started indoors six weeks earlier, outdoors once the danger of spring frost passes and the soil is warm. Similar to growing tomatoes, an ideal soil should be moist but well-drained and fertile.

CARE TIPS: After planting, apply a water-soluble, transplant fertilizer and water as needed to keep the soil moist. Fertilize with a balanced, granular fertilizer four weeks after planting. Mulching will help keep the soil damp and reduce weeds. Harvest the tomatillos when the husk becomes loose and papery and the fruit changes from green to a mellow yellow.

PROBLEM PREVENTION: Plant tomatillos in a place where no related plants—including tomatoes, peppers, eggplants, and potatoes—have grown recently.

 TOMATOES (*Lycopersicum esculentum*)
Appearance/Flavor: Bushy/sweet
Garden Color: Yellow flowers; red, orange, pink, or yellow fruit
Life Cycle: Annual
Temperature Preference: Warm
Sun and Shade: Sun
Spacing: 2 feet apart for compact types, 3 feet apart for full-sized types

GROWING GUIDELINES: Delicious, homegrown tomatoes—unrivaled in their taste—grow on undisciplined vines that can sprawl on the ground. For extra productivity, they can be pruned to a single stem and tied to a stake, or corseted together in an upright cage. There are determinate tomatoes, such as paste tomatoes, which stay compact, stop growing, and produce their tomatoes all at once—very businesslike. And there are the more leisurely indeterminate tomatoes—cherry tomatoes, for example—that keep growing all season, producing more new tomatoes all the time. Provide tomatoes with warm, fertile, moist, and well-drained soil. Plant seedlings outdoors after the last spring frost passes, starting seedlings indoors under lights eight weeks earlier. Bury the bottom portion of the tomato plant stem; it roots easily and will provide a stronger base for the plant. Water with a water-soluble fertilizer when transplanting.

CARE TIPS: Surround seedlings with supports—wire cages, decorative trellises or hoops, or four stakes forming a box that can be closed up with twine. Water as needed to keep the soil evenly moist and mulch to prevent the soil from drying out. In early summer, when flowering commences, add a granular fertilizer with a low nitrogen content and higher potassium and phosphorus levels. Harvest the tomatoes when they turn completely red. Pick them when they're still firm for slicing or let them get softer for cooking.

PROBLEM PREVENTION: Grow tomatoes in well-drained soil and rotate each year to a site that hasn't been used recently for growing related crops such as peppers, potatoes, eggplants, and tomatillos. Clean up old tomato debris and if unhealthy, bag and landfill it to eliminate disease spread. Select disease-resistant plants to avoid wilt, nematodes, and other problems. To prevent tomatoes from developing a brown blotch on the blossom end, maintain even soil moisture.

APPENDIX B: PLANT, SEED, AND SUPPLY SOURCES

W. Atlee Burpee Co., Warminster, PA 18974

The Cook's Garden, P.O. Box 535, Londonderry, VT 05148

Filaree Farm (garlic), Route 2, Box 162, Okanogan, WA 98840

Garden City Seeds, 778 Highway 93 North, Hamilton, MT 59840

Gardener's Supply Company (supplies and irrigation), 128 Intervale Road, Burlington, VT 05401

Goodwin Creek Gardens, P.O. Box 83, Williams, OR 97544

Harmony Farm Supply, P.O. Box 460, Graton, CA 95444

Johnny's Selected Seeds, Foss Hiss Road, Albion, ME 04910

Native Seeds/SEARCH, 2509 North Campbell Avenue, #325, Tucson, AZ 85719; (520) 327-9123

Nichols Garden Nursery, 1190 North Pacific Highway, Albany, OR 97321

Park Seed Co., Cokesbury Road, Greenwood, SC 29647

Peaceful Valley Farm Supply, P.O. Box 2209, Grass Valley, CA 95425

Pinetree Garden Seeds, P.O. Box 300, New Gloucester, ME 04260

Ronniger's Seed Potatoes, Star Route, Moyie Springs, ID 83845

Seeds of Change, P.O. Box 15700, Santa Fe, NM 87506

Shepherd's Garden Seeds, 30 Irene Street, Torrington, CN 06790

Southern Exposure Seed Exchange, P.O. Box 170, Earlysville, VA 22936

Territorial Seed Co., P.O. Box 157, Cottage Grove, OR 97424

Thompson and Morgan, Inc., P.O. Box 1308, Jackson, NJ 08527; (A good source of British seeds; order early for best availability.)

The Thyme Garden, 20546 Alsea Highway, Alsea, OR 97324

APPENDIX C: RECOMMENDED READING

Bradley, Fern, and Barbara Ellis, eds. *The Organic Gardener's Handbook of Natural Insect and Disease Control.* Emmaus, PA: Rodale Press, 1992.

Cooking with Herb Scents. Cleveland, OH: The Western Reserve Herb Society, 1991.

Daar, Sheila, William Olkawski and Helga Olkowski. *Common-Sense Pest Control.* Newtown, CN: Tauton Press, 1991.

DeBaggio, Thomas. *Growing Herbs from Seed, Cutting, and Root.* Loveland, CO: Interweave Press, 1994.

Gershuny, Grace, and Deborah Martin. *The Rodale Book of Composting.* Emmaus, PA: Rodale Press, 1992.

The Herb Companion Cooks. Loveland, CO: Interweave Press, 1994.

Lang, Jennifer, ed. *Larousse Gastronomique.* New York: Crown Publishers, 1988.

McClure, Susan. *The Harvest Gardener.* Pownal, VT: Garden Way Publishing, 1993.

———. *The Herb Gardener: A Guide for All Seasons.* Pownal, VT: Garden Way Publishing, 1996.

McClure, Susan, and Lee Reich. *Rodale's Successful Organic Gardening: Fruits and Berries.* Emmaus, PA: Rodale Press, 1996.

McClure, Susan, and Sally Roth. *Rodale's Successful Organic Gardening: Companion Planting.* Emmaus, PA: Rodale Press, 1994.

Raboff, Fran, and Renee Shepherd. *More Recipes from a Kitchen Garden.* Berkeley, CA: Ten Speed Press, 1995.

APPENDIX D: INSPIRATIONAL GARDENS

Burpee Trial Garden, Ambler, PA
Chadwick Arboretum, Columbus, OH
Chicago Botanic Garden, Glencoe, IL
Fetzer Food and Wine Center, Valley Oaks, CA
Iron Horse Ranch and Vineyard, Sebastopol, CA
The Kitchen Garden, Valparaiso, IN
L'Auberge Provençale, White Post, VA
Longwood Garden, Philadelphia, PA

Montague Inn, Saginaw, MI
Monticello, Charlottesville, VA
Mount Vernon, Mt. Vernon, VA
National Arboretum, Washington, D.C.
Rodale Institute Research Center, Kutztown, PA
Sea World of Ohio, Aurora, OH
United States Botanical Garden, Washington, D.C.

Index

Note: Page numbers in boldface denote photos

INDEX

INDEX

bean, 57; baby beet, 56; dilled potato, 86; leek, sautéed, 133; lemon cucumber, 86; mesclun, 57; potato and lima bean, 33; regal rainbow, 47; Swiss chard, 72; tarragon chicken, 136

Salt-Free Herb Mix, 98

Sandy soils, 4, 7; compost and, 6

Sapling fences, 26, **26**

Sauces: apple, 88; creamy dill, 49; fennel seed, 123; horseradish, 147; laced with lavender punch, 108; strawberry, 73; strawberry butter, 59; tomato, 125

Sausage-Stuffed Poblanos, 155

Sautéed Rolly Polly Squash with Marjoram, 47

Sautéed Cabbage, 144

Sautéed Leek Salad, 133

Savory, summer (*Satureja borensis*), 44; winter, (*S. montana*), **95**; growing, 182

Savory Pot Roast, 146

Scampi Primavera, 122

Scarlet runner beans, 79, **79**

Scented geraniums (*Pelargonium* spp.), Apricot, 104; Dr. Livingstone, 104; growing, 172; Lemon, 104; Rober's Lemon Rose, 104; Snowflake, **104**

Seed, saving, 78

Seeding, direct, 8

Seedlings, starting, 8, 9–10

Shallots (*Allum cepa*): French, 132; growing, 182

Shortbread: lavender, 110; rosemary, 99

Silt blends, 4

Sites, choosing, 2

Sitting areas, 20

Size, determining, 16

Small Garden of Baby Vegetables, xi, 23, 50–56; designing, 50, 52; locating, 18; sketch of, 51

Smothered Baby Eggplant, 58

Snap beans (*Phaseolus vulgaris*), 27–29; Blue Lake 274, 28; freezing, 28; growing, 161–62; Kentucky Blue, 28–29; Kentucky Wonder, 28; Provider, **27**, 28

Snappy Peas with Noodles, 48

Soil, 2; judging, 4–5

Soilless mix, 66

Sorrel, **3**, 55

Sorrel, French (*Rumex scutatus*), 132; soup, 135; growing, 182–83

Soups: dilled cheese with potato, 33; French onion, 134; French Sorrel, 135; Gazpacho, 153; pumpkin, 86

Sowing, direct, 8

Spacing, guidelines for, 8

Spaghetti squash, 116; Hasta La Pasta Hybrid, 120–21; herbed, 122; Pasta Hybrid, 120; Vegetable, 120

Spearmint, **105**

Spiced Winter Squash, 154

Spinach (*Spinacia oleracea*), 132–33; freezing, 28; growing, 183

Sprouts, pickled, 97

Squash, 152; Rolly Polly, sautéed, with marjoram, 47; spaghetti, 116, 120–21; spaghetti herbed, 122

Squash, summer (*Cucurbita* spp.), 31–32, 46, 69–70; dilled, 72; growing, 183–84

Squash, winter (*Cucurbita* spp.), 32; growing, 183–84; spiced, 154

Stakes, 11, **11**, 67

Stewed Cucumbers, 87

Stewed Tomatoes, 34

Stir-Fried Tomatoes and Herbs, 71

Stowell, Nathan, 83

Strawberries (*Fragaria* spp.): Alpine, 56; Apollo, 106; Brighton, 70; Chandler, 106; Earliglow, 106; growing, 184; minimelons with, 58; Pink Panda, 38, **38**, 40, 46; sauce, 59, 73; Surecrop, 106; Tribute, 70; Tristar, 70

Strawberry Sauce, 73

Structure, 18–19

Style, identifying, xi, 16–17

Summer savory, 44

Summer squash (*Cucurbita* spp.), 31–32, 69–70; Burpee Hybrid Zucchini, 32; Butterstick Hybrid, 70; dilled, 72; Gourmet Globe, 46; growing, 188–89; Kuta, 46; Seneca Prolific, 31–32; Sunburst, 32, 70

Sun, 2–4, 158

Sundials, 128

Sunflowers (*Helianthus annuus*), **27**; growing, 184; Lemon Queen, 32; Mammoth Russian, 32; Sunspot, 32; Velvet Queen, 32

Sunflowers, cutting (*Helianthus* x *multiflorus*), 190

Supports, 11, 116

Sweet corn, **29**, 82–83; Golden Bantam, 83; Stowell's Evergreen, 83

Sweet marjoram (*Origanum marjorana*), 44, 119; growing, 184–85

Swiss chard (*Beta vulgaris*), 30, 55; growing, 185; Rhubarb, 70; Ruby Red, 70

Swiss Chard Salad, 72

Syrups, lavender, 109

Tarragon, French (*Artemisia dracunculus* var. *sativa*), 133; growing, 185

Tarragon Chicken Salad, 136

Tarragon Vinegar, 137

Teas, sage, 99

Tepees, **12**

Texture, garden, 20–21

Thyme (*Thymus* spp.), 68, 81, 96, **107**; English, 107, 144; French, 133; golden lemon, 106; growing, 185–86

Tomatillos (*Physalis ixocarpa*), 152; growing, 186

Tomatoes (*Lycopersicum esculentum*), 2, **12**, 152–53; baked, 145; Big Beef, 32; Brandywine, **x**, 76; Celebrity, 46, 116; Chiapas, 153; Ciudad, 153; Currant, 56; dried, 36; freezing, 28; growing, 186; Green Grape, **x**; grilled, 34; Hungarian Italian Paste, 121; Italian Gold Hybrid, 121; Large Ribbed Zapotec, 153; Marmande, **x**; Mexicali, 153; Milano VF, 121; Oregon Spring, 71; Red Pear, 83, 84; Red Robin, 70; Roma, 121; San Remo, 121; staked, **11**; stewed, 34; stir-fried, with herbs, 71; Super Marmande, 144; supports for, 116; Sweet 100, 46; Tiger, 144; Tumbler Hybrid, 70; Viva Italia Hybrid, 121; Yellow Pear, 84; Yellow Ruffled, 153

Tomato Sauce, 125

Tortillas, black bean, 155

Trellises, 11, **12**; blackberries on, 104; crops for, 79–80; three-wire, **104**

Vegetables: freezing, 28; Mexican, 154

Victorian Courtyard Garden, ix, xi, 16, 17, 100–107; designing, 102–3; sketch of, 101

Vinegar: balsamic, 137; with chive blossoms, 109; cider, 137; distilled white, 137; herbal, 137, 138; with nasturtiums, 109; red wine, 137; rice wine, 137; tarragon, 137; white wine, 137

Violas, **60**

INDEX OF BOTANICAL LATIN NAMES